ABOUT THE AUTHOR

Mary McGrigor grew up in a Scottish medieval castle which inspired her love of history.

Married to Sir Charles McGrigor, she was first a soldier's, and then a farmer's wife.

She has four children, twelve grandchildren, and two great granddaughters.

The author of many books and magazine articles, she lives in Argyll.

King Henry's Sister Margaret: Scotland's Tudor Queen

Mary McGrigor

King Henry's Sister Margaret: Scotland's Tudor Queen

Joan and Howard
With much love from
Mary

June 2018

Vanguard Press

VANGUARD PAPERBACK

© Copyright 2018
Mary McGrigor
Cover image © Bridgeman Images

A CIP catalogue record for this title is
available from the British Library.

ISBN 978 1 7846 5320 0

Vanguard Press is an imprint of
Pegasus Elliot MacKenzie Publishers Ltd.

www.pegasuspublishers.com

First Published in 2018

**Vanguard Press
Sheraton House Castle Park
Cambridge England**

Printed & Bound in Great Britain

Acknowledgements

My deepest thanks to those who have so very kindly given so much time and gone to so much trouble in helping me with this book. In particular, Adrian Gibbs and Sian Phillips of The Bridgeman Gallery London, for the beautiful images they supplied, Roy Summers for his striking photographs of Scottish castles, Claire-Rose Charlton and the team of editors and designers at Pegasus Elliot Mackenzie Publishers in Cambridge and, as always, to the members of my family for their continual support and help with today's technology which I find so hard to comprehend!

Part 1

CHAPTER 1

Gold, glorious, glistening, dazzling the beholder's eyes. There were eighteen thousand of louis d'ors sent by the French King Louis XII to bribe King James IV of to Scotland invade England on his behalf.

It was almost more than Queen Margaret could endure. Her husband, the man she both loved and hated for his many infidelities, was being induced to take an army into the land of her birth to fight the brother, who, despite his indifference towards her, was her own flesh and blood. Why otherwise had she been married, sacrificed as a pawn, to the great sorrow of her father, to bring peace between the two countries when she was only twelve?

Margaret Tudor was now still only twenty-four, sixteen years younger than the man she had been forced to marry a long ten years before. Theirs was to have been the union to cement long lasting peace, which her father, King Henry VII, had so desperately desired. Now it was all to end, due to the despicable seduction of the man her brother, the eighth Henry of England, was fighting, Louis de Valois, King of France.

The gold had been brought ashore at Leith. Contained in a lead casket, it had been smuggled secretly from the harbour to its hiding place in Linlithgow Palace, which James now showed to his wife. It was the last act of reconciliation between them. James was still angry, suspicious that the manifestation of a monk robed in blue, who, in the adjoining royal chapel of St Michael, where he was attending evensong, had warned him of impending disaster should he invade England, prophesying that he would never return alive, had been a last desperate attempt by Margaret to dissuade him from his attempted campaign. It had long been a cause of discord between them, just one of the many continuous quarrels that had virtually torn their marriage apart during the last few years. Yet Margaret, despite their differences, was still his wife. Therefore she, above all people, should be entrusted with the knowledge of the hiding place of the gold. When James invaded England, Henry, if not conquered, would at least be distracted from France. Then James, with the promised French backing, would have the power both to rule his own country, free from the constant drain of poverty, as he had so long envisaged, and to lead a crusade most cherished of his dreams.

James had always needed money to escape the curse of his birth, so clearly foreseen by his father when he had barely been conceived. Wealth would provide the power to prove, not only his own authority, but to assuage the sin of that same father's mortality which even the constant chafing of the iron belt of chastity around his waist, made heavier with each succeeding year, could never be lifted from his mind. King James was beset by demons, relentless, persistent, something which his wife, during their ten years of marriage, had never learned to understand. Once the foray into England was completed, backed by King Louis' assurance of yet more financial aid from France, he would be able to lead his crusade against the Turkish infidels, pinnacle of the long established ambition to achieve redemption for his own unpardonable crime.

King James III of Scotland was a very frightened man. From the ramparts of Stirling Castle he looked down upon the bridge over the river Forth, defended so gallantly by William Wallace against the English King Edward nearly two hundred years before. To the west lay the field of Bannockburn, where his ancestor, Robert the Bruce, had so famously defeated another English invasion in 1314. To the more distant west rose the great mountain of Ben Lomond, its crest topped with snow, from which blew the bone-biting wind that chilled him through the thick, fur lined cloak that he wore over his doublet and the cuirass of steel, which, paranoid over fear for his safety, he always wore.

But it was not the physical cold which made the king's knuckles show white as he gripped the balustrade before him, but terror of what the great comet, clearly visible in the sky at midday, foretold.

Still haunting his mind was the memory of the dream in which he knew he was dying, his limbs being virtually torn apart. Returning to the interior of the castle, he sent a messenger to summon William Elphinstone, the bishop of Aberdeen, who like himself was interested in the study of the stars and planets in the sky. On the cleric arriving he asked him bluntly what the appearance of the great comet in connection with his dream might portend.

Presented with this question, Elphinstone rose slowly, with reluctance, to give his unequivocal reply.

'The royal lion of Scotland,' he said, 'through the course of time, would be torn by his whelps.'

Horrified, the king is claimed to have consulted witches, hoping they could give better news, but none could relieve his mind of the presentiment that the imminent birth of a child to his queen, the sixteen year old Princess Margaret of Denmark, would result in disaster for himself. Accordingly, when on St

Patrick's Day, 17 March 1473, the queen gave birth to a son, King James did not manifestly enjoy the celebrations accorded to the arrival of his heir apparent, a boy given his own name of James.

The child was sickly to the point where his father, thinking him to be a threat to his own existence, believed and indeed hoped, that he would not survive. In August, King James and Queen Margaret made a pilgrimage to the shrine of St Ninian in Galloway, after which, some four months later, a second son was born. Again they called him James, so that the name, now dynastic in the Scottish royal family of the Stewarts, would continue. A third son would follow, this time to be christened John.

But perversely, against all expectations, the eldest James survived. He was barely two years old when his father, always short of money, saw a way to embellish his coffers by making use of his heir. Prince James, now Duke of Rothesay, hereditary title of the heir to the throne, was barely a year old when his father began negotiations for his marriage to Princess Cecilia, youngest daughter of the reigning monarch in England, King Edward IV.[1]

The Parliament of May 1474, obedient to the king's wishes, decided to send 'ane honoable ambassat in Ingland' to work for 'frendshep and amitie and keeping of the pece in tym to cum' after which, on 15 June, King James empowered the ambassadors to propose a marriage of his eldest son to Princess Cecilia. Subsequently, on 29 July, Edward appointed commissioners to effect the suggested match.[2]

The idea of such an arrangement in fact suited Edward very well. He was just about to lead an invasion into France, and a

---

[1] *Calendar of Documents relating to Scotland* in H.M. Record Office Edinburgh. No 1414.

[2] Nicholson, Ranald. *Edinburgh History of Scotland*, Vol.2. p.478.

betrothal of his three year old daughter to the son of the Scottish king would ensure the maintenance of the truce with the country, pledged by an old alliance, to support the kingdom of France. Thus, the preliminaries once arranged, in what amounted to surprising haste, indentures were drawn up on the following day of 30 July.

No time was then wasted before English ambassadors, either on horseback or on board a ship, reached Edinburgh where, on 26 October 1474, they completed an indenture. Following this, in the Blackfriars Dominican Monastery (near to the High Street of today) the formal betrothal took place. Neither participant was present, Cecilia being five years old and James not yet two, but the Earl of Crawford and Lord Scrope, acting as proxies, joined hands and plighted their troth.

The actual marriage, as was stipulated, would not take place until both parties were of age. The dowry, however, was stated to be twenty thousand English marks, of which a first instalment of two thousand marks would be paid to King James within three months. Following this, a further two yearly payments of the same amount would be disbursed, after which the remaining fourteen thousand marks would reach the Scottish Exchequer at the rate of one thousand a year.

King James was totally delighted. He could not foresee, as could no one else at that time, that before his son could be married, two more kings would ascend the English throne.

CHAPTER 2

ENGLAND 1483

'The best laid plans of mice and men,' as Burns would later write, 'go aft agley.' How right he was is nowhere better illustrated than in those of James III of Scotland for the dynastic marriage of his son. Edward IV died on 9 April 1483 to be succeeded by his eldest son as Edward V. But, as is so well known, the boy's uncle, Richard Duke of York, in his capacity of protector of the kingdom, had him, together with his brother, imprisoned in the Tower of London where both of them mysteriously disappeared. Following this, on 25 June, virtually at Richard's dictation, an assembly of lords and commoners endorsed his claims that Edward IV's marriage to the beautiful Elizabeth Woodville had been invalid thus making their children illegitimate. As such the Princess Cecilia was no longer of political importance and moreover her lucrative dowry had disappeared.

King James, not to be beaten, then tried to negotiate a marriage for his son with the Lady Anne de la Pole, daughter of John, Duke of Suffolk and his wife Elizabeth, sister of King Richard III. According to the historian Bishop Lesley, Lady Anne, said to have been the king's favourite niece, 'was known as the Duchess of Rothesay at the court of the king of England, but when his untimely death took place, she lost that title as quickly as her cousin, Lady Cecilia, lost hers.'

Lesley, of course, was referring to the death of Richard III at the battle of Bosworth Field in August 1485.

The House of Lancaster, descended from the mighty John of Gaunt, the third son of Edward III, had ended, or so it had seemed, with the murder by suffocation of Henry VI in the Tower of London in May 1471.

But there was still a young man living in exile in France who, through his mother, Joan Beaufort, great-granddaughter of John of Gaunt, could claim an inheritance of the long disputed English crown.

Henry Tudor was the son of Edmund Tudor, made Earl of Richmond by his half-brother Henry VI in 1452, the mother of both of them being Catherine de Valois, daughter of Charles VI, famous as the 'mad king' of France. Catherine, as the wife of Henry V, had been queen of England and mother of the son who succeeded him as Henry VI. But, on the king's death, she had married the Welsh knight Owen Tudor, with whom she had three sons.

On his mother's death, Edmund and his next brother Jasper (subsequently the Earl of Pembroke) had been brought up by the abbess of Barking, Lady Katherine de la Pole, the pious eldest daughter of the Earl of Suffolk, before being summoned, thanks to her influence, by his half-brother, King Henry VI, to attend his court. Edmund was there when, in 1452, he was granted the wardship of Lady Margaret Beaufort, the nine year old daughter of the Duke of Somerset, whom he married three years later when she was twelve.

But the wars of the Roses, between the royal houses of York and Lancaster, had then begun. Edmund, a Lancastrian, was captured and imprisoned in Carmarthen Castle where, in November 1456, just a year after he was married, he died of the plague. He left behind him a widow just thirteen years old, pregnant with their first child. Both the baby and Margaret nearly died in what proved to be the traumatic circumstances of his birth, but miraculously they survived. Henry, with the dark hair of a Welshman, was brought up in Wales but when the Yorkists defeated Margaret of Anjou at the battle of Tewkesbury, after which his grandfather Owen Tudor was executed, he fled with his uncle Jasper for the coast from where they escaped to France. A gale forced them ashore in Brittany, then an independent duchy, where Duke Francis II gave them asylum. Henry's mother contrived to keep in touch with him, and Edward IV, assuring Duke Francis of his safety, tried to make him return to England offering the hand of one of his daughters as an inducement. But Henry, convinced he would be murdered, refused to leave Brittany, where, living on Duke Francis's charity, he learnt the value of money, later being accused of mendacity in scrutinising accounts. When Edward IV died and his brother, Richard III became king in June 1483, there were many in England who thought that Henry, the young Earl of Richmond, who, since the deaths of Henry VI and his son, had become head of the House of Lancaster, had a better claim to the throne.

In September 1483, Henry Stafford, Duke of Buckingham, who as the greatest protagonist of Richard Duke of York, had helped him to secure the throne as Richard III, rebelled against what he now perceived as the king's tyrannical rule. Writing to Henry Tudor, he invited him to come to England to free the country from the grip of the dictator that Richard had become. He told him that there would be risings in Wales, the West Country and the Home Counties, and that Henry would be acclaimed as a deliverer when he landed. But it all went wrong. The men in Kent rose too early giving Richard a chance to make plans. Buckingham intended to cross the river Severn to join up with the men, raised by his allies in Devon, but the river rose in flood, making it impassable, so that he had to retire to Shropshire where he was betrayed and executed in Salisbury in front of the king.

Henry Tudor meanwhile, held up by storms in the Channel, had returned to Brittany, where, in Rennes Cathedral, on Christmas Day 1483, he took a solemn oath that, once king of England, he would marry Princess Elizabeth, the eldest daughter of the dead King Edward IV and heiress of the House of York.

This seemed a faint hope at the time. The princess was living with her widowed mother, the famously beautiful Elizabeth Woodville, and her four younger sisters in sanctuary in the cramped cold crypt of Westminster Abbey.

Following the suppression of Buckingham's rebellion however, Richard persuaded Queen Elizabeth to come out of sanctuary, and having given sworn assurances for her safety, he sent Princess Elizabeth to Sheriff Hutton Castle in Yorkshire.

In April 1484, when Richard's only son died, he named his sister's son, his nephew, John de la Pole, the Earl of Lincoln as his heir, granting him the estates of Henry's mother, the countess of Richmond.

But although Buckingham's rebellion had ended so catastrophically, many of his supporters had survived to escape to France where they swore allegiance to Henry. Others, still in England believing that Richard had murdered his two young nephews, Edward V and Richard of Shrewsbury in the Tower, saw Henry as the saviour of the realm. King Richard, aware of this, increased his pressure on Duke Francis of Brittany, now aged and deranged, to surrender Henry, which the Duke's treasurer, tired of paying for the increasing number of his followers, agreed to do for a monetary bribe. But Henry was warned and escaped, dressed as a forester, across the border into Anjou. From there, with an increasing number of supporters, he reached Paris, where, after leaving hostages in security for a loan of sixty thousand francs from King Charles VIII, and with an army enlarged by French mercenaries, estimated at three thousand strong, he set sail for England from Harfleur.

This time, with a fair wind behind him, he landed a week later, at Milford Haven, in Pembrokeshire. The men of Wales rose to follow their own leader, Jasper, Earl of Pembroke and his nephew, to whom, although he spoke French better than English, they swore loyalty. It was not until 15 August that Richard III, by then at Nottingham, knew of the invasion force, marching across England from Wales.

The battle of Bosworth Field, fought a week later, on 22 August 1485, gave victory to Henry when both the Duke of Norfolk and Lord Stanley deserted from the king's side.

Henry was crowned king of England in Westminster Abbey on 30th October in that, for him, triumphant year, of 1485. Parliament then assembled on 7 November when both houses urged the king to honour his promise to marry Princess Elizabeth of York, by now his mistress, she having been returned on his order from Sheriff Hutton Castle immediately after Bosworth Field.

Subsequently, on the following 18 January, he married Elizabeth, by then pregnant with his child. On 20 September 1486, their first son, Prince Arthur, was born. Told of this happening in Scotland, King James could only hope that in due time a daughter might follow to renew his hopes of a marriage between a princess of England and his son.

CHAPTER 3

SCOTLAND JANUARY – JUNE 1488

In Edinburgh King James III sat in parliament, his nobles ranged on either side, foremost amongst them the Earl of Argyll, hereditary keeper of the royal household. Notable by their absence were any representatives of the powerful Border house of Home. Likewise Lord Hailes was nowhere to be seen. The reasons for this were obvious. In a previous parliament, of May 1485, it had been decided that envoys sent to the Pope should petition for 'ane ereccioun of Coldinghame to our sovereign lordis chapel.'[3] In plain terms this meant that the revenues of Coldingham Priory, hitherto owned by the Homes, would revert to the king who planned to build a collegiate kirk at Coldingham as a royal chapel. So furiously had the Homes protested at the loss of their ancestral rights, granted as requested by the Pope, that a later Parliament of October 1487 had enacted that anyone who defied the king's plans for Coldingham, would face punishment as a traitor.[4] Further to this, at the prorogued Parliament of 11 January 1488, warning was issued that during the forthcoming session, any prelate or lord who defied this edict, would incur the king's 'indignacioun and displesance.'[5] Then, significantly, on the same day of this announcement, the king's second son, James, like his elder brother, was created Duke of Ross.[6]

This caused speculation amongst those who heard the words pronounced. The king's aversion to his eldest son,

---

[3] A.P.S.,ii,171,c.7.
[4] A.P.S..,ii. 179,c.19.
[5] Ibid. 180,
[6] Ibid 180-1.

supposedly on the assertions of both Bishop Elphinstone and the witches, was well known. The heir to the throne lived apart from his father in Stirling Castle, virtually a prisoner, under the care of Sir James Schaw of Sauchie, appointed by the king as his custodian. His mother, the Danish Queen Margaret had died when he was only thirteen, after which his estrangement from his father had continued to the point where apparently, he had so far forgotten what his father looked like, that he could not recognize his face.

The Parliament was set to meet again on the following 5 May 1488. But this was not to happen. The witches had not been wrong. The herald sent to summon the Homes from their Border stronghold was attacked and injured, although he apparently survived. But in Stirling Castle, Lady Schaw of Sauchie, daughter of Lord Home, prevailed upon her husband to avenge the wrong done to her family by the king.

Details of what happened are obscure. Prince James, on his father's instructions, was held virtually a prisoner. But, on 2 February, perhaps under cover of darkness, Sir James Schaw released him to his father's enemies, who carried him off to Linlithgow Palace where again they held him captive in a fortress heavily defended.

They did so, they said, to save the prince from his father, who had become suspicious of him and was coming with a great army to put him in prison. King James, told of what had happened, took precipitate action. He announced that, on the advice of his Council, he had dissolved the present Parliament and ordered a new 'general' Parliament to meet in Edinburgh on 12 May. Then, on 18 February, doubtful of the Earl of Argyll's loyalty, he replaced him as chancellor with Bishop Elphinstone, a man on whom he could entirely rely.

Meanwhile those who held the prince in custody, determined to win the support of Henry VII, applied for safe conducts for the bishops of Glasgow and Dunkeld, the Earl of Argyll, Lord Hailes and amongst others, the master of Home, to go to England where they could put their case to King Henry and ask for his support.

It does not appear that they went. Instead ambassadors from England arrived in Scotland to declare that the kings of both England and France denounced the rising of the barons as 'verraye wickit and pernicious.'[7] Nonetheless despite these monarchs' disapproval there was open rebellion in Scotland by the month of March.

By then King James himself was virtually a prisoner in Edinburgh Castle, his enemies demanding that he abdicate in favour of his eldest son. Believing himself deserted by all but a few loyal men, he contrived to leave the castle undetected and (possibly in disguise) to board a ship ready to sail for Flanders lying in the Firth of Forth. The skipper was Andrew Wood, the Scottish sea captain who James had knighted and made his Lord High Admiral in 1495, being one of the few men he could trust.

His departure was soon discovered. Riding a fast horse, he was chased all the way to Leith. Some of his baggage, carried on pack horses, was seized by his enemies who used the gold they found packed into saddle bags, to hire men to fight as soldiers for their cause.

But King James himself eluded them, sailing down the Firth of Forth to land, not in Flanders as imagined, but on the north shore of the Firth in Fife. Riding on to Aberdeen to find his faithful William Elphinstone, the bishop of Aberdeen, he ordered the sheriffs of the shires through which he passed to call out their fencible men.

With the strength of all of the north behind him King James decided to fight. Determined to confront the rebels, who were holding his son at Linlithgow, he advanced to encamp at Blackness where supplies could be brought in by ship by Andrew Wood sailing into the Forth. From Blackness attempts were made for a peaceful settlement. James's envoys, who

---

[7] Bishop Lesley, Historie of Scotland.p57.

included Bishop Elphinstone, the earls of Huntly and Errol and the Earl Marischal, conferring with those of the other side who were headed by Bishop Robert Blackadder of Glasgow, the earls of Argyll and Angus, and the Lords Lyle and Hailes.

The rebels demanded that the king dismiss some of his councillors, in particular the envoys from England who urged the subjection of the realm. On King James abjectly refusing these demands Huntly, Errol and the Earl Marischal and Lord Glamis apparently left him and returned to their fastnesses in the north.

The king, thus largely deserted, was forced to hand over the earls of Ruthven and Buchan and two other hostages, as surety for his so-called agreement to the rebels' terms, before returning to Edinburgh Castle where he tried to carry on some form of government, as is proved by records of the time. Believing by now that he could trust no one, he was nonetheless persuaded – it is thought by Lord Bothwell – to leave Edinburgh to make a second attempt against the supporters of the son who his enemies planned to rule in his place.

Once more, in a ship captained by Andrew Wood, he crossed the Forth to Fife. Then riding on to Perth, he issued a call to arms of his supporters, men almost wholly from the north. Amongst them was Lord Lindsay of the Byers, according to the historian Bishop Lindsay of Pitscottie, a very rough man but nonetheless a good soldier who, on the strength of his reputation, the king made commander of his forces. Lord Lindsay arrived riding a fine grey courser of which, after jumping from the saddle, he made a present to the king.

Was this a wise move? Or one calculated to cause disaster? Seen in the light of hindsight, we shall never know. The king, as a leader, needed to be well mounted. A grey horse was conspicuous for all to see. But the king was not a good horseman so that the results of his being mounted on an animal, difficult to control as it was known to be, in the inevitable confusion of a battle, might well have been foreseen.

In the palace of Linlithgow, some forty miles as the crow flies to the south-east of Perth, beyond both the estuaries of both the great rivers of the Tay and Forth, the fifteen year old Prince James was talking to his advisers about the forthcoming campaign. Foremost amongst those gathered with him in one of the small rooms off the great hall in the building south side of the courtyard around which the palace stood, was the formidable Border magnate Lord Home. A man of imposing presence, once a close confidant of the king, the sequestration of the revenues of Coldingham priory, had turned him into one bent on revenge.

The prince, listening intently, but still unsure of what was being planned, put to him the important question which was so greatly troubling his mind. What, he demanded, would happen to his father in the event of his defeat. Assured that no harm would come to him, he listened, with increasing excitement, to what was being planned.

Because of the slowness of communication anywhere in the world at that time, Prince James had no way of knowing that his father was leading his army from Perth towards Stirling, riding at the head of the column of men, who, armed with everything from pikes to axes, trudged behind along the road where the mud and slush of winter had turned hard beneath the summer sun. Neither was he to know that his father, on reaching Stirling, was to be denied access to his own castle, place of his birth, by Sir James Schaw of Sauchie, the man he himself had appointed captain of the place he loved most of all others in Scotland. Moreover, most cruel of all insults, Schaw, from behind the portcullis, shouted that he now held the castle on the authority of Prince James.

Angry beyond all reasoning, the king turned the great horse's head away from the iron artifice, behind which he guessed that the garrison, watching with leering eyes, rejoiced at the temerity of their captain in defying their sovereign's command.

On 11 June the royal force was marching through Stirling, heading for the rebel headquarters at Linlithgow, when a scout reached the king with the news that Prince James, leading an army, had already crossed the River Carron. Battle could not be avoided. The wolf must fight his cub.

The two armies faced each other on flat ground beside the Sauchie burn about two miles south of Stirling. The king, wearing full armour, sat astride his huge grey charger in the centre battalion of his army with the men of Fife and Angus on one side and those of Strathearn and Stormont on the other. Beside him were recruits from the local districts, while the vanguard was composed of the Highlanders under the leadership of two of the men most loyal to him, his uncle the Earl of Atholl, and the Earl of Huntly.

Beside the king stood an esquire, also in full armour, holding the mighty sword of his ancestor Robert the Bruce, who had vanquished Edward II of England, almost on this very place, in the famous battle of Bannockburn in 1314.

This must be a good omen. In the minds of most of the army, if not of that of the king, lay the certainty that victory must lie ahead.

Opposing them were the men of the south of Scotland and the east with the Homes and the Hepburns conspicuous to the fore. Above them a standard bearer raised the royal banner, a red lion on a gold background, flying clear against the summer sky.

At sight of it King James knew terror together with a crushing sense of the inevitable as the words of Bishop Elphinstone's prophesy echoed through his mind. Convulsed with fear, he swayed in his saddle, his steel gloved hand clutching at the pommel, as he fought to forget the image while finding words of command. His distress must have been obvious for, according to Bishop Lindsay of Pitscottie, Ross of Montgrennan, riding close to him, urged him to leave the field.

The king apparently wavered, confused by what was happening, undecided what to do. But, as the armies advanced upon each other, fighting hand to hand, weapons clashing, men yelling and screaming in a deafening ground shaking roar, he appeared to be taking Ross's advice.

He may have decided to make for the Forth where lay the ship of his stalwart Andrew Wood. But, even as he tried to choose his direction, the great charger, petrified by the noise of the fighting, got its tongue over the bit and bolted. Through the village of Bannockburn it galloped until, reaching the Bannock burn, it drew back on it haunches for a massive leap. Unseated, the king, losing his balance, fell with bone-crushing force on the ground.

Stunned and badly bruised, James lay helpless, unable to move and almost suffocating under the weight of his armour, until, rescued by some local people who had seen him fall, he was carried into a nearby mill. Pulling down his vizier the miller's wife then asked him who he was.

'I was your King this day mourn,' he managed to tell her before, believing he was dying, as badly bruised he struggled for breath, he asked her to fetch him a priest.

The woman ran out crying, 'A priest, a priest for the King,' whereupon a man standing by, who seeing the great grey horse grazing had guessed what had taken place, told her, 'Here am I, am a priest, where is the King?' Following her he entered the mill where, the king, on seeing him, asked him to give him the last rites.

'That I shall do hastily', cried the so-called priest, and with that he pulled out his sword to drive it, four or five times into the heart of the king.

Following the battle the young Prince James asked anxiously for news of his father. Some thought he had escaped from the battlefield in one of the ships anchored in the Forth, but in fact it was Sir Andrew Wood himself, who went to find the prince to tell him what had occurred. James, much confused by the results of the battle in which he had been chased from the field by Ross of Montgrenan fighting on his father's side, was apparently bewildered at sight of the handsome, obviously important man who was ushered into his presence.

'Are you the king my father?' he is said to have asked him, before Wood, explaining his identity, told him, with the greatest sorrow, that his father, who he had served so faithfully, was dead.

CHAPTER 4

THE PALACE OF WESTMINSTER 1489

On 29 November 1489, in a room adjacent to the Painted Chamber in the Palace of Westminster, Margaret, the Princess Royal of England, first daughter of Henry VII and his wife Elizabeth of York, was born. The baby, with her fluff of red gold hair, plainly carried the genes of her father's family of the Tudors, descended from warriors of Wales.

She was christened the very next day, a custom not unusual when infant mortality was so high, but in this case dictated by her grandmother and godmother, Margaret, Countess of Richmond, from whom she also took her name. No one quarrelled with the countess, described by her contemporaries as the most powerful woman in England, who in this case dictated that the infant must be baptised on the 30th, it being St Andrew's Day, the patron saint of Scotland.

Whether she was prompted by premonition of the child's future will never be known. Margaret, Countess of Richmond, whatever her many attributes, was not famed as a seer. It is in fact more likely that, inspired by the great piety for which she was renowned, she chose the day of a saint for whom she had high regard. On a more practical note, it was observed that both she and her son, King Henry, were anxious to conciliate the Scots, the betrothal of their king to the aunt of the newly born child, Princess Cecilia, having been foregone. Likewise this may have been the reason for the baptism taking place in the nearby church of St Margaret, dedicated to the Scottish saint.

In the early dark of a November day, the little princess was carried from the palace in the arms of Lady Berkeley, followed by the earls of Arundel and Shrewsbury, robed in their full regalia, into the Whitehall. There, by the light of torches, the procession formed to proceed through the gate in the wall of New Palace Yard to the church, where the bishop of Ely waited, wearing his full robes of office. The silver font, used for the christening of all children of the kings of England, had been brought from Canterbury Cathedral to stand in the porch of St Margaret's, where the walls were hung with tapestry and the ceiling with beautiful embroidery. It was truly a magnificent setting for the tiny one-day old child.

Taking precedence amongst the attendants was another of her aunts, the Lady Anne of York, who, as the fifth daughter of Edward IV and his Queen Elizabeth Woodville, was now a lady in waiting to her elder sister Elizabeth, the baby's mother, the present queen. It was she who carried the white chrisom, a linen cloth anointed with holy oil laid over a child's face at baptism in the Roman Catholic ceremony. Behind her came Lord Welles, husband of Princess Cecilia, the baby's aunt – she who, betrothed as a small child to James IV, King of Scotland when daughter of the king of England, had eventually been married to a staunch Lancastrian, John, Viscount Welles, the maternal half-brother of the countess of Richmond – carrying the salt in a great gold salt-cellar, another custom at baptisms. A magnificent silver chandelier, glinting with burning candles, was borne before him, while unlit wax tapers were carried by all the congregation, who included officers of the royal household. Margaret Countess of Richmond herself, austere with her high head-dress, from which fell a white veil, gave the child's name to the bishop, she being the chief godmother, the Duchess of Norfolk the other. Doctor John Morton, Chancellor of England and Archbishop of Canterbury, then foremost advisor to her father the king, stood as godfather to the tiny princess.

Despite the coldness of the season, the new-born infant was totally immersed in the font, where, hopefully the water was heated. Then, perhaps as she howled, all the tapers were lit before the Princess Royal was carried back to Westminster Palace, this time below a canopy held by four bannerets who had won their spurs in her father's great victory of Bosworth Field. Amongst them was Edward Stanley, brother of her grandmother's fourth husband, Sir Thomas Stanley, now made Lord Derby in honour of his deserting King Richard to join his stepson, Henry Tudor, in that battle.

Leading the procession were trumpeters, 'sounding merrily' and men carrying the baby's christening presents including a lovely gold aspersoir, adorned with precious stones, for sprinkling sweet water, the gift of her godfather, the Archbishop, while Lord Welles carried the silver chest, heaped with gold coins, from the grandmother and godmother who was to play such an important part in her early life, Margaret, Countess of Richmond.[8]

The little Princess Margaret was to spend much of her childhood in the Palace of Sheen, standing beside the Thames in what is now Richmond Park. Said to be her mother's favourite home, it had also been that of Anne of Bohemia, first wife of Richard II, who, devastated when she died there of the plague, had it pulled down. Rebuilt by Henry V, it was renamed Richmond Palace by Margaret's father, Henry VII, in token of his earldom of Richmond in Yorkshire. When Henry held a great tournament there in 1492, Margaret, his eldest daughter, said to be his favourite child, was probably allowed to watch, she being at that time just three years old. In 1498 she was nearly ten when, just before Christmas, for some unstated reason, the great house caught fire. Precious possessions, including the children's gifts were destroyed. But the family, and it would seem all their servants, survived.

King Henry rebuilt the palace in the Gothic style, with many towers making it one of the finest buildings in Europe of its day. Margaret grew up there, exploring the many towers

---

[8] For further details, see, Strickland, Agnes, *Lives of the Queens of Scotland and English Princesses,* VOl.1. pp.3-4. Pub/ BiblioBazaar,LLC.

with her brother Henry, two years younger than herself, and playing under supervision in the park where deer, kept there for hunting, roamed in what was then open countryside.

But it was her grandmother, rather than her parents, who proved the prime influence in Margaret's life.

Born in 1443 on 31 May, Lady Margaret Beaufort was the daughter and heiress of John, 1st Duke of Somerset and his wife Margaret Beauchamp of Bletsoe. Her father, great grandson of Edward III, and grandson of that king's third son, John of Gaunt, was thus the main descendant of the House of Lancaster.

Following the death of her second husband, Edmund Tudor, Margaret and Henry, the son she had borne with so much risk to both their lives, had lived with her brother-in-law, Jasper Tudor (created Earl of Pembroke by Henry VI) at Pembroke Castle. Then, two years later, she had married her third husband, Sir Henry Stafford, son of the Henry Stafford who was made 1st Duke of Buckingham. They had been married for thirteen years before, in 1471, Stafford, fighting for the Yorkists, had been fatally wounded at the fog-bound Battle of Barnet in 1471.

A year later, Margaret had married as her fourth husband, Thomas Stanley, the Lord High Constable of the Isle of Mann of which he was briefly known as king. As his wife, although still called the countess of Richmond, she had returned to the court of Edward IV and Elizabeth Woodville, whose lady-in-waiting she had become. Then, following Edward's death, she had served in the same capacity to Anne Neville, Richard III's queen, holding her train at her coronation.

But even when acting in this capacity, she had been secretly plotting with Edward IV's queen, Elizabeth Woodville, at that time living in the sanctuary of Westminster Abbey, and she had certainly conspired with the Duke of Buckingham in his failed rebellion against King Richard. Then when Elizabeth Woodville's sons, 'the Princes in the Tower' as they were named, had disappeared, believed to be dead, it had been agreed that Margaret's son Henry be betrothed to Elizabeth Woodville's eldest daughter, Princess Elizabeth of York.

Margaret's fourth husband, Thomas Lord Stanley, had famously stood aside at the Battle of Bosworth Field while his brother, Sir William Stanley, had changed sides to fight for King Henry at the crucial moment when Richard III, in a final act of desperation, had charged onto the field to be killed. But it was said to have been Lord Stanley who, finding the circlet of gold worn on Richard's helmet under a thorn bush, placed it on his stepson, Henry's head.

Henry, once king, had rewarded his step-father with the earldom of Derby and made him Lord High Constable of England, after which his mother had become styled as the countess of Richmond and Derby.

But Margaret, once her son held the throne, considered herself a queen, signing her letters Margaret R. Wearing robes as magnificent if not more so than her daughter-in-law, Queen Elizabeth, she walked only half a step behind her and insisted on being waited on at table as royalty, by servants on bended knee.

However, it was not for her titles, nor her grandeur, that, by the time of her granddaughter's christening, Margaret had become so renowned. Always devout, she would rise at five o'clock every morning to begin her sequence of devotions, which lasted throughout the day. Although crippled and in constant pain from arthritis, to the point where it reduced her to tears, she spent long hours kneeling on stone floors. Her portraits show her wearing dark robes, with a white wimple and headdress like those of a nun, concealing the hair shirt which she wore next to her skin. Now known as 'My Lady the King's Mother,' she devoted her time to religion and was later to re-found and enlarge Christ's College, and to found St John's College in Cambridge where many years later, the first women's college would be named after her as Lady Margaret Hall.

This was the woman then, who during their childhood, at the newly built Richmond Palace, would have the strongest influence over her grandchildren's lives.

Not surprisingly, in view of her own academic persuasion, 'Lady Margaret the King's mother' was determined that the grand-daughter named after her, should follow the excellent example of devotion to learning and religion throughout her forthcoming life.

This was something, however, with which the young Princess Margaret, had no intention to comply.

Margaret was certainly no scholar, however much her grandmother wished her to be. Whereas 'Lady Margaret, the King's mother,' wrote fluently with the running hand of the old English black character, Margaret could only trace letters and her spelling left much to be desired. Seen in retrospect she may have been dyslexic, a condition at that time undiagnosed.

Nevertheless, studious in learning as she certainly was not, she made up for it by being athletic and a graceful dancer as was noticed when, at her brother Arthur's wedding to the Spanish Princess, Catherine of Aragon, the courtiers applauded with delight as she and her younger brother Henry danced together. It was Arthur, three years older than herself, to whom Margaret was most close. Arthur was more gentle than Henry, who, two and a half years younger than Margaret, was aggressive and forceful in character from the moment of his birth. Margaret, in fact, seems to have been a bit of a tomboy, incurring her grandmother's displeasure by riding and watching their hawks fly with her brothers, instead of studying the books of divinity chosen for her to read.

She was certainly musical. Her mother's lists of expenses include fees for 'Giles the luter' for teaching her, and the purchase of lutes and lute strings suggestive that the lessons continued for some time.

She was painted, together with her two younger brothers, Henry and Edmund, who died when he was only four, by Jan Gossaert, a Flemish artist, more commonly known as Mabuse, a rather dissolute forerunner of Hans Holbein, in about 1496 or 7, when Margaret would have been seven to eight years old. His portrait of the three children, which hangs in the long gallery at Hampton Court, is not flattering. It shows a rather serious looking little girl in a plain dress, her lovely hair covered by a hood, and her pink and white complexion dimmed by the fading of the colours which he used. Margaret was then about eleven, therefore it must have been in 1500 that the young Sir Thomas More, on King Henry's instruction, took Erasmus to visit the royal children at Sheen, as to some people the newly built Palace of Richmond was known. Margaret and Henry entertained them, their parents being absent that day and they particularly noticed the baby of the family Mary, beautiful as a child, as later she would be a woman, playing amongst the rushes on the floor.

They did not spend all the year at Richmond. As in all large houses where a great many people lived, the buildings, after a few months of occupation, had to be left to be cleaned. The royal children moved with their parents in a peripatetic progress throughout their many domains. King Henry had no less than three residences in his capital and five in the Home Counties which, usually together with his family, he visited on a regular basis throughout the year.

The oldest was Westminster Palace, transformed by Richard II, who had built the hall with its famous hammer beam roof, and which Henry now extended over its site on the north bank of the Thames. Visits to the royal apartments in the Tower of London were short, the rooms, largely unchanged from Norman times being both cold and small. By far the more comfortable in comparison were those in Baynard Castle, also by the side of the great river, the main thoroughfare of the day. Greenwich Palace, which the young Margaret Tudor, later in her life, would learn to know so well, had been built by Humfrey, Duke of Gloucester, the younger brother of Henry V, who had ruled as regent during his son's minority following the king's death. When Humfrey died, it had been taken over by Margaret of Anjou, queen of his nephew Henry VI, who had changed it considerably, adding many windows and pillars to the outside, carved with her own emblem of the marguerite, and even changing its name to Placentia or Pleasaunce, as was the word in French. Now Henry changed it again, this time to Greenwich, which, as the palace most associated with him, it has subsequently remained.

Of the other palaces, Eltham, in Kent, surrounded by its moat, was too small for a great many people and kept mainly as a hunting lodge. Windsor Castle, in contrast, was large enough to hold an almost unlimited number of courtiers and visitors alike, while Woodstock, in the grounds of the present Blenheim Palace, was again used only when the king himself had a reason to find himself in Oxfordshire.

While time in the other palaces was quite frequently spent, it was Richmond, built so newly round its courtyard, where the royal quarters were embellished with no less than fourteen turrets, and where the children could climb up a hundred and twenty steps to the top of the main tower to see what must have seemed to them, half of England spread out below them following the course of the Thames, which they looked upon as their main home.

On 28 May 14 1493, King Henry VII commissioned the bishop of St Asaph, Sir William Tyler and two other ambassadors to negotiate 'a real peace' with the king of Scotland, if possible for the life of both princes, and also to try to arrange a marriage between King James, now in his twentieth year, with the Lady Katherine, daughter of the countess of Wiltshire. King James, however, was having none of it. He would marry only a princess of royal blood. Furthermore he would agree to a truce lasting just to the end of April 1501.

In July 1495, King James sent Lord Elphinstone and other Scottish ambassadors to the court of the Austrian Holy Roman Emperor Maximilian. They asked him to form an alliance with Scotland against England, and for the hand of his daughter as a bride for their young king. Also they assured him that their king supported the young man, claimed by the Duchess of Burgundy, a sister of Edward IV, and widow of the Duke known as Charles the Bold, to be the son of her late brother King Edward, one of the two boys supposed to have been murdered in the Tower.

CHAPTER 5

THE CUCKOO IN THE NEST

It had been in the autumn of 1491 that a Breton merchant, called Pregent Meno, had sailed into Cork harbour in Ireland with a cargo of silk and other fine fabrics. One of his crew was a young man, called Master Perkin Warbeck from Tournai, the son of a boatman on the Scheldt, who he used as commercial salesman to show off and sell his wares. So splendid did he appear that the people of Cork thought that he must be royal, and soon the rumours were spreading that he was either the Earl of Warwick or Prince Richard of Shrewsbury, younger son of King Edward IV, who had vanished so mysteriously in the Tower of London. Finally it was decided that he must be the latter and so, said the young man later 'they made me to learn English and taught me what I should do and say.'[9] Soon there was support for his pretensions from the kings of both France and Scotland, the Austrian Holy Roman Emperor Maximilian and most importantly, Margaret, Duchess of Burgundy, who, as sister of both Edward IV and Richard III, delighted in causing trouble for Henry Tudor, the man who had seized her brother's crown.

When Warbeck returned to Burgundy, Margaret refused to surrender him, whereupon Henry vetoed all trade with Flanders for the space of two years, greatly to the detriment of merchants on both sides of the English Channel. The duchess, who claimed that she saw a great resemblance to her dead brother Richard, in the face of his supposed son, insisted that he was treated as royalty, giving him a personal bodyguard dressed in the York livery of the White Rose. Henry, told of this, discovered the identity of most of his supporters in

---

[9] Williams, Neville, Henry VII. Pp.72-4.

England who included, to his astonishment, both Sir William Worseley, the Dean of St Paul's, who had been Steward of the Royal Household, and even more amazingly, his chamberlain, Sir William Stanley, the younger brother of his mother's husband, the man who had swung the day for him at Bosworth Field, and without whose aid the battle might have been lost. Totally disillusioned, feeling that there was no one he could trust, Henry ordered the execution of Stanley, making him the scapegoat as a warning of what others might expect.

Despite this, encouraged by the Duchess of Burgundy, to whom he promised the town and castle of Scarborough if he won, Warbeck, with a party of mercenaries, set sail from Flanders to land off Deal, in Kent, in July 1499. [10] An advance party, sent ashore, was quickly overcome and Warbeck sailed on westward through the Channel to land once again in Ireland, this time in Munster, where, with his followers, he joined the Earl of Desmond who was sympathetic to their cause.

Henry, however, had sent Sir Edward Poynings, one of his most experienced soldiers to Ireland, as Deputy Governor, so that when Warbeck sailed into Waterford harbour, with a fleet of eleven ships, he met with such fierce resistance that, after an attempted siege, he gave up and sailed for Scotland across the Irish Sea.

Warbeck reached Scotland in November and made his way to find King James, who, believing that he could manipulate him against King Henry, welcomed him with open arms.

The royal silver plate was brought to Stirling where, on 20 November, Warbeck arrived to be received by James as the prince whom he claimed to be. Shortly afterwards the king summoned the Great Council to win the support of its members to an attempt to invade England in the name of the supposed Duke of York.

---

[10] Ibid.

Meanwhile the Scottish king was discovering, that in Warbeck, he had found a kindred spirit, a man who shared his passion for falconry and who loved red wine, pretty ladies and good company as much as he did himself. Such was his liking of Perkin that within two months, he had arranged his marriage to his own distant cousin, the beautiful Lady Katherine Gordon, daughter of the Earl of Huntly.

The wedding was followed by a tournament, for which James dressed the bridegroom in purple damask over his armour. Taking part himself, the king was wounded in the hand. Then, not content with paying all the expenses of his army, a rag tag assembly of ruffians said to number one thousand four hundred in all, he gave Perkin a pension of one thousand three hundred and forty four pounds a year. Following this, in May 1496, he sent a summons to the men of the north of Scotland and the Isles to assemble in arms at the Border town of Lauder with the aim of invading England. But he then postponed the attack.

The reason for this, it would seem, was that James himself had fallen in love with Margaret, eldest daughter of John Lord Drummond, of Drummond Castle in Perthshire, near the little town of Crieff. [11]

In the words of a contemporary poet, anonymous by name,
'Joy was within and joy without
Under the unlenkest waw,
Quhair Tay ran down with stremis stout
Full srecht under Stobshaw.
To creatur that was in cair
Or cauld of crewelty,
A blicht blenk of her visage bair
Of baill his bute micht be…
The blosummes tha wer blicht and brycht
By her were blacht and blew

---

[11] C.T.S. =*Compota Thesoriorum Scotorum*, Accounts of the Lord High Treasurer of Scotland.. Vol.1. p.269.

Scho gladit all the foull of flicht
That in the forrest flew;
Scho mycht haif comfort king or knyct
That ever in cuntre I knew..."

James installed Margaret Drummond, first in Stirling Castle and then Falkland Palace. In fact she was not his first mistress. Already Margaret Boyd, daughter of the laird of Bonshaw, had borne him a son, Alexander Stewart, who eventually would become the archbishop of St Andrews.

But the king, much as he loved his new mistress, was still determined that he must have a princess for his queen.

James had sent Bishop Robert Blackadder of Glasgow to the court of King Ferdinand and Queen Isabella of Spain where, in 1495, he arrived to ask for a Spanish princess as a bride for Scotland's king. They received him graciously enough, but the hand of their youngest daughter, Catherine of Aragon, was already bespoke, promised to Prince Arthur, King Henry of England's eldest son.

Following the French invasion of Italy in the previous year, Spain had joined Maximilian, the Holy Roman Emperor and the rulers of Venice and Milan in a Holy League against France. But England remained neutral and only with English support could they hope to overcome the common enemy, this being the reason why their one unmarried daughter had been used as a bribe, promised to King Henry's son.

One great stumbling block emerged to confront them in their plan. Henry would never leave England to fight France if Scotland was invading from the north. The Spanish king and queen prevaricated, promising a Spanish princess if not actually giving her a name. At the same time an envoy was sent to the Pope, asking him to make Blackadder a Cardinal, a position of great authority in the church, which he greatly desired.

With him, when he returned to Scotland, came two Spanish ambassadors, with instructions to procure a peace between

Scotland and England, so that King Henry could go to war with France.

The Spaniards failed to convince James of the necessity of maintaining the peace with England, but he sent Blackadder back to their country to insist on the marriage with an infanta and to try to bribe Ferdinand and Isabella with a promise that, in the event of this happening, he would make a permanent peace with England and abandon his protégé, the-so called Duke of York.

Blackadder returned from Spain to say that Ferdinand was still indecisive; no firm agreement had been reached. But with him came a new ambassador, the dashing and charismatic Don Pedro de Ayala, in whom James found a companion much after his own heart.

Yet, despite his assurances to the king and queen of Spain, that he meant to maintain peace with England, and even at the risk of losing King Henry's offer of the hand of his seven year old daughter Princess Margaret, King James decided that the chance to invade England on behalf of the pretended Duke of York was too good to miss. With Perkin he struck a bargain that, in the event of victory, he would not only return the town of Berwick – taken by Richard II, when as Duke of York, he had commanded the English army in 1482 – to the Scots, but provide the Scottish Council with one hundred thousand marks, a sum which Perkin beat him down to fifty thousand, payable in two years.

On 14 September, while the king and Perkin knelt side by side before the high altar at Holyrood, the great guns, dragged down from Edinburgh Castle, were pulled by teams of oxen through the town of Haddington and on over the Lammermuirs to the assembly point at Ellem.[12] With them went a host of labourers carrying spades, picks and mattocks for use in the

---

[12] C.T.S. Vol 1. pp.296-9.

forthcoming campaign. Then on the 20th, James together with Perkin and Ayala, crossed the Tweed into England.

The Scottish soldiers soon began raiding, rounding up herds of cattle and sheep, fattened by the summer grass, from the valley of the Till, to the great distress of Perkin, who implored the king not to do any more harm to 'his own English' people. James retorted by saying that none of these so-called subjects seemed ready to raise a finger on his behalf and Perkin, much offended, returned to Scotland on 21st September.

De Ayala remained as James laid siege to Heton Castle, near Cornhill. The Spanish ambassador, watching, noted his skill and failings as commander, particularly his exuberance when pitching in to a fight.

''He is courageous, even more than a king should be,' he wrote afterwards. 'I have seen him often undertake most dangerous things in the last wars'. But then he added more ominously, in presentiment of what was to come.

'He is not a good captain, because he begins to fight before he has given his orders. He said to me that his subjects serve him with their persons and goods, in just and unjust quarrels, exactly as he likes, and that therefore he does not think it right to begin any warlike undertaking without being himself the first in danger.'[13]

On 24th September the castle was mined, raising it almost to the ground, but the king, warned that an English army was approaching from Newcastle, left the battlefield in darkness and returned across the Border into his own land.

Back in Edinburgh he still planned to continue the war, but by now he had seen through Perkin, no longer believing him to be the Duke of York, but the imposter he is known to have been. In October he provided a ship to take his followers, whose upkeep was proving ruinous, to take them back to Europe or anywhere clear of Scotland's shores. Perkin himself

---

[13] Cal. *Of State Papers*, Spain, vol.1 No 210.

lingered on, James still paying his pension until, in the summer, the king, losing his patience, hired a ship, aptly named the Cuckoo, in which, together with his lovely wife, Perkin sailed again for Ireland, from the Scottish port of Ayr.

CHAPTER 6

King James had broken the truce and King Henry was determined to make him suffer for his breach of trust. When his Parliament met in January 1497, the members present were united in granting the king the then unprecedented amount of money, raised from taxes, of £one hundred and sixty thousand to pursue what Cardinal Morton, the Archbishop of Canterbury and Lord Chancellor of England, described as 'the perfidious Scots.'

Most areas of England were compliant, but the men of Cornwall rose in rebellion against what they considered to be exorbitant demands. The trouble began in the west where a man called Michael Joseph, described as the smith of St Keverne, led a deputation of local men to complain about the unfairness of the taxes. Then a lawyer from Bodmin, called Thomas Flamank, with a great gift for oration, incited people to fury by proclaiming that Henry's war with the Scots was only an excuse 'to pill and poll the people.' To the Cornish tin miners he put the question of why should they, 'who grubbed under the earth' and the small farmers who struggled to exist by scratching the poor soil, be 'grounded to powder for 'a little stir of the Scots soon blown over'?'[14]

Furthermore, having studied old law books, he claimed that it was even illegal for the men of Cornwall to have to pay for the king's war against Scotland. Between them Flamank and Joseph managed to raise a force of no less than fifteen thousand discontented men, with whom they said they were going to march peacefully to London, to demand the resignation of the king's financial advisers, Cardinal John

---

[14] Williams. pp.78-9.

Morton, and the man who had actually found Richard III's crown in the thorn bush and handed it to Lord Stanley to put on Henry's head, Sir Reginald Bray. Claiming that they were coming to rescue the king from his evil advisers, they marched to Taunton, where they killed the local tax collector, before continuing to Wells, in Somerset, where Lord Audley, who had quarrelled with Henry, took command of the army, as it converged upon London, to lay protests before the king.

King Henry arrived in his capital in May 1497 to find people living in terror. He himself guarded Henley Bridge to stop the rebels from crossing the Thames, while ordering Edmund de la Pole, Earl of Suffolk, to defend the village of Staines. Lord Daubeney then stationed his men in St George's Fields, to defend London as the rebel army converged upon the capital from Blackheath.

Despite these precautions, afraid for his family's safety, Henry sent Queen Elizabeth and their children, probably by boat from Westminster, to the stronghold of the Tower of London, to be guarded in the royal lodgings of the White Tower.

Built originally by William the Conqueror, the Tower was used largely for housing political prisoners. It was here, only twelve years before that the two little princes, sons of Edward IV and his wife Elizabeth Woodville (parents of the present queen) had so mysteriously disappeared. It was the younger of the two, Prince Richard, who the king of Scotland and the Duchess of Burgundy amongst others, were now claiming to have escaped and to be living, no longer in Scotland but, as had recently been discovered, in Ireland.

Did Queen Elizabeth, their sister, and her children, their nieces and nephews, think of them as they slept, perhaps even in the same rooms that those boys had occupied where, as two little faces looking from the windows, they had last been seen alive? They can hardly have failed to think about them when there was still so much speculation as to whether there was truth in the rumours of Richard being the young man who, largely on the word of his supposed aunt, the Duchess of Burgundy, was still at large and alive.

It is probable, however, that, under the circumstances, with their father waiting to meet the rebel army converging upon London, that thoughts of the fate of those two young princes, claimed at the time of disappearance to have died of natural causes, were driven out of their minds. Not even the roaring of the lions in the menagerie attached to the Tower can have diverted them from the very real threat of danger in which they stood. Prince Arthur, now eleven, was ready to draw his sword to defend his mother while Margaret, aged eight and her younger siblings Henry and little Mary, must have realized from the anxiety of their mother and her servants, constantly watching from the windows and hastening to the door to get news from guards and messengers as they heard feet running up the stairs, that they had reason for fear.

Soon they were to be told, that the Lord Mayor had called out the craft guilds to defend London Bridge and that a fierce fight was taking place between the Cornish bowmen and the king's forces led by Giles, Lord Daubeney. They waited, all now peering down at the river from the overlooking windows, to see if the people on boats and barges going up and down gave any clue as to what was happening, before a man sent by their father, came running to tell them that the state of emergency was over. The Cornishmen and their allies had all ceded defeat.

Henry joined his family in the White Tower, from where he visited the three rebel leaders in their cells. All were summarily executed, although Henry spared the lives of the rank and file of the insurgents, provided they returned home, where they would be fined before receiving a pardon.

In July the king, his coffers now enriched, sent Richard Fox, the bishop of Durham and William Warham, Bishop of London, to King James in Scotland to negotiate the surrender of Perkin Warbeck. But, by the time they arrived, the cuckoo had sailed – the bird had flown.

Perkin had in fact reached Cork in Ireland, only to be chased out again and pursued by five ships from Waterford. He had only just managed to escape. Subsequently, on 7 September, he landed near Lands End in Cornwall, at Whitesand Bay.

Henry, aware of his movements, was ready for him. Daubeney was sent west to command the levies, raised by the Duke of Buckingham in Gloucestershire, who were joined by men from all of the counties of south-west England. The Earl of Devon was to hold Exeter, while Henry himself mustered his main army at Woodstock, near Oxford.

Perkin, who had left Katherine Gordon, his Scottish wife and their son at St Michael's Mount, marched on to Bodmin where he had himself proclaimed as Richard IV. With three thousand men he attacked Exeter but, after hard fighting, they were driven from the town. Next they made for Taunton where Perkin, to his horror, heard that Daubeney with his army was only twenty miles away. Losing his nerve he fled to Beaulieu Abbey, hoping to find a ship in Southampton Water in which he could escape. But the whole coast was closely guarded and realizing his position to be hopeless, he threw himself on the king's mercy and surrendered.

Perkin, together with his wife and child, was taken under close guard to London where, in front of the Parliament, he made a full confession. Thanks to his foreign birth, he was found not guilty of high treason and Henry, having pardoned him, allowed him to live at court. His wife, the lovely Lady Catherine, reverting to her maiden name, together with her little son, were lodged in the queen's household.

It is easy to imagine how eagerly Queen Elizabeth waited to meet Perkin Warbeck, in the hope, the very faint hope, to which since his emergence from Flanders she had always clung, that he might be her little brother, taken away seventeen years ago, from the crypt at Westminster Abbey, where with their mother they had been living in sanctuary, to join his brother Edward in the Tower. But, although similar in feature, she knew that it was not the boy, whose fate she would now never know.

Perkin certainly did resemble Prince Richard, at least to some extent in looks. It is thought that in fact he may have been an illegitimate son of Edward IV, which, had this been the case, he would have been a half-brother of Henry's queen. But Perkin was never acknowledged. Dissatisfied he escaped from Westminster Palace to hide in the Priory at Sheen. But found there, he was taken back to London, this time, to be held in the Tower.

There he discovered a fellow prisoner, with whom he made contact to the extent of his becoming a friend. This was Edward, the Earl of Warwick, who, as the son of Edward IV's deceased brother, the Duke of Clarence, was considered a danger to King Henry being heir to the House of York. Together he and Perkin and some other Yorkist prisoners, in what seems to have been a foolhardy scheme, tried to escape. Captured, both he and the simple-minded young Warwick, who had spent nearly all his life a prisoner, were executed.

For Katherine Gordon it all ended more happily, for she married not once, but twice, some say four times again. Henry VII looked after her, giving her clothing including, in November 1501, 'clothes of cloth of gold, furred with ermine, a purple velvet gown, and a black hood in the French style.' [15] An admirer wrote of her as 'the brightest ornament in Scotland' and Henry VIII, while a young man, 'still marvelled at her beauty and amiable countenance and sent her to London to the Queen.'[16]

---

[15] *A Calendar of Documents relating to Scotland,* 1357-1509, ed. Joseph Bain, Vol.4 (Edinburgh H.M. Register House,1888), nos.1677.1685,1688, (and in Latin pp.419-421, no.36)

[16] Wikipedia, the free encyclopedia.

CHAPTER 7

SCOTLAND 1498
'THE EARS OF THE WOLF'

At the beginning of 1498 James ratified the treaty for a peace to endure, both for his own lifetime and that of Henry and afterwards for a year. Hardly was the ink dry on the paper, however, before a party of Scottish raiders were driven off, with some loss of life, by the English garrison of Norham Castle in Northumberland, one of the garrisons placed strategically to guard the Borders, standing high above the River Tweed.

Told of it, James swore that 'by sweet Ninian' he found nothing on earth more uncertain than a peace with England.

Once, not long before, this would have been enough to go to war but James was warned by de Ayala that 'he had seen the ears of the wolf.' Pacified, he sent the Marchmont Herald to England with letters demanding redress. If this was not granted he would consider the treaty null and void.

Henry replied with conciliatory words, promising that the men of the garrison would be punished. This did not satisfy James. But Henry did not want war. Instead, in November, he sent Bishop Richard Fox, in whose diocese lay Norham, to meet James in the great Abbey of Melrose.

James was by now aware, as were most others in his kingdom, that only three lives lay between the Princess Margaret and the English throne. By marrying her it was not inconceivable that he might become king of England himself.

With that enticing prospect in view he allowed de Ayala to go as his ambassador to England to Henry's court.

The Spaniard was more than willing to do so. King Ferdinand and Queen Isabella were still urging him to try to effect the peace between England and Scotland that they so urgently desired. Their enemy Charles VIII, the king of France had died and his successor, Louis XII, had not yet sent an envoy to Scotland to try to renew the 'Aulde Alliance'. Therefore this was the moment to act.

So, in the Abbey of Melrose, where men still worked on the rebuilding after the destruction by fire of an army of Richard II over a hundred years before, King James conferred with Bishop Fox, to whom he explained that he would be willing to sign a treaty of perpetual peace with England were Henry to grant him the hand in marriage of his eldest daughter Princess Margaret. Fox hastened back to London with the news which, according to Polydore Vergil, (recently arrived in England as an agent of Cardinal Castellesi) 'delighted King Henry in a wonderful degree, for there was nothing dearer to him than peace.'[17]

Henry, always careful with money, hated war for what it would cost. Nonetheless he prevaricated, unwilling to commit himself entirely to an agreement which distressed both his wife, Queen Elizabeth and his over-riding mother, Lady Margaret, who, in view of her own experience, demurred largely on the count of Margaret's age, she being only nine and therefore sixteen years younger than the Scottish king. Moreover, word had already filtered down through ambassadors and others frequenting Scotland, that the king had the reputation of a womaniser, known to have kept several mistresses.

It was perhaps just as well that they were unaware that King James had in fact a new paramour, in the form of Lady Janet Kennedy, who he seduced from her former lover Archibald, 5th Earl of Angus, more famously known for his hanging of James II's favourite Robert Cochrane, over the Bridge of Lauder, as 'Bell the Cat.' Little could anyone, far less King James, have guessed that this was an insult to the powerful family of Douglas that would result in avengement, against not only himself, but the English princess, his future wife.

---

[17] Polydore Vergil, *Historia Anglia*, vol.11. p.1539.

CHAPTER 8

THE SPANISH BRIDE

Bishop Fox had already been involved in procuring a royal bride. In March 1488, while still bishop of Winchester, he and Giles Daubeney, recently made a Knight of the Garter, were sent by Henry VII to negotiate a treaty with King Ferdinand and Queen Isabella of Spain, which would include the marriage of his then infant son Arthur, the Prince of Wales, to Princess Catherine of Aragon, youngest of their five children.

In the following year the arrangement was confirmed by the Treaty of Medina del Campo, signed near Valadolid. There was, however, much argument over the princess's dowry. Henry, parsimonious as usual, demanded two hundred thousand crowns, as well as much jewellery, while Ferdinand protested that he had four daughters, and if all their prospective husbands were so avaricious, it would be better if they remained unwed. Equivocation continued. Henry was afraid that Catherine would marry King James of Scotland, known to be seeking her hand, and Ferdinand that Prince Arthur would marry a Habsburg princess. Despite their mutual distrust however, in October 1496, a new marriage treaty was signed and ratified during the following year.

Behind it was the influence of the Spanish ambassador to England Dr Rodrigo de Puebla, who with Don Pedro de Ayala, the ambassador he had advised Ferdinand to send so successfully to James IV, had helped to enforce the truce between England and Scotland. A formal betrothal was made at Henry's palace at Woodstock, after which a marriage by proxy took place in London in the summer of 1498 with de Puebla representing the bride, Henry then declaring 'by his royal faith that he and the Queen were more satisfied with this marriage than with any other in Christendom.'

Arthur then had to go through a second ceremony on WhitSunday 1499, in the chapel of the royal manor of Bewdley where de Puebla, described as a deformed old man, again represented the young Spanish princess. Arthur took his arm saying clearly that he rejoiced at the contract, in obedience to the Pope and to his father, and also for 'his deep and sincere love for the Princess, his wife.' De Ayala, who came down from Scotland, recognised Henry's impatience for the Spanish princess's arrival for this raised the King's own status. 'He likes to be spoken much of and to be highly appreciated by the whole world' he wrote, adding that 'Prince Arthur was much loved by the people.'[18]

As for Catherine, when, after crossing the Bay of Biscay in a storm, she arrived at Plymouth at the beginning of 1501, she was met with rapturous joy, one of her train reporting that 'she could not have been received with great rejoicings if she had been the saviour of the world.'[19] Escorted by a party of local squires and nobles and by Don Pedro de Ayala, she rode eastward in easy stages, stopping at Exeter, where the bells that had rung for Perkin Warbeck, now peeled out joyfully for her. At Amesbury she was welcomed by Thomas Howard, Earl of Surrey, the Lord High Treasurer, and from there she set out on the next stage of her journey towards Basingstoke where, waiting to receive her, was the bishop of Bath.

But by then, unknown to her, King Henry with Prince Arthur and a bevy of the most important people in the country, were riding from Richmond to meet her. Told of his coming, Catherine's chief attendants, the archbishop of Santiago and Dona Elvira Manuel were horrified. It was contrary to Spanish etiquette for the bridegroom or his father to set eyes on the princess before the wedding service. De Ayala was sent off to tell them so. But Henry, jumping off his horse, with Arthur behind him, entered her dressing room and to his great delight

[18] Williams.pp.88-9
[19] Ibid. pp.90-1

and surprise saw her face unveiled. The portrait of Catherine, painted at the time of her wedding, shows her as the very pretty, sweet faced young woman, fair-skinned and with her brown hair tucked into a snood, looking down demurely as the artist caught the likeness, which proves her to have been as beautiful as was claimed. Arthur was delighted, telling all those around him that 'he had never felt so much joy as when he first saw her sweet face.' Progressing on to London they were married on 14 November 1501, in St Paul's Cathedral where Prince Henry, now aged ten but of a stronger build than his brother, gave Catherine his hand as she walked down the aisle to the altar steps. It was afterwards, following the wedding banquet, that he and his eleven year old sister Margaret so delighted all those who applauded them dancing together, the two red gold heads so alike, as they twisted and turned in performing the sequence of complicated steps.

Watching them, on that day of great celebration, most of the wedding guests knew that Margaret, whose twelfth birthday was to fall at the end of the month, would herself be a bride before long. It was now well known to most of them that the Scottish ambassadors, who were amongst them on this most auspicious of occasions, had come, not only to offer the congratulations of their king, but to arrange what he hoped would be his own marriage to the eldest of Arthur's sisters who danced so merrily on that day.

It had been just over a month before the wedding, on 8 October, that King James of Scotland had sent the much travelled Robert Blackadder, Archbishop of Glasgow, together with Andrew Forman, the bishop of Moray and the Earl of Bothwell to King Henry to organize both the perpetual peace treaty and his marriage to the Princess Margaret. The Scottish ambassadors, with a train of a hundred horsemen, had ridden into London to join in the celebrations following Prince Arthur's wedding to his spanish Princess. Much as they enjoyed the entertainment, they had to come down to serious business when, on 28 November, King Henry commissioned Thomas Howard, Earl of Surrey, son of the Duke of Norfolk, and Robert Fox, now the bishop of Winchester, to confer with them over the arrangements for the marriage of the king of Scotland to the Princess Margaret.

With them was William Dunbar, known for his poetry, as 'the Rhymer of Scotland,' who, overcome by the pageantry and wealth, which he found in London, called it 'the floure of Cities all'. Rising to his feet at a banquet, he proclaimed a poem in the city's praise, for which King Henry duly flattered, gave him £13.6.8.

The celebrations, the jousting, the feasting and the masques which followed the wedding of Prince Arthur to his Spanish bride, lasted for a month during which time, Margaret enjoyed herself enormously, loving any form of entertainment, as she is known to have done.

Her father, King Henry, wrote to Catherine's parents, Ferdinand and Isabella, that 'great and cordial rejoicings have taken place.' He was putting it mildly. Such celebrations in the whole of Europe had seldom before been seen.

For the first time, a tree of chivalry, on which the challengers hung their shields, was erected in the lists in front of Westminster Hall. Then, as a procession of knights and their servants entered, spectators cried out in amazement as Lord William Courtenay came in concealed as a dragon escorted by a giant. The Earl of Essex appeared in a car resembling a green mountain and spectators held their ears as others followed in a float like a ship with sailors firing cannon.

This was just the beginning. There were banquets and music and dancing and pageants in the hall transformed by Master William Cornish, a gentleman of the Chapel Royal, into fairyland. One masque consisted of twelve lords, hidden in an arbor, while the twelve ladies with whom they would dance, entered in a transparent lantern. Another had a tower pulled into the hall by seahorses escorted by mermaids, all of them sweetly singing, while a third, more elaborate than the others, consisted of three scenes in a castle occupied by ladies, to which a ship arrived carrying knights errant, who reached the castle across a ladder after which they all climbed down to dance together.

Such were the rejoicings for Arthur's wedding which Margaret, although saddened by the thought that this, her favourite of brothers, would soon be leaving their parent's court to found one of his own, so greatly enjoyed.

Together they had shared so many childhood adventures laughing surreptitiously at the piety of their grandmother, 'Margaret the King's mother', who was always reproving them for running headlong along the corridors of the palaces, for talking too loudly and above all, for not studying the Latin texts and prayers they were forced to learn with the devotion that she herself showed.

Thus it was with mixed feelings of pride in her handsome brother, now a man at sixteen years old and a personal sense of loss, that Margaret said goodbye to him and his new demure Spanish wife with her halting, often confused words of English, before they both rode away to live in Ludlow Castle in Shropshire, on the outskirts of Wales, from where Arthur, as Prince of Wales, would govern the principality in their father's name.

On 14 January 1502, the details of the treaty were finally concluded. Margaret, at her father's expense, was to be conducted to Lamberton Kirk, on, or before 1 September 1503, and her marriage would take place within the next fifteen days. As a wedding gift from her husband, she would receive lands and castles in Scotland with a rental of £two thousand sterling, amounting to £six thousand Scots. With her to Scotland would go, no less than twenty-four English attendants. King James would maintain her, at his own expense, in the state befitting the wife of a king and the Princess Royal of England, and in addition would give her an allowance of £one thousand Scots every year. Her father would give her a dowry of ten thousand angel nobles, amounting to about £ten thousand sterling or £thirty thousand Scots, in three yearly instalments, unless, that in the event of her dying childless, before three years had gone by, he was to keep the unexpended balance of the money.

Thus the terms were settled of the marriage of the king of England's daughter to the king of Scotland, to be immortalised by William Dunbar, ecstatic over its happening, in his poem 'The Thistle and the Rose.'

Written in the form of an elegy, the poem presented as a dream, celebrates the marriage of James, depicted as the thistle which had appeared on Scottish coins since the reign of his grandfather James III, and the rose, coloured red and white, representing the joining of the Lancastrian and Yorkist factions of the Plantagenet dynasty, as represented by Henry VII's marriage to Margaret's mother Elizabeth of York.

It begins, rather charmingly with a description of spring, recognisable in the present day.

'Quhen Merche wes with variand windis past
And Appryll had with hir silver schouris
Tane lief at Nature with ane orient blast,
And lusty May, that muddir is of flouris,
Had maid the birdis to begyn their houris,
Amang the tendir odouris reid and quhyt,
Quhois armony to heir I was delyt.

The sleeping poet dreams that he is visited by May.

'Me thocht fresche May befoir my bed upstude'

'Slugbird' schoe said,'Awalk annone, for schame'

May then leaves him to enter a beautiful garden to which the poet follows her to find Dame Nature holding court to a company of mythical creatures, the lion amongst them, 'Reid of his collour as is the ruby glance…saying

'the King of beistis mak I thee,
And the chief protector in the woddis and schawis,
Onto thi leigis go furth, and keep the lawis.'

The lion of course is the king of Scots, whom all the other beasts proclaim.

'All kind of beistis into their degre´
At onis cryit lawd. Vive le roy!
And till his feit fell with humilite,
And all thay maid him homage and fewte.'

Dame Nature then crowns the eagle as the King of the birds before, turning to the plants,

'Upone the awful thrissill scho beheld
And saw him kepit with a busche of speiris.
Concedring him so able for the weiris,
A radius croun of rubeis scho him gaif.'

She tells the thistle to go into the field to defend the smaller plants, implying James's determination to protect his kingdom. She then advises him, obliquely to abandon his mistresses 'And sen how art a king, thow be discreit...'

'And lat no nettill vyle and full of vyce
Hir fallow to the gudly flour defyce.'

Dame Nature then speaks to the rose, and after praising her beauty asks her to come forward and be crowned, on the 9th of May. Then the birds all join in a chorus of praise.

'Then all the birdis song with sic a schout,
That I annone awoilk quhair that I lay,
And with a braid I turnyt me about,
To se this court, but all wer went away.
Than up I lenyt, halflingis in affrey,
And thuss I wret, as ye haif hard to forrow,
Of lusty May upone the nynt morrow.'

Yet despite the general rejoicing not everyone was happy.[20] Margaret's brother, Prince Henry, two years younger than herself, probably influenced by his tutor, a man named Skelton, who openly detested the Scots, when told to

---

[20] Strickland, Agnes, Lives of the Queens of Scotland and English Princesses, vol 1. P.9

congratulate his sister, flew into a violent rage. The ambassadors, de Ayala amongst them, drew back in both astonishment and fear, as the red-headed boy rolled on the floor in fury and then was convulsed with which one of them, Cardinal Cajetan, described as several fits of ague brought on by 'excessive displeasure of the prince at his sister Margaret's betrothal to James IV.'

CHAPTER 9

WESTMINSTER 1503.

The Spanish ambassador Pedro de Ayala, possibly bored with
Scotland, persuaded James to send him to London to treat with
King Henry. His was the influence behind the marriage of the
Princess Margaret to the king of Scots. He must have been
satisfied to see the results of his diplomacy enacted when, on
25 January 1502, in the newly refurbished palace of
Richmond, the Princess Margaret, before her parents, King
Henry VII and Queen Elizabeth and a congress of churchmen
and nobles, 'wittandly and of deliberate mind, having twelve
Yeares compleat in Age', made a solemn promise to take the
king of Scots for her husband while the Earl of Bothwell,
speaking as procurator, took her as wife and spouse for his
sovereign, and vowed that he would forsake all other for her
during his natural life.

'That don, the Trompeters standing on the leds at the
Chamber End, blew upp, and the lowd Noise of Minstrells
played, in the best and most joyfullest manner.'[21]

At the same time the marriage was announced by a
clergyman at St Paul's Cross and a *Te Deum* sung in the
cathedral. Then in the early darkness of the January night
bonfires blazed throughout the city and beside twelve of the
biggest of them hogsheads of Gascon were set, the which wyne
was not long in drinynking'.[22]

As the whole city rejoiced, no one was happier than King
Henry, hating war for its cost in both lives and money as he

---

[21] *Narrative of John Young, Somerset Herald,* in Leland,
Collectanea, vol . 1V. pp 528-62. See also Mackie R..L. *King James
IV of Scotland*, p.97.

[22] Kingsford, Chronicles of London, p.255.

did, that now the ever present threat of invasion from Scotland had finally disappeared. Content with what had been arranged, even though it meant the inevitable unhappy parting from his favourite child, he was not to know, in this moment of triumph, any more than could those of his subjects, so happily drinking and dancing around the bonfires, at the tragedy that loomed ahead.

In February, one of the coldest months of that year, there was an epidemic in Ludlow of influenza, or as some claim the dreaded sweating fever, which could kill within hours. Catherine caught it and was ill for some time, but then Arthur succumbed to it, probably catching it from her, and on 2 April, apparently from a lung infection, which could have been tuberculosis, he died.

Arthur had been just sixteen, smaller in height than most of his family, but noted for his looks and his charm. The four months of his marriage had been happy ones. Catherine was devastated by his death.

His parents as well as his siblings, his sisters Margaret and Mary and his surviving brother Henry, were all overcome by grief. Arthur had always seemed so strong, so robust in health with his red hair and vibrant energy, that it was almost inconceivable that he had so suddenly died. Inevitably there were rumours of poison but, while today antibiotics would almost certainly have saved him, it would seem that he succumbed to a lung infection worsened by the cold and damp of the castle in which he had been sent to live.

A courier rode fast to London, taking the dreadful news which was broken to Henry by his confessor. Hardly able to comprehend what had happened, he sent for his wife, Queen Elizabeth and told her that they 'would take the painful sorrow together' for now, devastated by the loss of the eldest son on whom he had set such score, he depended on her love and support. If, as her Spanish relations claimed, the coming of

Catherine had been hastened by Edward Warwick's execution, the tragic end of her marriage was seen as a form of retribution.

For Margaret, the favourite sister to whom he had been so close, his fondness for her was demonstrated by his will, made either before or during that last illness, in which, as he lay gasping, his strength failing, he guessed at the approach of death. To, it would seem her great surprise and as it would prove to the subsequent annoyance of Henry, her surviving brother, it was found that Arthur had left most of his possessions of value, including both gold and valuable jewels, to Margaret.

In Scotland, however, a different attitude prevailed. There were many who now realized that the loss of his eldest son to King Henry meant that their own king, pledged as he was to marry Henry's eldest daughter, was one step nearer to his throne.

In Richmond Palace the number of people in the household increased with the return, from Ludlow Castle of Arthur's now widowed Spanish queen. Catherine came back from Shropshire with the ladies, all of them hardly speaking English, who had come with her from Spain, as well as the high born English women, chosen by Henry to be part of her entourage.

Catherine had lost her own adored brother, the Infante Juan, who like herself had been married for only a few months to Margaret of Austria, the eldest daughter of the Emperor Maximillian, before, he too had died very suddenly of a fever such as had killed Arthur, although, in his case, after a lingering illness, over a greater length of time. Now in this time of mourning, the intensity of their grief made a bond between Catherine and Margaret to whom Arthur had been, not only dearest brother, but also beloved friend. That an attachment developed between them seems proved by the kindness, and the gifts given to Margaret, by Catherine in the years to come.

The similarity of their circumstances was another common factor between the two princesses, in addition to the sadness which they shared. Margaret would shortly be leaving her childhood home to go to a strange country, to marry a man she had never met, just as, so recently, Catherine had done. Catherine must have advised her, to some extent what to expect, both in the kingdom to which she was going, a wild place so it was said, and perhaps more intimately when she got there, in the marriage bed.

CHAPTER 10

SCOTLAND 1501

It was two years before this, when, on an early summer morning of the year 1501, a lone horseman had ridden up the wide strath of the River Earn. Dawn was just breaking, foxes and other predators, still on their stealthy prowl. Deer, grazing on the new grass by the river, raised their heads to watch as the man and the horse went by. Had they been humans they would have wondered, why, on this rainless morning, the rider was so heavily cloaked. Only he knew, that below his enveloping plaid, was, not only a sword and a dagger, but a packet strapped to his side.

The man rode on as the sun began to rise until before him, on the crest of a ridge above the valley, he saw what he knew to be Drummond Castle, the place he had been given such clear directions to find.

Still following those instructions, he dismounted and hobbled his horse, before, hidden behind trees, leaving it to graze. Then he walked quietly round the back of the square tower of the castle to unstrap the packet, held in a leather pouch round his waist, and to hand it to the man waiting to receive it without saying a word.

It is largely due to Pedro de Ayala that we believe that King James was actually already married at the time of his betrothal to Princess Margaret. The Spanish ambassador to Scotland wrote that:

'When I arrived, he was keeping a lady with great state in a castle. He visited her from time to time. Afterwards he sent her to the house of her father, who is a knight, and married her. He did the same with another lady by whom he had a son.'[23]

King James had several mistresses. The first known, Mariot Boyd, daughter of the laird of Bonshaw, as already mentioned, certainly bore him the son, Alexander Stewart, who was later to become the archbishop of St Andrews.

The lady mentioned by de Ayala, however, was presumably Janet Kennedy, daughter of Lord Kennedy and Lady Elizabeth Gordon, a daughter of the Earl of Huntly. Having enticed her away from Archibald, Earl of Angus, famously dubbed 'Bell the Cat', by whom she had had a daughter, James eventually installed her in Darnaway Castle in Morayshire on condition that she remained unmarried. [24]Some accounts say they had no less than three children, but it is known that the king later created their son, James Stewart, the Earl of Moray.

Most famous of all his mistresses, however, and the one whom he really loved, was Margaret Drummond. The eldest of five daughters of the first Lord Drummond, she was evidently renowned for her beauty. De Ayala may not have been referring to her, as she is known to have had not a son, but a daughter with the king, who is certainly believed to have secretly married her sometime before 1501. However, the fact of their being distantly related, due to common descent from Annabella Drummond, wife of King James I of Scotland, meant that to legalise the marriage, dispensation must be obtained from the Pope.

Travel, in those times, invariably being slow, the Pope's permission had not arrived when de Ayala went to England, as one of the ambassadors, to arrange the betrothal of King James to the daughter of Henry VII.

---

[23] Calendar of State Papers, Spain, Vol1. (1862) no.210

[24] Accounts of the Lord High Treasurer of Scotland , vol.2 (1900) xxxiii.297.

There were many in Scotland determined that the much vaunted union with England should take place. Amongst them was Archibald Earl of Angus, no doubt with his own axe to grind, and who, as the head of the great house of Douglas, omnipotent in the south of Scotland and elsewhere, was regarded as the leader of what was commonly thought of as 'the English Party in Scotland' as opposed to that of the French.

It is known that many people of influence in Scotland feared that because of his infatuation with Margaret Drummond, the king did not mean to marry the Princess Margaret as was being arranged. Mystery, however, surrounds the identity of the man, or men, who decided that, in view of the importance of the alliance with England, Margaret Drummond must die.

But die she did, together with two of her sisters, Euphemia and Sibylla, of poison (probably arsenic which is tasteless) administered in meat eaten for breakfast, or as others say, in sugared fruit. Alternately the fatal substance may have been put into the communion wine, which the sisters drank at mass. All three lie buried before the altar in the choir of Dunblane Cathedral below stones of unmarked blue granite marking the position of their graves.

Naturally, at the time, there was much speculation as to who had killed, not only the king's great love Margaret Drummond, but two of her four innocent sisters. Suspicion immediately fell on the Kennedys, obviously angered by James's repudiation of Janet for his new love. But years later, James's own wife, by then his widowed queen, was to accuse Lord Fleming, who she believed had considered his wife Euphemia expendable in the saving of his country, from losing an alliance with England dependant on King James's marriage to that country's young princess.

Because of the frail health of her mother, Queen Elizabeth, Margaret's wedding did not take place in the splendour of Westminster Abbey, but in her mother's own apartments in Richmond Palace. Now in the last month of her seventh pregnancy, Queen Elizabeth hoped fervently for a son to replace her beloved Arthur for whom, eight months after his death, she still so deeply grieved.

It was John Young, the Somerset Herald, who left a first-hand description of the details of the ceremony that took place.

'At the King's royal manor of Richmond, on St Paul's Day, January 24, 1502-3, were performed the fiancels of the right high and mighty Prince James IV, King of Scots, and Margaret, eldest daughter of our sovereign lord Henry VII, King of England and France, and Lord of Ireland, as ensueth – The King and Queen, and all their noble children, having heard mass, and a notable sermon preached by Richard Fitzjames, Bishop of Chichester, the Queen, after service, received the whole illustrious company in her great chamber. She was attended by her daughter the Princess Margaret, and by the little Lady Mary, her youngest child; likewise by her own sister, the Lady Katherine of Devonshire, and most of the great ladies of the court.'

Young's sharp eyes at once espied the beautiful Lady Katherine Gordon (now returned to her maiden name) who he called the widow of Perkin Warbeck, amongst the courtiers, describing how 'on account of her nearness of kin both to Kings of England and Scotland, she took rank next to the royal family, although Lady Bray, wife of the chief minister was present.'

Young also noticed how even Prince Henry behaved with perfect decorum, apparently reconciled to the marriage of his sister to the Scottish monarch whom he held in such disdain.

'Then was introduced Patrick Hepburn, the Earl of Bothwell', Young continues, 'who acted as proxy for the King of Scotland his sovereign; and the other procurators for the marriage being the Archbishop of Glasgow and the elect Bishop of Moray.'

Then the Earl of Surrey stood forth, and with very good manner right seriously declared the cause of that fair assembly being met together.'

This is the first mention of the man who was to play such a large part in the lives of both Margaret and her future husband King James. Now a veteran of sixty, and greatly renowned as a soldier, Thomas Howard, only son of the 1st Duke of Norfolk, had begun life as a henchman of Edward IV, being severely wounded fighting for him against the Earl of Warwick (backing Henry VII for the throne) in the battle of Barnet in 1471. When Edward died in 1483, Howard had supported Richard III, bearing the sword of state at his coronation. Granted land by the king, he had been made Earl of Surrey, his father becoming Duke of Norfolk at the same time. Together they had suppressed the rebellion of King Richard's erstwhile favourite, the Duke of Buckingham and had fought for Richard at the Battle of Bosworth, in which the Duke of Norfolk had been killed and Surrey wounded and taken prisoner to languish in the Tower of London for the next three years. Then, after proving his loyalty, by refusing a chance to escape, Henry VII had restored him to his earldom and most of his lands. Sent to subdue a rising in Yorkshire, Surrey had subsequently become Lieutenant of the North, proving his competency to the point where, two years before Margaret's wedding, in 1501, her father had made him Lord High Treasurer and a member of the Council before involving him in the negotiations of Prince Arthur's marriage to Catherine of Aragon. Now, as King Henry's most trusted servitor, Surrey was to take charge of his daughter Margaret on her journey to be married to King James. Little could anyone have guessed at that point how much he was to become involved in the catastrophic future of that Scottish king.

The Pope's dispensation read out, Robert Blackadder, the archbishop of Glasgow, demanded both of King Henry and Queen Elizabeth as to whether they knew of any impediment regarding the marriage of their daughter to King James. On receiving an answer to the negative, the bishop asked the same question of Margaret who again gave a satisfactory reply.

King Henry, for his part, plainly informed of the rumours regarding James's past mistresses, then very pointedly asked the same question of Bishop Blackadder, reminding the august clergyman that James had at one time been plighted to Margaret's aunt, the Princess Cecilia and informally to her cousin Ann, daughter of the Duke of Suffolk.

On the archbishop swearing, in knowledge of the death of Margaret Drummond, that the king was free to wed, he then asked the Princess Margaret whether she was 'content and of her own free will, and without compulsion, to wed his master.'

Margaret, speaking with her young clear voice, replied 'If it please my lord and father the King, and my lady mother the Queen, I am content.'

Kneeling, she received the blessing of both parents, after which the archbishop proceeded to read out the words of the betrothal, first to the Earl of Bothwell, who replied on behalf of his sovereign, and then to the Princess Margaret, who, turning towards Bothwell, answering very clearly on her own behalf, concluded with the promise:

'I take the said James, King of Scotland, unto, and for my husband and spouse, and all other for him forsake during his and mine lives natural; and thereto I plight and give to him in your person, as procurator aforesaid, my faith and troth.' [25]

With that the royal trumpeters 'blew up their most inspiring notes and a loud noise of minstrels answered in their best and joyful manner.'

---

[25] Strickland, Agnes, *Lives of the Queens of Scotland*, Vol.1. p.13.

Elizabeth of York, taking her daughter by the hand, then led her to the banquet set out in her private rooms to place her at a table as if she had been a queen.

The king adjourned to his own rooms to entertain the Earl of Bothwell and Bishop Blackadder before, in the afternoon there was jousting amongst the nobles, the Duke of Buckingham, Lord William of Devonshire and Lord Brandon amongst them, who 'distinguished themselves remarkably by the spears they brake, and the right goodly gambades they made.'

The following morning, after the king and queen had breakfasted, the young Queen of Scotland came into her mother's great chamber where she thanked all the men who had taken part in the jousts held in her honour. Particularly she mentioned a visiting French knight called Rayne de Shezelle, and Charles Brandon before finally, turning to a Scottish knight, John Carr, and Lord William of Devonshire, she thanked them best of all.

After Margaret had distributed prizes to all her champions, 'a goodly pageant entered the hall, curiously wrought with fenestralis (windows) having many lights burning in the same... Also a very good disguising of six gentlemen and six gentlewomen, who danced divers dances.'

Then followed a voide or banquet when the Earl of Bothwell gave the gown of cloth of gold he had worn at the betrothal ceremony to the English officers-of-arms.

Another day of jousting followed before, at a supper, King Henry gave cupboards of gold and silver plate, both to Archbishop Blackadder and the Earl of Bothwell, while the Lord Lyon, principal herald of Scotland, received a purse filled with a hundred soleil – crowns and a goodly satin gown.

It was only a few days later, even as the last preparations for Margaret's departure for Scotland were being made, that the joyous time of celebration came suddenly and unexpectedly to a tragic end. Queen Elizabeth, whose health had not been good during her pregnancy, had chosen the royal apartments on the upper floor of the White Tower of the Tower of London, next to the little chapel of St John, for her lying in. Here, in the last week of January, she gave birth, not to the longed for son, but to a daughter who was hastily christened Catherine before she died. Then, just a week later, on 3 February 1503, to the overwhelming grief of her husband and her family, Elizabeth herself died from weakness and complications following the birth.

CHAPTER 11

SCOTLAND 1503

Meanwhile, north of the Border, preparations for Margaret's arrival were going on apace. At Stirling Castle from where, what has been described as 'the King's brood of illegitimate children,' had been removed to other quarters, masons and craftsmen worked day and night on completing the alterations on what the king was determined should be a castle fit for a queen.

Already the wall head of the Forework, the old frontispiece, the innermost of three barriers on the south-east side of the castle had been completed and the Princes' Tower, the rectangular tower at its end had been finished by 1501. In 1503, when Margaret was already travelling north, the chief mason, John Yorkstown, was working on the Kitchen Tower (now the Elphinstone Tower) at the north-east end of the Forework.

At the same time another mason, John Lockhart, was building the central gatehouse above which the portcullis would be installed, before the king arrived with his bride. Work was also going on in the chapel, already erected into a collegiate church some two years before, while on the flat ground below the west side of the castle, the barras, or tilting grounds were being repaired.

But by far the greatest achievement, its significance perhaps unrecognized at the time, was the building of the Great Hall of Stirling Castle. With its soaring hammer-beam roof, constructed from locally felled oak trees, as the largest banqueting hall, at that time seen in Scotland, it rivalled the Great Hall of Westminster. Two high windows lit the dais, on which he and his queen would sit, while five enormous fireplaces heated the whole of the room. James is believed to have built it largely to impress his young bride. But there may have been another reason, even closer to his heart.

This was the dream of the architect, Robert Cochrane, the mason turned architect who the king's father, James III, had raised to power and dearly loved, but had been unable to save when his enemies, headed by Archibald Earl of Angus, had hanged him over the Lauder Bridge. James had no reason to venerate the memory of a man he probably disliked. But for the sake of his father, of whose death he was constantly reminded by the chaffing of the chastity iron belt, he may have wished to try to exonerate some of the guilt lying so heavily on his mind.

CHAPTER 12

ENGLAND 1503

As the thudding of hammers echoed throughout Stirling Castle, the king's bride, for whom it was intended as a palace to rival her father's own, was beginning her journey to Scotland up the great road leading to the north.

On the first part of the way, Margaret was escorted by her father. Riding from Richmond Palace on 16 June, she left the home of her childhood, which, however exciting the future, she must have been sad to leave. Slowly, through the English countryside, in the full glory of mid-summer, they began the long journey, the king riding a beautifully caparisoned horse, with Margaret beside him, sitting side-saddle on one of the two snow white ponies he had given her as a parting present. Behind them came some of the courtiers, well mounted and gaily dressed in honour of their sovereign's daughter, now herself a queen. Still farther back were the wagons, loaded with Margaret's trousseaux of the finest dresses and capes, chosen by her mother shortly before she died.

The roads were dusty with the summer heat, but beside them the meadows were green with new grass on which, at night, the horses could be loosed. Eleven days it took to make the first stage of the journey to Colleweston, in Northamptonshire, where her grandmother and namesake, Margaret, the still formidable 'mother of the king', now lived.

Four years had passed since when, in 1499, with the permission of her fourth husband, the Earl of Derby from whom she was estranged, the countess of Richmond as she still was known, had made a vow of chastity and moved to live without him, first at Woking, where she had shared her house with twelve aged paupers whom she cared for herself when they were ill, and then at Collyweston, the royal manor within its surrounding park, granted to her by her son the king, where she lived in the state accorded to her rank.

Arriving there, on 26 July, her son and granddaughter were welcomed with all the entertainment, which this indefatigable lady could devise. But, inevitably, sadly, the day of departure drew near. On 8 July all those related to the royal family, who were within riding distance of Colleweston, gathered in the great hall of the manor to say goodbye. Finally, kneeling before them, Margaret received the blessing of both her father and the grandmother who had supervised so much of her childhood. Then having risen to her feet she made her last sad farewell. Her father, plainly emotional, after giving her a short lecture on how she should in future behave, gave her the beautifully illustrated book of prayers, on one page of which he had written

'Remember y^r kynde and loving fader in y^r good prayers.'
Henry R.

The silence, respectful and solemn, as all within the great hall recognized the pathos which this parting would entail, was suddenly broken as, with a loud clattering of horses' hoofs, appeared the members of Margaret's escort, the Earl of Surrey at their head, stalwart, grey haired and upright in the saddle for all of his sixty years.

With the bodyguard were several ladies, the countess of Surrey amongst them. A cousin of her husband's first wife, the former Agnes Tilney she was mother of the last seven of the eighteen children he is known to have fathered in all. Now chosen as the chief of Margaret's attendants, the arrangement made with King Henry, was that both she and her husband, on arrival in Scotland, could stay there or return according to the wish of King James, an agreement which, for reason of their family commitments, it seemed they would urge the latter choice.[26]

The sad parting over, Margaret set forth 'riding in a rich riding dress' as described by the Somerset herald, John Young. Before her rode Sir David Owen, also very splendidly dressed, on her left was Bishop Nix of Norwich, and on her right, in the place of honour, Andrew Forman, King James's much travelled bishop of Moray. Three footmen always walked close to whichever of the queen's two ponies she was riding, while 'a gentleman mounted' came behind leading the other one. Also in close attendance was Sir Thomas Wortley, her Master of the Horse.

Margaret, however, did not sit on horseback all of the time. Approaching a town she would dismount to enter a litter, carried from both front and behind by two horses, and with a footman, in the royal liveries of white and green, with the arms of Scotland and England, parted with red roses and crowned portcullises, walking either side, from which she could wave to the crowds pressing forward to see her, without the fear of being crushed. Her ladies, however, followed on their palfreys, squires riding on all sides to protect them, 'a right fair sight' for all to see. Next in the procession came, what the herald calls a chariot, which carried four ladies of Margaret's bedchamber throughout the journey, their own female servants riding behind.

Spectacular as was all this to the spectators, pressing forward in their eagerness to catch a glimpse of the king's daughter as she passed, their delight was enhanced by the music, of Johannes and his company of musicians, minstrels and trumpeters blowing loudly, under banners raised above their heads.

---

[26] John Lesley, Bishop of Ross, The History of Scotland from the death of James I in the year 1436 to the year 1561, Bannatyne Club Edinburgh 1830. p.71.

It was indeed a splendid company that, in the long days of summer, rode with the Princess Royal of England on her journey to wed the Scottish king. For the first stage went none other than Lord Derby, Constable of England, (he, who, as Sir Thomas Stanley, at the battle of Bosworth, had placed the crown on her father's head) the fourth husband of her grandmother, from whom he was estranged. But only a mile beyond Coleweston, he kissed Margaret on parting, a privilege allowed him as her next of kin.

Nearing Grantham, Sir Robert Dymock, the High Sheriff of Lincoln, with thirty horsemen in his retinue, rode out to meet her, holding a white wand in his hand. Hailing her as queen, he rode with her as far as the border of Lincolnshire, the first of all the sheriffs of the counties who would pay her the same honour as she passed.

So on she went with bells ringing to welcome her in all the towns and villages through which she either rode or, to prevent too many people pressing forward to see her, was carried in a litter. In Grantham, where a long procession of dignitaries rode out to meet her and the mendicant friars received her singing praises, she was lodged in the house of a gentleman called Mr Hiol. Newark was the next stop where 'it was a fair sight to see the people thronged on the windows and streets... and the Queen was lodged at the Hart.'

The next day's journey ended at Tuxford where she slept in an inn called the Crown. Then it was on to Scrowsby where, on the night of the 12 July, she stayed in the manor house of the archbishop of York before, after entering Doncaster in procession, she spent the next one in the convent of the Carmelite nuns. From Doncaster she continued to Pontefract, where she was met by Sir John Milton, with seven riders, all pulling their horses back on their hocks to make the leaps called gambades. 'Very fair was the array when she entered that town,' but Margaret avoided Pontefract Castle with its sinister connections as the place where, not only had Richard II reputedly starved to death, but her mother's uncle Lord

Rivers and his son Lord Richard Gray had been killed. Shrinking from the grim scene of so much fear and suffering, she lodged instead in rooms attached to the church.

But, while people throughout the length of England had welcomed the little queen with joy, nothing could outdo the reception she received when she arrived at York. The Lord Scrope of Bolton met her after she left Tadcaster, 'riding in great state with his lady richly beseen,' their son following with an army of Yorkshire chivalry being joined by the sheriffs of all the West Riding and their men. A mile from the city of York, Margaret dismounted to change her dress in her litter where she was hidden by screens. Then, as the York gates opened, 'a grand procession of civic magistrates and gallant Yorkshire cavaliers poured forth to welcome the train.'

Most splendid of all was Henry Percy, the Earl of Northumberland, a young man of twenty-six, who brought up in the court of Margaret's father, had been knighted by him on the occasion when his friend Prince Arthur had become the Prince of Wales. Now, dressed from head to foot in crimson velvet, every item of clothing, down to his boots of black velvet being embroidered with gold, he rode towards Arthur's sister whom he had known as a small child. His horse, a magnificent charger, its harness embellished with gold, made many gambades to the great delight of the crowd, before, with minstrels singing and trumpets blowing, he escorted Margaret to the city, where people from all over Yorkshire were waiting to see her arrive.

On the morning following her arrival, when received in his palace by the archbishop of York, Margaret drew gasps of admiration in her gown of cloth of gold, belted with a girdle studded with precious stones reaching down to the ground, while her necklace caught everyone's attention being of large eastern gems.

Leaving York on 18 July, she said goodbye to some of her escort, the bishop of Norwich amongst them, who had come with her so far. She then proceeded, first to Newburgh and then

Allerton, where she was met by Lord Lumley and his son. The next stop was at Hexham from where she went on to Darnton, near Leeds, before, on the morning of 20 July, arriving at Durham to be welcomed by Sir Richard Stanley (brother of her grandmother's husband) and his wife.

This time the Earl of Northumberland appeared in 'a gown of goodly tinsel furred with ermine and with gold and little bells on the harness of his horse which tinkled every time it moved.'

Queen Margaret lodged in the castle at Durham until, on the 24 July, she once again took the road for Newcastle. Again there was great rejoicing, children dressed in white, the streets hung with tapestry, and even the ship's tops in the harbour crammed with people anxious to get a glimpse of King Henry's daughter on her way to wed Scotland's King James, the festival of whose patron saint St James fell on the 25th of the month.

In the evening the Earl of Northumberland 'treated her to a goodly banquet... Thither from the north came Lord Dacre (hero of Bosworth Field and now Warden of the Western Marches) 'with a mighty train in his livery and there were dances, sports and songs... lasting until midnight.'

Margaret set out again next day (26 July) to stay the night at Morpeth Castle. Little could she guess at that time of such festivity that the castle, standing above the River Wansbeck, would one day be a place of refuge from enemies as yet unknown.

From there she rode on to Alnwick Castle, the major fortress along the English Border of Scotland, held by the Percy family for two centuries, seat of its head, the Earl of Northumberland, who rode out to meet her and escort her through his park, where she 'killed a buck with her bow' before being taken to the castle to be warmly welcomed by her host who, on her last night in England, 'made her very good cheer.'

Then it was on to the town of Berwick so long disputed between the two countries, which now, because of her marriage, she was due to unite. At the gate of Berwick Castle she was received by Lady Darcy, wife of Thomas Lord Darcy, the captain of Berwick, a man well known to the Earl of Surrey with whom, six years earlier, he had laid siege to Norham Castle and chased King James back to Scotland.

Now, in a more festive mood, he entertained the young princess, whom the Scottish king was to marry, with bear baiting by dogs and loud shooting of guns, enjoyable perhaps to himself but hardly to a girl of twelve. She was, however, allowed to rest for two days, for the strain of the long journey, in the heat and dust of the summer, was taking its toll, not only on Margaret herself, but on the men and women of her escort and the horses on which they rode. Presumably Euphemia Darcy found washerwomen and seamstresses to mend torn clothes, for, as reported by the herald, both Margaret and her entourage, were 'rested and cleansed from the toils and stains of travel, and all attired in new garments [when] the Scotchgate of Berwick was flung open, and the bridal escort began to defile from under its grim portals into the northern kingdom.'

The earls of Surrey and Northumberland with their retinue of squires and men-at-arms, led the way through the Scotchgate into Scotland. Following came the archbishop of York and the bishop of Durham with their attendants in ecclesiastical robes, with behind them the Lords Scrope, Gray and Latimer, and a great many young nobles all splendidly dressed. Most particularly was the herald entranced by the horses, 'frisking of their own accord,' to make the bells attached to their harness – some of them silver and some gold– make 'a sweet chiming when they took leaps and gambades at their pleasure.'

Margaret herself, gorgeously robed and bejewelled, sat in her litter as it passed below the arch of the gateway (from which hopefully the heads of miscreants had been removed) into the new country of which she was now the queen. Beside her rode Sir Thomas Wortley, her master of the horse, leading one of her white ponies. Behind came Lord and Lady Darcy who would ride with her to Edinburgh, as before them the van of the Scottish chivalry of the Border, led the way.

Never before in Berwick, its walls so often besieged, had been seen such a gay cavalcade. Immediately in front of Margaret's litter rode Johannes and his players, amongst them the chief trumpeter, Harry of Glastonbury, and his mates, blowing their lungs out to the sky. At the back of the procession the sergeants of mace were followed by what the herald wrote were 'English Border troopers, to the amount of two thousand men-at- arms…. such was the fair order of the bride queen's entry into Scotland; and it was a joy not only to see, but to hear.'

Lammermuir was the first stop of the great procession as it wound its way over the hills. At Lamberton Kirk the archbishop of Glasgow, 'with a good company of Scottish nobles were waiting to receive the Queen' dressed, as John Young rather waspishly remarked, 'without gold and silver on their doublets' made only of plain or cloth. However, there were 'five trumpets or clarions of the King of Scotland that blew right merrily, which melody was good to see and hear.'

As the queen approached, the bishop of Moray and the Scottish lords knelt down before her on the grass before she was 'kissed by the said lords who led her into a pavilion where 'there was plenty of bread and wine disposed and everyone was content.'

Margaret, sitting side-saddle on her white pony, then made a formal farewell to the 'chivalry of the English Border' who had escorted her from Berwick. Led by the Earl of Northumberland, his horse responding to his spurs leaping about, they rode away as about a thousand of the nobility of the Scottish Marches and their followers came to take their place.

With her Scottish escort surrounding her, a local guide leading the way, Margaret rode on through a stretch of wild land of rock and bog and down a steep hill into the Giant's Pass of fable, known as Cockburnpath before reaching the coast at St Abb's Head. There, on a promontory, stood Fastcastle, a fortress literally rising from the waves that crashed against the rocks of its foundation. Defiant against all enemies, it was later to become famous as the Wolf-Crag of Walter Scott's *Bride of the Lammermuirs,* but to Margaret, on her first day in Scotland, it must have been an awesome sight.

Walking across the natural bridge formed by a ledge of rock across a cleft between the cliffs, Margaret was warmly received by Lord and Lady Home, keepers of the castle which was in fact part of her jointure in the contract of her marriage to King James. Little could Margaret have guessed, on that night when, in the fire-lit hall, she sat at the top table fêted as the king's bride, at the unpropitious circumstances in which she would again meet Lady Home.

Next morning, after leaving Fastcastle, Margaret re-joined her escort at Coldingham. From there, as they journeyed north, the roads became so bad that men had to be sent ahead to level them to allow her chariot, the first form of wheeled carriage ever seen in Scotland, to proceed. Passing the town of Dunbar, she was told that King James was currently repairing the ancient fortification, on its sea girt ridge of rock, from where the legendary Black Agnes had so famously defied the Earl of Salisbury from its walls. Now it was lying, purposely left derelict, to prevent English occupation, since forfeited from the Earl of March, nearly fifty years ago. Because of the castle's current state of ruination, Margaret did not visit it, but she heard cannons fire in her honour as, with her train of attendants, she passed it by.

Heading west up the sea-coast they reached Haddington, where, on the night of 2 August, while Margaret and her ladies slept in a convent, the gentlemen of her escort lodged with the Grey Friars.

Then it was on to Dalkeith Castle, seat of the Douglas Earl of Morton, head of the Douglases of Dalkeith, whose father had been granted the title on his marriage to Joanna, the dumb daughter of James I. Now although not involved in politics, thanks to the value of his land, he was one of the richest men in Scotland.

Shortly before reaching Dalkeith Castle, Margaret once again dismounted to be dressed in the privacy of her litter in one of her most magnificent gowns.

The Earl of Morton was waiting to meet her at the gateway where he gave her the keys of the castle, before, between the two gateways of the courtyard, his wife Lady Morton with an entourage of local people, received her on bended knee. Raising her to her feet, Margaret kissed Janet Morton before she was taken to the grandest rooms in the castle all specially prepared for her coming.

After so many miles of travelling, she must have been thankful to be ushered in to a chamber filled with many items of comfort to welcome her. In particular the sight of the four-poster bed with its tapestry hangings and the goose-feather filled mattress must have been welcome after the convent's austerity. But hardly did she have time to appreciate all that had been prepared for her, before, as of the clattering of many hoofs rang up from the courtyard below, a maid came rushing in, breathless in her excitement, to say that the cause of the commotion was that the king himself had arrived.

CHAPTER 13

SCOTLAND AUGUST 1503

Margaret just had time to wash the dust from her face and let her maid brush the worst tangles out of her hair, before she heard feet pounding up the stone stair. Going to the doorway of her bedroom she met James, the man she was to marry, not as she expected a dignified figure robed in velvet and fur, but a young man, his hawking lure flung over the shoulder of a velvet jacket, rather worn and whose hair and beard curling naturally, were both in need of a trim.

James, renowned as the handsomest monarch in Europe, was a man few women could resist. On meeting Margaret, a small figure beside him, he swept off his bonnet and bowed, while she, her mind confused in her surprise, just managed to make a deep curtsy. Then, taking her hand to raise her, he kissed her before saluting all her delighted ladies in turn.

The king said he was hungry, having been hawking all day, so supper was immediately served. Having washed their hands together from a bowl held by a page, James and Margaret sat down together at the head of the table beside Lord and Lady Morton, their hosts. Then afterwards as 'the minstrels began to blow', Margaret danced with Lady Surrey to the great delight of the king, who retired back to bed in Edinburgh, thoroughly pleased with all that had happened on this most important of days.

Margaret also went to bed only to be woken up by screams and the smell of smoke. A fire had started in the stables which threatened to engulf the house. Wrapped in a plaid, she was taken down to the courtyard where people were gathered anxiously watching men with leather buckets, hurling water into the flames. Then above the noise she heard horses stamping, whinnying in terrible fear. Frantically she tried to run towards them, shouting to all within earshot in the darkness to save her ponies, but women behind her held her back, grabbing her arms to hold her, assuring her that they would be safe.

But they were not. Fortunately no person was injured, the fire being quickly put out, but Margaret's two lovely white ponies, which had carried her so many miles, were both found to be dead, killed as they lashed out struggling to escape, by the thick, suffocating smoke.

King James, when told that Margaret had cried all morning, immediately sent a message that she must go to Newbattle Castle, close by, where everything had been made ready for her to stay for four days. He would come himself he said, that same afternoon, whereupon, Lord Surrey, the archbishop of York and several others set out to meet him. But James missed them, coming another way to Newbattle where he found that Margaret, despite her sadness, was playing cards. This time, more formally attired in a black velvet jacket, bordered with crimson velvet and edged with white fur, he once again kissed her and all the other ladies, before, as he and Margaret were talking together, the men who had ridden out to meet him, returned.

The king, having greeted them most warmly, the minstrels again began to play. Margaret danced, again with Lady Surrey, before, to her great delight, James himself began to play, first on the clavichord and then the lute. Sir Edward Stanley, the high sheriff of Lancaster (fifth son of the Lord Derby, fourth husband of Margaret's grandmother) then sang some ballads for which the king gave him good thanks. James, having again kissed Margaret, said farewell to the company, John Young the herald amongst them, who came to watch him vault into the saddle.

'James of Scotland did leap on his horse, without putting his foot in the stirrup; and the steed was a right fair courser;

and forward the King spurred, let follow who might,' wrote the Somerset Herald.

The next day the king turned up looking even more magnificent, in a tan coloured velvet doublet lined with the much prized black otter's fur, while below it his shirt was stitched with gold. After Margaret had played on the lute, they sat down to supper with James at the head of the table in the chair of state. But noticing that Margaret, perched on a stool beside him, looked uncomfortable, he gallantly made her take his place, while at the same time, summoning Lord and Lady Surrey to join them at the high table.

Afterwards, James and Margaret talked together as the minstrels played. Then, having kissed her goodnight, he was on the point of leaving, vaulting into the saddle as before, when Lord Surrey chose that moment to give him the noble courser, sent to him as a present by Henry VII., which, as described by the herald, was 'well-appointed with damask housings of the Tudor colours green and white, which hung to the ground with great buttons of silk,' even the reins of the bridle being coloured to match. This magnificent animal was ridden before him as James returned to Edinburgh for the night.

The next day, being Sunday 6 August, Margaret, wearing a dress of cloth of gold, accompanied by her English household, went to mass at the chapel of Newbattle Castle. Then, after dinner and more dancing, she and her ladies spent the afternoon in games and conversation before the king appeared for supper this time wearing 'a gown' of black velvet, furred with martin, to dance with Margaret as the minstrels played.

Then, on the Monday, dawned the day when the queen was to enter Edinburgh. The king had sent more ponies, all wearing new harnesses, to replace the two killed by the fire. But Margaret, on this occasion, 'very richly dressed' as the herald wrote, 'in a gown of cloth of gold, with cloak of black velvet and a necklace of pearls and precious stones,' chose to sit in her litter. Thus she set off until, half way to Edinburgh, King James was seen advancing, in full magnificence, with a concourse of nobles in his train.

This time the king had outdone himself. Again according to the herald, his very horse was trapped with gold, a deep gold fringe round its neck, the saddle and harness of gold and a bridle and headgear of burnished silver. Astride it the king was a splendid figure decked out in a jacket of cloth of gold, lined and bordered with lilac velvet and black otter fur, a waistcoat of violet satin, a shirt embroidered with pearls and gems, and finally scarlet hose. Thundering along at full gallop, driving his horse with gilt spurs, he rode towards his bride before, just as it seemed he must either jump over or collide with her – her ladies by now screaming with fear – he pulled it back on its haunches, to leap off and kiss her in her litter, before vaulting back into the saddle.

Excitement then subsiding, a gentleman usher unsheathed the sword of state from its scabbard of purple velvet, to carry it in front of the procession in regal fashion.

King James rode beside the litter until, just before they reached Edinburgh, one of his gentlemen appeared on 'a fair courser', 'trapped in cloth of gold, with crimson velvet interlaced with white and red.' The idea was for Margaret to ride pillion behind James as they entered the city, but, the horse proving too fresh, James had to content himself with mounting a quiet palfrey with Margaret sitting pillion behind him.

Thus they came to a green meadow where, before a pavilion, a mock tournament took place. This was followed by the hunting of a tame deer, netted in Holyrood Park, from where it had been conveyed in a cart to be let loose and a greyhound unleashed to give chase. However, jinking and swerving, it managed to escape, and guided by homing instinct, outran the chasing dog to reach the sanctuary of Holyrood Park

By this time a vast crowd had gathered to see the arrival of the queen into the capital. From the city came the Greyfriars in procession, carrying a cross and some relics, which the royal couple had to kiss. The queen's minstrels, headed by Johannes, joyfully heralded their approach, joined by Scottish musicians, who, again as the herald noticed rather spitefully, did not have new banners to wave over their heads. He was more impressed by the 'gate with two tourelles which stretched across the entrance into Edinburgh. In the tourelles were windows, where vested angels, sang joyfully at the coming of so noble a lady; and at the middle window was another angel, who flew down and presented the keys of the town to Queen Margaret. Then, in procession, came the college of the parish of Saint Giles, richly vested, as they brought the relic of the arm of their saint, presented to their King to kiss.' But, continues the herald, 'he courteously refused to take precedence in this ceremony of his royal partner, sitting on the pillion behind him, and Queen Margaret had the privilege of kissing the arm of St Giles before her lord.'[27]

Then, suddenly, perhaps to divert her from the grizzly relic, the king began to sing the *'Te Deum Laudamus*, his voice loud above the others as all the churchmen joined in.'

To the sound of bells ringing joyfully, the procession moved up the West Bow, below houses hung with tapestry, to the newly painted Mercat Cross. Beside it a fountain ran copiously with wine, while nearby, on a stage, were depicted the Judgement of Paris, the Annunciation and the Marriage of the Virgin. From there the company proceeded down the High Street to the Nether Bow Port, where images of the Virtues, Justice, Force, Temperance and Prudence, stood triumphant over Nero, Holofernes, Epicurus and Sardanapalus writhed at their feet. Then it was on to Holyrood, to the church of the Holy Cross, from whence came James's brother, the

---

[27] Leland's Collectanes. Narrative of Young, Somerset Herald. Anstis MS.

archbishop of St Andrews, to present both himself and Margaret with yet another cross to kiss. James, having dismounted, put his arms round Margaret to lift her from the saddle before, after entering the church, he led her to the high altar where they knelt together on cushions of cloth of gold.

All of the aristocracy of Scotland were present, the Earl of Huntly, the Lord Constable the Earl of Errol, the Earl of Argyll, Steward of the Household and the Earl of Lennox Chamberlain amongst them who, as she passed them, bowed low to the royal bride. King James then walked through the cloisters, his arm round Margaret's small waist, as he led her to the great chamber of Holyrood, where the bishop of Moray waited to introduce to her all of the high born ladies of the land. Afterwards, the king withdrew to his own rooms and she to hers. After supper he went to see her to dance some more dances together before, after this most momentous of days, the thirteen year old girl, retired, it must seem thankfully, to bed.

On 8 August 1503 Margaret was married to King James. As usual the herald John Young was in attendance to describe how the king stood, bonnet in his hand, as the lords filed past him. Foremost amongst them was the Earl of Surrey, magnificent in a long gown of cloth of gold, the collar of the Order of the Garter around his neck. James then asked the English peers, sitting on a bench before him, to cover their heads as he himself took his seat on a chair of crimson velvet below a canopy of blue velvet figured with gold.

The bishop of Aberdeen escorted the English lords to the queen's chamber where she stood ready to be led by them to the church. For this most auspicious of days, she wore a robe of red and white damask, bordered with crimson velvet and lined with white sarcenet. On her head was a magnificent crown, made for her by Currour and a collar of pearls and precious stones circled her neck, but what most caught the herald's eye, was her hair, the gorgeous red gold tresses, falling, so he avers, down the whole length of her body.

Led, on the right hand, by the archbishop of York, and on her left by the Earl of Surrey, Margaret was followed by her ladies, the countess of Surrey carrying her train, to stand near the font in the church. Then came the king and his brother, the archbishop, with their cousin, Lord Hamilton, bearing the sword of state before them both. Passing the queen he bowed to her, as she sank low in a curtsey.

James, dressed for his wedding, was a splendid sight in a gown of white damask figured with gold, a jacket with slashes of crimson satin bordered with black velvet, a waistcoat of cloth of gold and a pair of scarlet hose. His shirt was embroidered with gold thread, his black velvet bonnet looped up with a balsas-ruby, his sword strapped to his side.

The marriage ceremony itself was performed by Robert Blackadder, the Archbishop of Glasgow, together with Thomas Savage, Archbishop of York. 'The trumpets then blew up with joy' as the king, bareheaded, his own hair falling to his shoulders, holding his queen by the right hand, passed through the assembled company to the high altar where they knelt, side by side on the cushions covered with cloth of gold. At the Gospel they made their offerings, and after the queen was anointed, the king gave her the sceptre to hold. Then, as the choir burst into the *Te Deum,* with two prelates holding a canopy over the royal pair, the whole company celebrated mass.

At the wedding breakfast which followed, Margaret, on her husband's command, was served first before him. The first course of a wild boar's head, was succeeded with 'a fair piece of brawn' which in turn was followed by a ham. Then came at least fifty-two other dishes, including roast crane, swan, and a jelly decorated with the arms of Scotland and England, all served up in gilt vessels to the king and his queen. [28]

---

[28] Guildhall MS Great Chronicle of London, fols.300 v-i.

The herald describes how the state chamber was hanged with 'red and blue and cloth of gold', representing the history of the town of Troy, while painted glass in the windows showed the arms of England and Scotland bi-parted by a thistle and a rose interlaced through a crown. He then notes, most interestingly that, 'in the same room was a rich state bed and dresser (side cupboard) set out in the manner of the country.'

Dinner over, the minstrels played as one of them, perhaps Johannes himself, sang the song, of which, five centuries later, the words in their original form, can be found in the British Museum.

'O fair, fairest of every fair,
Princess most lovely and preclare,
The loveliest that on-live there been,
Welcome to Scotland to be Queen!

Young tender plant of pulchritude,
Descended of imperial blood,
Fresh fragrant flower of fairhood sheen,
Welcome to Scotland to be Queen!

Sweet lovely imp of beauty clear,
Most mighty monarch's daughter dear,
Born of a Princess most serene,
Welcome to Scotland to be Queen!

Welcome the rose both red and white,
Welcome the flower of our delight,
Our sprite rejoicing from the spleen,
Welcome to Scotland to be Queen!'

As the song ended, a hall was cleared and James and Margaret led the dancing. A conjuror entertained the assembly and bonfires lit up the streets. [29]

---

[29] Mackie.p.111.

Then the king went to evensong alone before coming back to the palace to take off his marriage robes and give them to the English heralds and officers-of-arms. After which, putting on, what sounds like his dressing gown, of black velvet furred with martens, he ended the long day.

CHAPTER 14

The wedding was only the start of the festivities which continued for four more days. On the first, in the palace courtyard, an acrobat gave a display of rope dancing which the king and his guests watched from the windows. Then later, the countess of Surrey and her daughter, Lady Grey, for clipping the royal beard, were given presents, the countess fifteen ells of cloth of gold, her daughter the same length of gold damask.

That evening, so the herald writes, 'the Queen sent her wedding gown to the heralds and officers-at-arms of Scotland.' The next morning, however, she sent fifteen nobles to the Marchmont Herald to retrieve it and return it to her wardrobe.

On the second day, following mass, the king tapped forty-one men with his sword on their shoulders before telling the queen 'these are your knights.' Then followed three days of jousting in the courtyard, judged by the old soldier Surrey, and the Earl of Bothwell, from a scaffold on which they stood. The celebrations ended on Sunday 13 August when James made his cousin, Lord Hamilton, the Earl of Arran; Lord Graham became the Earl of Montrose and Lord Kilmaur Earl of Glencairn.

Margaret did not attend mass but stayed resting in her room. Then there was more jousting and the queen appeared in great state sitting in the great bay window of her chamber at Holyrood, surrounded by the Scottish ladies in what the herald describes as 'the garb of their country,' presumably hand woven plaids. That evening she entertained the king in her great presence chamber. She danced with her husband, and the herald noticed that 'they seemed to spend their time in marvellous mirth and gladness.' But then it was time for many of her English escort, including Sir Edward Stanley to say goodbye to her before starting their journey home.

With them, in a sealed packet, went a letter to her father which proves that, however, in public, she kept a brave face, Margaret was lonely and unhappy, feeling herself badly used. Plainly she resented Lord Surrey's great friendship with her husband, something which, as a young girl, still unfamiliar with the world, she could not recognize as being natural to men of similar interests to whom she, herself, was still a child. Far less could she even guess at the tragic, unforeseen circumstances in which this relationship would end. Dictating to a secretary, she added only her name at the end of a screed loaded with bitterness and regret.

'My most dear Lord and Father

In the most humble wise that I can think, I recommend me unto your Grace, beseeching you of your daily blessing, and that it will please you to give hearty thanks to all your servants, the which, by your commandment, have given right good attendance on me at this time, and specially to all the ladies and jantilwomen which hath accompanied me thither, and to give credence to this good lady, the bearer hereof; for I have showed her more of my mind than I will write at this time.

'Sir, I beseech your Grace to be good and gracious lord to Thomas, which was footman to the Queen my moder, for he has been one of my footman hither, with as great diligence and labour to his great charge of his own good and true mind. I am not able to recompense him except by the favour of your Grace.

Sir, as for news, I have none to send, but that my Lord of Surrey is in great favour with the King, here, that he cannot forbear the company of him at no time of the day. He and the Bishop of Murray ordereth everything as nigh as they can to the King's pleasure. I pray God it may be for my poor heart's ease in time to come. They call not my Chamberlain to them, who, I am sure, would speak better for my part than any of them that be of that council. But if he speak anything for my cause, my Lord of Surrey hath such words unto him that he dare speak no further. God send me comfort to his pleasure, and that I and mine, that he left here with me, may be well entreated.

For God's sake Sir hold me excused that I write not myself to your Grace, for I have no leisure at this time; but with a wish I were with your Grace now, and many times more. And for this that I have written to your Grace, it is very true, but I pray God I may find it well for my welfare hereafter. No more to your Grace at this time; but our Lord have you in his keeping. Written with the hand of your humble daughter.

Margaret.'

Five hundred years later the pathos of that letter from a girl, forced away to live in a strange country from which she longed to come home, still reaches one's mind. Margaret was plainly discontented: feeling herself isolated and misunderstood amongst people, largely older then herself, with whom she had little in common, Lady Surrey, described as her governess, clearly being one.

Whatever the truth of her list of complaints to her father regarding her treatment, Margaret's claim that she did not have time to write letters herself, was indeed a genuine excuse, for in the days of celebration following her marriage she had little time to spare.

The festivities continued until, on Sunday 13 August, a farewell feast was held for the few of her English escort who remained. Margaret was led to church by the Earl of Surrey a man who she quite plainly disliked. Once again the faithful Somerset Herald was in attendance, describing how, on this occasion, she wore 'a gown of purple-figured velvet, bordered with gold thread and furred with ermines, made with great rebras, large trumpet-shaped sleeves. Round it she wore a rich girdle and above a necklace of gems. Lady Surrey carried her train and behind came the King and his chief officers of state.'

James too was splendidly dressed, in cloth of gold furred with marten, a doublet of crimson satin lined with cloth of gold, and a shirt embroidered with pearls. Three Scottish lords, presented by the Marchmont Herald at this ceremony, were created earls, as in the words of the herald, 'the King of Scotland girdled them with their swords above their shoulders. Then the King took the Queen's hand and led her to the company; but because it rained, her Grace passed through the King's chamber to her own.'

Dinner was followed by a morality play performed by John English and his company before, after more dancing, the king went off again to even-song, a service which Margaret, apparently bored with so much church going, noticeably did not attend, 'therefore the making of some knights, who were to have been made for the love of her, was put off until the next day.'

This was the last episode described by the perspicacious John Young, who must have returned to England with the Earl of Surrey the next day. Sadly the English visitors had not appreciated James's generosity–during their visit he had spent £two thousand two hundred on wine alone – instead 'they returned to their country, gevynge more prayse to the manhoode, than to the good maner and nurture of Scotland.'[30]

---

[30] Rotuli Scotiae. Vol. xii, p.181.

CHAPTER 15

REBELLION

Sadly the Somerset Herald was not there to describe Margaret's coronation, which took place in Edinburgh in the Parliament Hall. Neither was he in attendance when the king made a tour through the southern part of his kingdom to introduce his subjects to his bride. It was left to Bishop Lesley, the Scottish historian, to tell how well they were entertained at the great Border abbeys and how generously the royal couple contributed to the funds of the churches they visited, giving them purses of gold.

James was notoriously kind-hearted, this being one of the reasons why, in Scotland, he was greatly loved. Margaret's eight English musicians were beneficiaries, receiving no less than forty crowns on his wedding day. A love of music was one of the few things that this notably disparate couple, separated by so many divergent interests as well as by years of age, were known to share. On one night James gave his winnings at cards to Margaret's harpers and a few days later a man with the unusual name of Bountax, described as a cornet player, who played in Queen Margaret's chamber, received twenty-eight shillings, before being given new whistles.[31]

Amongst men who benefitted from his benevolence was the foreign dog-handler, a man called Jean Caupene, who was not only maintained with his servants and dogs while in Scotland, but given £two hundred and a letter of recommendation to Louis XII when he returned to France.

Margaret was soon to learn that life with James, if unpredictable, was never tedious. In 1504 he bestowed the

---

[31]Accounts of the Lord Treasurer, Register House Edinburgh,

Abbey of Tungland in Dumfries and Galloway to what has been described as 'a mysterious French Leech' John Damian, who convinced him that he could make gold of other metal 'quhilk science he callit the quintessence; quhairupon the King maid greit cost, bot all in vaine.'[32]Men pumped away with bellows at lumps of metal, heated above a roaring fire, but despite their frantic efforts the secret of the Philosopher's Stone eluded them and the metal, if changed in shape, remained as lumps of lead.

Disappointed at this outcome, James, ever the optimist, then agreed to support Damian's next experiment of flying back to France on a pair of wings. The whole court gathered in excited expectation as Damian took off from the battlements of Stirling Castle only to land in a midden piled against the foot of the wall. Bruised and crestfallen, but fortunately still alive, Damian assured the king that his attempt had only failed because the wings were made of the feathers of a barnyard fowl which wanted to return to its natural habitat. Had he used those of an eagle he would, assuredly, have crossed the sea to France.

King James, if described as the handsomest monarch in Europe, was certainly the most restless. In January 1504, after celebrating Christmas with Margaret at Holyrood, he was off to Falkland Palace, to ride out from the courtyard with some of the fellow spirits amongst his courtiers, to hunt, a hooded falcon on his wrist, on the low lying land of the Howe of Fyfe and the slopes of the Lomond Hills. Returning only as it grew dark, he spent the evenings gambling and drinking wine, as the minstrels played to entertain him before a huge open fire.

---

[32] Lesley.John The History of Scotland from the death of King James I in the year 1436 to the year 1561, Bannatyne Club London 1830. p 76.

At the end of January he left Falkland to ride to St Andrews for the funeral of his brother, James, Duke of Ross, Archbishop of St Andrews, who had died two weeks before. Then at the beginning of February he was back in Edinburgh, playing golf on the links at Leith with the Earl of Bothwell before going to Stirling and then Biggar, and then riding all the way down to Dumfries. Generous to a fault, it was here, that on leaving, he left money for the cook's boy who had broken his leg, and paid for his surgeon's fee. On another occasion, moved by the sight of a man standing disconsolately beside his dead horse, he stopped to give him fourteen shillings.

Returning to Holyrood, summoned by a messenger with disturbing news, James found himself faced with a national crisis. Rebellion had broken out in the north-west Highlands and the Isles. The situation was soon so serious that, on 11 March 1504, Parliament was summoned in Edinburgh to take emergency measures to deal with the problems on hand.

This was not the first time that James had been forced to deal with a rising in the north and far west of his kingdom since becoming king. Ten years earlier, in January 1494, when he had just reached his twentieth year, John, fourth and last Lord of the Isles, without a legitimate son to succeed him, had retired into a monastery, surrendering his lands and titles to the crown.

Thus, it would seem had the great dynasty of the Lordship of the Isles, founded by the half Norwegian Somerled, vanquisher of the Vikings, three hundred years before, come to a peaceful end. But John of the Isles had left a grandson, son of his own natural son Angus, who the Islesmen claimed to be their lord. The boy, named Donald Dubh for his dark colouring , taken prisoner by his maternal grandfather the Earl of Argyll, had been held in captivity on Argyll's castle of Innischonnell on an island in Loch Awe for many years –legend says till his hair went grey– but rescued eventually by some daring

MacDonalds of Glencoe, he had become a figurehead for a rising led by his uncle, Torquil MacLeod of Lewis.

James and his new young wife were celebrating Christmas at Holyrood when the island clans, under Donald Dubh, raided and laid waste to the Earl of Huntly's lands of Badenoch.

The measures taken by parliament, summoned to meet the emergency, included the calling out of what was termed the 'fencible' men, those of military age of the whole kingdom north of the rivers Forth and Clyde. The earls of Argyll, Huntly and Crawford, the Earl Marischal, chief of the Keiths, and Lord Lovat, were to lead the force against the Islanders, while letters were sent to many of the chiefs of the Isles, ordering them to join with the other forces against the rebels. Then on top of this, Lauchlan Maclean of Dowart [Duart] and Ewin Allanson of Locheil, for proclaiming Donald Dubh as Lord of the Isles, were amongst those declared as traitors, their lands forfeited to the crown.

With parliament prorogued the king went to Stirling to be given a great number of pike for Lent before going back to Edinburgh to spend Easter, which fell on 7 April in 1504. In the same month, on the directions of the parliament, the royal army assembled at Dumbarton from whence all kinds of artillery, including 'gun stanes' or stone bullets, were sent for a siege of Carneburg, the fort on a small island off the west coast of Mull. James himself, went twice to inspect the ships that were preparing to sail, and on leaving, with his usual generosity, gave fouteen shillings to the pipers of Dumbarton before, on his way back to Edinburgh, giving the same amount of money to 'the seik folkis at the toun end of Strivelin' [Stirling] where a blind man at the gate got another fourteen pence. In June James visited the ruined priory on the Isle of May at the entrance to the Firth of Forth, then, together with Queen Margaret, with twenty-four carts trundling behind them carrying her clothes, he went to Linlithgow. Leaving her there, he was off again to Bothwell Castle to see his mistress where he ordered a requiem mass to be sung for Eleanor Jones, one of Margaret's ladies-in-waiting, with whom, if he enjoyed a relationship, it was not publicly known. From there he rode back to Linlithgow, but only to go on to Stirling, taking a white peacock he had somehow acquired on the way.

Then he conceived another plan, this time to subdue the cattle raiders of Eskdale with Lord Dacre, the governor of Berwick's help. With him went his falconers, his minstrels and his master cook, all of them stopping in Dumfries, where James paid the man who had hanged some thieves, adding another eight pence for the cost of buying the rope. Proceeding then to Canonby, he watched the execution of some of the cattle thieves before going once more to Lochmaben to enjoy flying his hawks. Leaving there in mid-September, he went to Dunfermline where, in the royal residence attached to the monastery, he was joined by Margaret who had come from nearby Linlithgow with her clothes and those of her ladies packed into thirty-five carts.

It was now the end of September, when surely, by anyone's standards he had travelled enough for one year. But James, forever restless, was once again on the move, making a pilgrimage to the shrine of St Duthac on the north side of the Moray Firth in Tain. Again the falconers went with him and this time a Moorish drummer and a horse carrying silver plate. Returning he stopped at Darnaway Castle, near Forres in Moray, where Janet Kennedy, the mistress he had stolen from the old Earl of Angus, and who bore him three children, was installed. Then he rode down the East coast and through Perth to reach Falkland on 8 November, just six weeks after setting out on a journey which, even for a man of just forty, as was James at that time, was a test of both stamina and strength.

But even then he was restless, driven by some inner compulsion that kept him forever on the move. Crossing the Forth, he escorted Margaret back from Dunfermline to Edinburgh before going down to Melrose for more hunting with his hawks. However, he did return to Holyrood to spend

Christmas with Margaret, to find the walls hanging with tapestry from Linlithgow, and silver brought from Stirling glittering in the hall.

CHAPTER 16

RISING OF THE LAST LORD OF THE ISLES.

Fear spread throughout lowland Scotland, where the men of the Highlands, lawless savages, murderers and robbers to a man, unintelligible with their Irish language, were regarded as a race apart.

As the state of emergency continued, command of the northern division of Scotland was conferred on the Earl of Huntly, and while James's namesake and cousin, James Hamilton (who, on the day of his wedding to Margaret he had created Earl of Arran) was given two commissions against the Isles, the Earl of Argyll, MacIan of Ardnamurchan and MacLeod of Lewis kept in constant touch with the king. James had learned some Gaelic, the only Scottish king known to have done so, and was thus able to converse with the messengers; wild looking, long haired, bearded men, who came, very often in darkness, to find him wherever he might be.

James, who shortly after his accession, when still in his early twenties, had led two successful naval expeditions against the rebellious Islesmen, taking several of the chiefs hostage against future insurrections, did not in this instance take part. Instead, officially for the first anniversary of their marriage, but in reality for her safety, he took Margaret to the Earl Marischal's fortress of Dunottar near Stonehaven in Aberdeenshire. The castle, standing on a small plateau, above perpendicular cliffs, connected by only a thin strip of land to the shore, was virtually unassailable, surrounded as it was on three sides high above the North Sea.

It was here, in the month of August that the king kept court. Generous as usual, he gave yet more money to Margaret's musicians, twenty-seven shillings to two English songstresses, while the child who played on the monochord got eighteen.

Still better paid were Pate Harper, who played the clarcha, the English boy Cuddy and Souter, the luter, who was given enough money to get his lute out of pawn. In addition, four Italian minstrels, perhaps over-staying their welcome, were paid 'to clear them of the town' while Hog, the taleteller, obviously more welcome, got thirteen shillings for the stories and legends that he told.

By this time the ships sent to besiege Carneburg had returned to Dumbarton, the fortress apparently subdued. But sporadic fighting continued so that a second fleet sailed from Dumbarton in the spring of 1405. According to Donald Gregory, King James, in person, invaded the Isles from the south and Huntly from the north,[33] In December Torquil Macleod, the main agitator, charged with treachery, was summoned to stand trial, but, secure in his fortress in Stornoway, predictably did not appear.

Maclean of Duart, however, from his castle in Mull, surrendered Donald Dubh in exchange for a restoration of his lands. This proved the end of the rebellion. Donald Dubh, the last Lord of the Isles, as his followers still claimed him to be, held prisoner in Stirling Castle, was to remain in captivity for thirty-eight long years.

---

[33] Donald Gregory History of Scotland and the Western Isles, p.194

CHAPTER 17

OF ARCHITECTS AND DESIGN.

It was from the early years of his reign, that with the threat of civil war in Scotland and of likely invasion from England always paramount in his mind, that James had begun the huge project of restoration of the fortresses in his kingdom which would remain throughout many centuries as a legacy of his reign. First and foremost in importance was the rebuilding of the great fortress of Dunbar, the former castle of the earls of Dunbar, defended so magnificently by Black Agnes against the Earl of Salisbury but later, after the forfeiture of George de Dunbar, 11th Earl of March, destroyed to prevent occupation by the English. James, when he rebuilt Dunbar Castle, standing like a lone cormorant on a ledge of rock above a vast sea cave, could not possibly have guessed how, at a time of great danger, it would one day prove a place of refuge for his granddaughter Mary Queen of Scots.

Other castles which were strengthened in the early years of the king's reign, were the Royal Castle of Tarbert, on the eastern side of the isthmus dividing Knapdale from Kintyre, and the castle of Loch Kilkerran, former stronghold of the Lord of the Isles, near the present town of Campbeltown at the southern end of the peninsula of Kintyre.

But it was not only fortresses, which James, transformed. Most importantly it had been for Margaret's long awaited arrival in Scotland in between her betrothal and her marriage, which had inspired the king to make great additions to Holyrood in the form of the barbican, the chapel, the great hall and most importantly the long gallery, the first of its kind seen in Scotland, to impress his English guests. The building programme, had in fact continued, during the first years of the king's marriage, when the Tower, in what is now the north-west wing of the palace, was finally ready for occupation.

But it was in Stirling Castle, the citadel so beloved of his father and place of his own birth, that James set the seal of his hallmark much as it remains today.

Standing on a high rock, with views in all directions for miles around, it was built as a fort, traditionally by Kenneth MacAlpine King of Scotland after he had vanquished the Picts, to guard, what in earlier times was the lowest downstream crossing of the River Forth. More factually it is known that, early in the 12th century, Alexander I built a chapel here, in what was by then a royal residence, where Alexander III laid out a deer park below the castle in about 1260. It was the death of that king, without a direct heir, that had led to the War of Scottish Independence, when Edward I and his son so famously and so futilely tried to subjugate the Scots. Following this, it was during the 14th century, in the reigns of the Scottish Kings Robert II and III that the first existing buildings had been built.

The king's Old Building comprised a vaulted basement, above which the royal rooms were reached by one of the spiral stairs, so practical as being easily defended by a single man with a sword. The entrance, through a porch, led to the king's halls and bedchamber. James is believed to have built the Forework, the old Frontispiece of the castle running from one side of the Castle Hill to the other, towards the end of his reign. The Prince's Tower, above the Lower Terrace, constructed of four storeys rising to a parapet walk, is also attributed to him, but it is the Great Hall, already described earlier, which, even if James had built nothing else in his life, will always commemorate his name.

Built to one side of the Upper Square, adjacent to the Chapel Royal, the Hall sadly dilapidated through time, it has now been restored by Historic Scotland to the glory of its original form.

It is logical to think, that because James felt himself to some extent responsible for his father's cruel death, he determined to carry out the project that had been so dear to his murdered sire as part of the retribution for what he believed to have been his own participation in the crime.

Alternately it is conceivable that James built the Great Hall at Stirling, to prove to the English nobles, who escorted Margaret to Scotland, that his reputedly wild country in the north, contained buildings as fine as anywhere in Europe.

But palaces and fortresses were not the only projects that James now had in mind. In 1505 he ordered the carrack, or great ship, to be known as the *Great Michael*, the largest vessel ever planned, to be built in the dock specially made for the purpose at Newhaven in the Firth of Forth. Sir Andrew Wood, the master-mariner in whom James III had placed such trust, both designed the ship and oversaw her construction. At two hundred and forty feet in length and thirty-five in width, she would, without doubt, be the largest ship afloat. According to the historian Pitscottie all the woods in Fife were cut down to build her, while loads of timber were brought in both from other parts of Scotland and from Norway to make her virtually unsinkable, with oak walls ten feet thick.

At the time this was considered to be display on the part of the Scottish king, noticeable for his eccentricity, of his wish to control the seas. Few of those even close to him, probably not even his wife, knew that behind this show of bravado lay an ulterior motive, for James had an all-encompassing dream to lead a crusade against the Turks.

His ship was called the *Great Michael*, specifically in honour of the archangel, and it was in her that he planned to lead an expedition against the Ottoman Empire, which became, as the years progressed, the absorbing ambition of his life.

Margaret had been married for over two and a half years, before, on 10 February 1506, when she was just sixteen, she gave birth to a son. She herself nearly died, but James was so ecstatic over the birth of his heir, that he gave a cup of silver, heaped with a hundred gold pieces, to the woman who brought him the news.

Then he was off to Whithorn, to the shrine of St Ninian to give thanks. Walking on foot over hard, most likely frozen ground, he outdid the four Italian minstrels–perhaps the ones sent off from Dunottar – who were so exhausted on arrival that they had to be returned to Edinburgh on horses.

Miraculously, it was discovered afterwards, that Margaret had begun to recover just as James had reached the shrine. She was certainly told of this, but probably not that he had used this opportunity to visit his old love.

Janet Kennedy was the mistress who James had enticed from her husband, Archibald Earl of Angus (forever known for his exploit of killing the architect Robert Cochrane as 'Bell the Cat') an insult for which Angus waited for a chance to wreak his revenge. That James's association with Janet had been of long duration, is proved by the fact that James Stewart, the son she had borne him, was by this time old enough to be studying under the theologian Erasmus in Rotterdam. Later, thanks to his father's influence, as archbishop of St Andrews, he would hold high office in the church.

When Margaret was fully recovered, she too made a pilgrimage to Whithorn, but not in the manner of her husband. There was no walking for her. Instead no less than seventeen pack horses were needed to carry her baggage. Even her chapel plate and furniture had to be transported in two huge coffers. In contrast James's clothes and belongings needed only three horses to transfer them, but the long caravan of people and animals moved so slowly that the pilgrimage lasted twenty days.

Margaret, vexed with sickness that year, travelled to the Galloway coast. The causes of her illness are not specified but it is known that her physical symptoms were worsened by the great sorrow of losing her first born son when, on 17 February 1507, in Stirling Castle, the little boy died when just over a year old.

Another reason for her apparent malaise and discontent, would seem to be that she had few real friends, with whom she shared common interests, amongst the lords, ladies, knights and lairds of her husband's court. Reading between the lines, from the works of contemporary historians, it would seem, that brought up, as she had been, in the strict and pious regime of her grandmother, the countess of Richmond's household, she found the people who always flocked around James, many of them plainly sycophants looking for free board and lodging, to be both bawdy and uncouth. James, with his inherent generosity, never turned anyone away, shutting a blind eye to louche behaviour, particularly of the young men, preening themselves in their doublets and over-tight breeches, who with little to do, but always looking for favours, amused themselves by making amorous advances to the maids-of-honour and behind closed doors, the servant girls whom they looked upon as ready game. No such behaviour had been tolerated by her grandmother and Margaret, if not a prude as later her own behaviour would prove, was certainly unprepared for the laxness of morals, and general impropriety, that she found in the Scottish court.

Despite the sadness of both his parents over the loss of their child, Christmas that year was 'spent merrily at Holyrood' according to accounts of the time. The king, as usual, was outstandingly liberal, ordering thirty dozen of little bells to be delivered to Thomas Boswell for the dancers at the revels on New Year's Eve. He seems to have gone to great lengths to raise Margaret from her state of depression, for, St Valentine's Day in February, was celebrated with music, minstrels and mummers. Then he himself went off to fetch a female minstrel known as *Wantonness*, paying her thirteen shillings, on two separate occasions, to sing in the queen's chamber. On top of this, a man called O'Donnel, an Irish harper, was given £seven.

James only waited until the roads were clear of the winter rain and frost before, at the beginning of April 1508, setting off once more on a pilgrimage to Whithorn on the Galloway coast. His reason for making it was genuine enough – James was certainly devout – but the chance to see his mistress, then living at Bothwell Castle, home of her father Lord Kennedy, seems to have added inducement to a visit to the far-off shrine.

Margaret, meanwhile, left at Holyrood, received an unexpected delegation of ambassadors from her father's court. Leading them was Doctor West, who tired of waiting at Berwick for a safe conduct, had probably taken the chance of James's known absence, to ride north. How happily Margaret welcomed them, eager to hear every detail of the doings and state of health of her family, in particular the father that she loved.

But the news of King Henry was bad. Always reclusive in character, since her mother's death he had become virtually a hermit, prone to bouts of depression in the loneliness of his self-imposed exile from the court. Doctor West had in fact come to Scotland to explain why King Henry had arrested James's cousin, James Hamilton, whom he had made Earl of Arran, and his brother Patrick Hamilton while travelling through England without a safe conduct.

James on his return was furious, rudely informing Doctor West that he was too busy superintending the making of gunpowder to give him an audience. Then to crown everything, Patrick Hamilton, who must have somehow escaped, returned to tell Margaret, in front of both James and

Doctor West, that his brother had been very cruelly treated by her father. [34]

This is probably the first recorded altercation between Margaret and James, she saying that the allegations of mistreatment were fictitious; he, on the affirmation of Patrick Hamilton, swearing they were true.

If Margaret was unhappy and angry, James, despite their differences, was nonetheless on top of his form, popular with his people who loved him for his eccentricity, and who saw no fault in a man who kept mistresses as well as a wife! Another excuse for the revelry, which he at least so plainly enjoyed, came in the month of May 1508, when the king of France, Louis XII, sent a party of ambassadors to Edinburgh to try to solicit his aid against the Holy Roman Emperor Maximilian V.

Once again, the capital city of Scotland became a scene of festivity as splendid entertainments took place.

Most exciting were the jousts, when an unknown knight called 'the Wild Knight,' surrounded by savage men, overcame all the French challengers in the lists. Queen Margaret, roused out of her apathy by excitement, joined in the applause for the ferocious 'Wild Man' who, when she presented the prizes, turned out to be none other than her husband King James!

The French ambassadors then returned the hospitality with a grand festival called a Round Table of King Arthur. King James was so impressed that he determined to call the child Margaret was carrying, Arthur, should it prove to be a boy. The idea was much favoured by Margaret for whom the name would remind her of the much loved brother she had lost. In the autumn she went with James to the castle, built on a peninsula in Lochmaben in Annandale, where the child, which proved to be a girl, died on the day that she was born. Again the king, distraught as was his wife, did his best to cheer her

---

[34] *Cotton Manuscripts*, Caligula B. viii.f.181. British Library.

by paying fourteen shillings to the crooked vicar of Lochmaben to sing to them both at Lochmaben on 17 September 1508.

CHAPTER 18
OF PIRACY AND POLITICS

HOLYROOD 1509

Margaret was again at Holyrood when a messenger rode from England to tell her that, on 21 April, at Richmond Palace, her father had died of tuberculosis, the then incurable disease. This meant that her brother Henry, the red-haired impetuous boy, who had raged so furiously against her marriage, was now the king of England, Henry VIII. Shortly afterwards came news that the grandmother, who had held such predominant influence over Margaret's young life, had also died. Joan Beaufort, who through her first marriage to Edmund Tudor when only a girl of twelve, had become the Countess of Richmond, had been known both as the most pious and most powerful woman in the land. Her hold over her son, King Henry, Margaret's father, had been such that she had been the only person he would speak to after his wife, Margaret's mother, had died. Such was her omnipotence that she had ruled as regent following her son's death. But now, on her own demise, it was her grandson Henry who held the full reins of state.

Two months later, on 11 June, King Henry, the necessary papal dispensation having been acquired, married the Spanish princess, Catherine of Aragon, widow of his brother Arthur, who had died now seven years before.

On 20 October 1509, at Holyrood, Margaret's second son was born. In accordance with her special wish, the boy was baptised Arthur and proclaimed prince of Scotland and Lord of the Isles.

Margaret had cause to remember her elder brother not only for his name. Just before his premature death, Arthur had

113

willed her all his most precious possessions including some valuable jewels. Her father had not sent them to her despite her repeated requests. Now it seemed that her brother Henry was proving to be equally obdurate in refusing to part with the legacy, left to their sister, on Arthur's specific word.

The name itself appeared to be unlucky, for the little Prince Arthur of Scotland died in Edinburgh Castle in the following July when only nine months old. Again the bereaved parents were desolate and Margaret physically ill.

Leaving Edinburgh immediately, they returned to Holyrood in October to watch a play in which one of the performers was the later much acclaimed poet, Sir David Lindsay of the Mount, wearing a dress of blue and yellow taffeta, given from the royal stores, in which to act his part.

King Henry's reluctance to part with the jewels bequeathed to his sister was not the only issue which worsened his relationship with James. Henry was a different man to his father, the peace loving Henry VII. In the summer of 1511 he found cause to take action against piracy in the North Sea.

The culprit was none other than Andrew Barton, eldest of the three brothers, Andrew, Robert and John, ship owners and shipmasters in Leith. The Bartons had long ago quarrelled with the Portuguese over acts of piracy, which had ended in the imprisonment of Robert for capturing a Portuguese ship. Andrew Barton, in high favour with King James, who had given him letters of marque, then used his brother's treatment as an excuse to pretend that the king of Scots was at war with Portugal and that all the goods, which he seized off English ships, were in fact Portuguese.

The merchants, robbed of their cargoes, naturally complained to King Henry who ordered Sir Edward Howard, the admiral of England, and his brother Lord Thomas Howard, to put to sea at once to destroy his enemy as he claimed Barton to be. Lord Thomas Howard was lying off the Downs when he sighted the *Lion* sailing north for Scotland. With a faster ship he overhauled her, coming alongside so that English sailors, jumping aboard, swarmed onto her decks. In the fierce fight that followed, Sir Andrew was fatally wounded, before his crew surrendered when at last overpowered. The men on the *Lion* were still fighting as Admiral Howard pursued the Barton's other ship, the *Jenny Pirwin,* which he took as a prize after killing most of the crew. The two ships were then taken into custody where the Scottish sailors who survived were imprisoned in a building belonging to the archbishop of York.[35]

James, furious and humiliated by the death of the great seaman to whom he had given land in Fife, immediately invoked the statute of 1509, whereby if an Englishman killed a Scot within the English Marches, his English counterpart was bound to arrest the culprit and bring him before the next Warden Court. Henry, however would have none of it, instead sending Richard Fox, the erstwhile bishop of Durham and now of Winchester, to question the Scottish prisoners. His methods of extracting evidence are not recorded, but the captives, whether or not under torture, soon admitted to piracy, a crime usually punishable with hanging. In this case however, a priest amongst them begged for mercy and Fox, with unusual leniency, released them on the promise that they would leave England and pray for its king. But this was not the end of it. Henry then seized the chance to send an insulting message to James telling him that 'if he had shown justice instead of mercy, Barton's men would have been as dead as Barton himself.'[36]

James retaliated to this insult by sending six commissioners, who included the Earl of Argyll, Lord Drummond and the Justice Clerk to meet Lord Thomas Dacre and Sir Robert Drury at the next Warden Court. Henry then responded by sending an army to the north. The Border

---

[35] Mackie. R.L. pp.209-10.
[36] *Hall's Chronicle*, edited by Sir H Ellis, London 1809. p.525.

garrisons were to be put in readiness for battle, and Lord Darcy appointed captain of Berwick.[37] The dogs of war were straining at the leash.

King Louis had promised to send James both ships, soldiers and money towards his crusade against the Turks if he would launch an attack into England to divert King Henry from invading France. But James could not do as Louis asked without breaking the truce with England which would result in excommunication by the Pope. He complained in a letter to Pope Julius, that Henry himself had invoked the truce by ordering the death and imprisonment of Scottish seamen but the Pope, unwilling to be drawn into the controversy, did not reply.

Andrew Forman, the Bishop of Moray, who James had sent as ambassador to King Louis's court, was then despatched as an envoy to the Pope in Rome. Arriving there in September, Pope Julius sent him back to the king of France with an order to that monarch that he must abandon his attempt to take Venice and withdraw from Bologna and Ferrara which he had already over-run. However, aware as he was of the French king's antagonism, in the following month of October, Pope Julius formed a treaty of alliance, known as the Holy League, with both Venice and Spain. King Henry VIII then joined the League and on 17 November 1511, both he and King Ferdinand of Spain, with the intent of returning that province to England, agreed to send a combined army, six thousand strong, into Aquitaine before the end of April 1512.

King Louis sent Forman back to the Pope, this time offering to surrender both Bologna and Ferrara if Julius would withdraw from the Holy League. But the Pope ignored this suggestion so Forman left Rome for the French city of Blois.

Meanwhile James prepared for war. His flagship, the *Great Michael*, the largest vessel afloat, lay at anchor in the harbour

---

[37] Letters of Henry VIII. vol.i. PT.I. No.833(65)

at Newhaven in the Forth. Traders were bringing guns and gun metal into Leith. Forges were red hot in Edinburgh Castle, where gunsmiths from France were hammering the metal to form the cannon that would stand on the ramparts ready to be hauled down for use.

Encouragement came when, during the mid-winter of 1511-12, King Louis sent Doctor Peter Cordier to Scotland to tell James that, in the event of an English invasion of France, Louis would help him to conquer England. At the end of January, James sent Cordier to continue his journey by sailing from Leith to Denmark to explain the situation, both in France and Scotland, to the king of that country, his uncle King John, and in the event of a war with England, to ask for his support.

Meanwhile Andrew Forman, Bishop of Moray, returning from France, was instructed by King Louis to obtain an audience with King Henry and to try to persuade him, not only to settle his differences with King James, but to join forces with him in supporting Louis against the Pope.

In his brief visit to the English court, Forman learned that Henry, by a formal treaty, was now allied to the enemies of France. Returning to Scotland in February 1512, the ambassador told James that there could now be no reconciliation with Henry and that Scotland must abide with the Aulde Alliance made over three hundred years before with France.

Hardly had Forman returned to Scotland, however, before the Pope's ambassador, Octavian Olarius, arrived in Edinburgh with an order to James to join the Holy League and to abandon his loyalty to France. Then Leonardo Lopez, the Spanish ambassador in London, reached the Scottish city with a letter with the same request.

But James listened only to Forman, and on 6 March he made the irrevocable decision to send the Unicorn Pursuivant to France to renew the long standing alliance between Scotland and France.

Hardly had James's ambassador left before King Louis's envoy, Jehan de la Motte – his ship probably passing the Unicorn's – arrived in Scotland, to tell James that King Louis expected an invasion from England. Most urgently, he wanted to know what help might be forthcoming from Scotland and Denmark. With him he brought a large post-dated cheque to induce James to fight his cause.

James was in a difficult position. Through his marriage to Margaret, while her brother remained childless, he saw the possibility of inheriting the English throne, something which, in no circumstances whatever, was he willing to forgo. De la Motte carried back his answer to Louis, asking him not to make war with England without his consent but, at the same time, requesting money, provisions and arms and suggesting that the pension of fifty thousand crowns, which Louis paid to Henry, could be usefully diverted to himself.

The French king's answer to these demands were conveyed to James by the bishop of Ross on 21 April 1512. Louis was hedging his bets. While promising to help James, in regard to his claim to the throne of England, he would come to no terms with King Henry without his consent. Nonetheless, he asked James to send ships to France with all possible speed. As for the so-called pension paid to Henry, this was in fact the return of money lent to England by the government of Brittany which was paid back to Anne, Duchess of Brittany, who, married to Louis, was queen of France.

De la Motte, returning from France in June, captured several merchant ships and fishing boats on the way, which, on landing, he sold to the citizens of Ayr. He came with the news that Louis was prevaricating over certain items of the original alliance so that finally, after discussion, the fifth article became an agreement, that neither James nor Louis would make a contract with Henry without the other's consent. Finally, at Blois, the treaty was confirmed by Louis on 12 September 1512.

CHAPTER 19

THE HEAVEN'S PROMISE

In the early spring of 1511 a comet had appeared in the sky, reputedly as bright as the sun, visible night and day for a period of three weeks. Just as such a phenomena had occurred before the birth of King James, terrifying his father into believing it to be an ill omen for the child that his wife was carrying at that time. Now James believed, that inevitably, his own hope of having a child that survived for more than a few months was doomed.

Desperate to avoid whatever fate awaited them, James sent Margaret on a pilgrimage to one of his own favourite venues, the shrine of St Duthus, in Easter Ross. The saint must have been benevolent for, on 11 April 1512, in her favourite Palace of Linlithgow, Queen Margaret gave birth to 'ane fair Prince'. Immediately baptised James, this was the boy who would live to survive his father as the fifth King James of the Stewart line.

The significance of the birth of a son to the king of Scotland was not lost on King Henry, who did not as yet have one of his own. As things stood, in April 1512, the newly born prince of Scotland was second in line to his throne.

In May, Queen Margaret moved to Stirling Castle where, on the evening of 4 May, Doctor Nicholas West, King Henry's indefatigable envoy, was summoned to her presence. On Margaret demanding to know if King Henry had sent her the jewels bequeathed to her by their brother Prince Arthur, West replied that he had been instructed to hand them over, but only if her husband, King James, would agree to keep the treaty of peace.

'And not else? 'asked Margaret.

'No', replied Doctor West, 'and if the King of Scots, your husband, persists in war, the King of England, my master, will not only keep the legacy, but take from him the best towns he has in Scotland.'

Then the conversation ended abruptly as James came into the room.

The beautiful child who Doctor West so greatly admired, was by then in the charge of Sir David Lindsay of the Mount, appointed by the king as his guardian or 'gentleman usher,' to use the then topical term. It would seem that it was largely due to Sir David's devoted personal care that the young James survived the period of early childhood in which three of his siblings had died. Later Sir David himself was to write to his charge, by then King James V:

'I take the Queen's grace, thy mother to witness, likewise my Lord Chancellor, your nurse and your old governess, how, when you slept, it was mightily close to my cheek, how often in the day, I bore your Grace on my back, even as a packman. But sometimes you bestrode my neck, dancing and jumping with many a nod and smile. Nay, the very first syllables you lisped were meant as my name, being Pa Da Lyné, and this you said that I might play on my lute to divert you.' Whereupon he continues to describe how he snatched up his lute and played 'twenty springs' (tunes)

'From play thou never let me rest,

But Ginkerton thou likest the best.'[38]

A version of one of Sir David's most famous poems, translated from ancient Scots, describes, rather charmingly, how he cared for his precious charge.

'I entered to thy majesty

The day of thy nativity;

I pray thy grace for to consider,

Thou hast made many lords and lairds,

And given them many rich rewards,

---

[38] Ginkerton = an old Scottish melody found in Ancient Scottish Melodies, pub. for the Maitland Club.

To them which were full far to seek,
When I lay nightly by thy cheek,
 I take the Queen, her Grace, thy mother,
My Lord the Chancellor and other,
Thy nurse and thy old mistress (governess)
I take them all to bear witness.
Old Willy Dale, were he alive,
My life full well he would describe,
How, as a packman bears his pack,
I bore your grace upon my back.
Sometimes you strode upon my neck,
Dancing with many a bend and beck.
The first syllabs that thou didst mute,
Were Pa Da Lyné on the lute.'

By the time that Doctor West reached England, the situation in Europe had already dramatically changed. On 11 April 1512, King Louis' army had captured Ravenna, but only ten days later, the Lancaster Herald had arrived in France to tell King Louis that King Henry had decided to support the Pope, and was ready to send an army of invasion against France. Then, two months later in June, the French army, defeated by the combined forces of the Holy League, had been driven back across the Alps.

An English force, commanded by the marquis of Dorset, having raided in Brittany, left France after the king of Navarre, his own country invaded by King Ferdinand of Spain, failed to join in what was planned to be a united campaign. But then, on 19 November of that fateful year of 1512, the Austrian, Holy Roman Emperor Maximilian added his strength to King Louis' enemies by joining the Holy League. Louis was determined on another invasion of Italy in the forthcoming year, but to do this he must contrive to make James invade England to invoke Henry into countering the attack.

On 19 November 1512, the evening of St Andrew's Day, the people living near the Firth of Forth heard the sound of guns. Then a strange ship was seen coming in to Leith to anchor not far from the shore. Word spread to Edinburgh where, as the alarm bell rang for hours, the citizens grabbed their swords before it was discovered that this was no invader but the French envoy, Jehan de la Motte, coming again to confer on behalf of King Louis with King James.

Lying off Leith the French ship, which had conveyed Jehan de la Motte to Scotland, dragging her anchor in a gale, was driven up to Blackness to lie beside the *Great Michael,* towering like a colossus above her decks. Regardless of the strength of the wind, still lashing the sea, James had himself rowed out to his ship, on board of which he received the ambassador, who had brought him the final version of the treaty cementing the Aulde Alliance between Scotland and France. Signed by King Louis, it came with his personal thanks to James 'for the great affection and love he had shown.'

De la Motte came with presents, thirty tons of wine for the king and eight lengths of cloth of gold for the queen. More importantly the hold of the ship was crammed with armaments, two hundred gunstones of iron, eight lasts of gunpowder, and eight serpentines of brass for the field. With them he brought his sovereign's message that 'it was now necessary to diminish the arrogance of the English, who had joined with the Pope and with Ferdinand of Spain, the contriver of a faction very dangerous to Christendom which he called the Holy League.' [39]To encourage James to help him he promised him, not only a subsidy of fifty thousand francs, to be raised by a tithe levied throughout France, but soldiers, guns, ammunition and a fleet of ships to transport them, to be standing by in readiness to join the strength of his crusade.

It was more than James could resist!

---

[39] Mackie. R.L., pp.226-7.

CHAPTER 20

THE WAR TO WIN A CRUSADE

Margaret found herself living with a man obsessed by a dream. The war with England would soon be over. King Henry would withdraw his troops from France, and Louis, in undying gratitude, would give James all that he needed to lead his crusade against the Turks. His excitement increased when, at the end of the year, Pope Julius' legate, Octavian Olarius, made a renewed visit, this time with a letter from the Pope, dated 1 July 1512, in which he asked James most urgently to 'lead an expedition against those most pestilent Turks.'

James did not need any more encouragement. But then came a crisis as the plague broke out in Stirling in January of the new year. He issued a proclamation, carried by riders from town to town, making it a capital crime for anyone sick of the plague to go to church, or market, or any other public places, or to import infected goods into the country. Nevertheless, despite this national emergency, the illusion of defeating the Turkish infidels in cohesion with the king of France continued to dominate the king's mind.

On 12 January he wrote to his uncle, King John of Denmark, explaining the situation, and that fear of imminent invasion from England had driven him to renew Scotland's alliance with France. He asked him to send his fleet of ships to Scotland and to urge the merchants of the Hanse towns to despatch and equip other vessels as well. His letter was carried by a young man, nephew of the chancellor of Denmark, who had been educated at the Scottish court. But King John was destined never to see it before, on 21 February 1513, he died.

But by this time the dice was cast. On 14 February, just a week before King John's death, Jehan de la Motte and James Ogilvie, had embarked on a French ship the *Petite Louise.*

With them they took another letter, this time from King James to King Louis, telling him that the decision had been made. James would invade England at midsummer.

Sharing the danger of the voyage, now threatened by attack from English ships, was the Pope's envoy, Octavian Olarius, also with a missile from King James, telling the Pope that although, as he put it, 'he had laboured for peace,' Henry had continued to attack Scottish ships and kill seamen in blatant aggression that was impossible to forgive.

But once again he was too late. Pope Julius died on the same day as King John of Denmark, 21 February 1513.

The election of the new Pope, Leo X, did not in itself affect the situation in Europe where other forces were at work. King Louis had begun to negotiate with Spain, and on 1 April signed a truce to last a year with King Ferdinand. Meanwhile, the Venetians, hostile against the Emperor Maximilian, deserted the Holy League to form an alliance with France. [40]

Back in Scotland, while James and Margaret and their infant son, and as far as known all the courtiers, escaped the dreaded plague, the royal household seethed with discontent. James raged against Henry for causing the death of Sir Andrew Barton, while Margaret, in the early stages of pregnancy, was both unwell and furious with her brother for failing to send the legacy, left to her by their eldest brother Prince Arthur, as he was dying, now eleven years ago.

King Henry was warned by Lord Dacre that James was preparing for war. He told him that there were eighty workmen, toiling day and night in Edinburgh Castle, forging cannons and making gunpowder, arrow-heads, lance staves and other armaments on the orders of the king. Likewise, at Newhaven, ship-wrights were preparing the *Great Michael* and James's other ships to put to sea.

---

[40] *Letters of Henry VIII.*, vol.1. Pt. 1. No. 1703.

Desperate to avoid a war with Scotland, which must, inevitably, disrupt his French campaign, Henry sent Nicholas West once more to Scotland to try to settle his differences, both with his sister, clamouring for her legacy, and far more importantly, his brother-in-law.

West rode from London, most likely with studs in his horse's hoofs to stop it slipping on frozen roads. Reaching Berwick, he wrote to Henry, on 13 March 1513, telling him that King James would probably not go to war were his ambassadors allowed safe conducts and their merchants safe passage by sea. Henry was doubtful about the latter, replying to West, on the 20th that it might be a ruse to let the Scottish fleet sail safely to France.

Doctor West arrived in Edinburgh on Sunday 20 March 1513. His arrival coincided with that of the Unicorn Pursuivant, who, with John Barton, sailed into Leith from France bringing a cargo full of gunpowder, cannonballs and wheat. They also brought word of Pope Julius' death.

King James was in Stirling whither went Doctor West. On Good Friday, 25 March, after attending mass in the Chapel Royal, he was received by the queen at which time he gave her the letters from her brother, sympathising over her illness and promising to send the legacy left by their brother, Arthur, as soon as an opportunity occurred.

Delighted she cried out, ' If I were now in my great sickness, this were enough to make me whole.'

On Easter Sunday, when West saw the king briefly just before he celebrated High Mass, he took the chance to tell him that the Pope was dead. Then, in the evening, when he dined with the queen, he gave her the news that she least wished to hear, that her brother meant to go to France to command his army himself. Seeing her reaction, distressed as he had known she would be, he begged her to use her influence on James to prevent him from attacking England on behalf of the king of France.

On the next day, Easter Monday, when West at last succeeded in obtaining a long interview with James, the king explained to him the extent of the difficulty with which he now found himself placed. The late Pope Julius had threatened him with excommunication should he attack England and James, devout in his faith, wished by any means possible, to be reconciled to his successor. To this purpose he wrote a letter to Pope Leo, explaining that he had sent Bishop Forman to Rome to further the cause of peace.[41] He also wrote to King Louis, telling him that he had declared war on England, both on land and sea, despite the fact –pointing out his own great loss in doing so – of forgoing Henry's promise, that in the event of his remaining childless, he would inherit his crown. Asking for men, armaments and ships, he reminded Louis of his own promise that, in the event of his going to war with England on his behalf, he himself would not make peace with England until he had placed the crown of that country on James's head. [42]

West was soon to discover that further discussions with James were fruitless, the king becoming extremely angry and demanding to know why his wife's legacy was not paid. However, shortly before departing, West tracked him down in the Chapel Royal, where James began to talk about his great obsession of leading a crusade against the Turks. He showed West some papers sewn together, which proved to be the secret articles which Louis had given to Bishop Forman in the previous year, offering, not only a fleet but an army with which to fight his crusade once, thanks to James's intervention, his own war with England had ended and Henry's army driven from France.

'Now', said James, delighted to have made his point clear to West, 'you can see wherefore I favour the French king and

---

[41] Ibid.No 1707.
[42] Flodden Papers, pp.72-9.

wherefore I am loth to lose him, for if I do I shall never be able to perform my journey.'

West, amazed and indeed confused by the naivety of a man of otherwise intelligent mind, pointed out that it was quite inconceivable that King Louis would keep his word. But James, bedazzled it seemed by the prospect of his crusade, refused to believe that the French King would not honour his promise of assisting his glorious campaign against the infidels of the east. For several days he prevaricated, while West pressed for a definite assurance that, at least during Henry's absence in France, he would maintain the peace with England. Eventually, on 1 April, West was allowed to attend the Council when Archibald, Earl of Argyll, the Lord High Chancellor of Scotland, gave the definite assurance that Scotland would keep the peace if England would do the same. Argyll, however, would not put the pledge in writing, as neither would the King.

Later that same day, Nicholas West received a letter, brought by a courier from King Henry, asking for a loan of the *Great Michael,* which James promptly refused on the grounds that he had already promised the ship to the king of France.

The court then returned to Edinburgh from where, on 3 April, West went down to Newhaven to find men working on the *Margaret* preparing her to go to sea.

On 9 April, in the chapel at Holyrood, he made a last appeal to James for a written declaration that, while Henry was in France, he would not go to war. James prevaricated, protesting that Henry would dishonour himself if he tried to hinder the crusade. Seeing that to argue further with him was useless, West then asked permission to depart, to which James readily agreed, but asked him to visit the queen and their infant son at Linlithgow. Margaret, he said, had tokens for him to take to her brother and Queen Catherine.

'Subsequently', wrote Doctor West:

'On Sunday afternoon I rode to Linlithgow, and came thither by four o'clock. As soon as I alighted, her Grace,

Queen Margaret, sent Sir John Sinclair for me. Howbeit, she told me she had done the best that was in her power, and would continue to do so. And without further communication about her legacy, or any other matter, she delivered to me the tokens for your Grace, the Queen and the Princess (Margaret's sister Mary.) Queen Margaret then commanded that I should be taken to see the Prince, and so I was. Verily, he is a right fair child, and a large one for his age'.[43]

West left Linlithgow with letters from both Margaret and James in his saddle-bag. Plainly she was referring to her father's promise that the jewels and other items, left to her by her brother Arthur, would be sent to her when she wrote, or rather dictated, the letter to Henry for West to take on his return.

'Right excellent, right high and mighty Prince, our dearest and best beloved brother.

We commend unto you in the most hartlie wise. Your ambassador Doctor West, delivered me your loving letters, in which ye show us that, when ye heard of our sickness, ye took great heaviness.

Dearest brother, we are greatly rejoiced that we see ye have respect to our disease; we give ye our hearty thanks, and your writing is to us good comfort.

We cannot believe that of your mind, or by your command, we are so unfriendly dealt with in our fader's legacy, whereof we would not have spoken nor written, had not the Doctor spoken to us of the same in his credence. Our husband knows it is withholden for his sake, and will recompense us so far as the Doctor shows him. We are ashamed therewith, and would God never word had been thereof. It is not worth such estimation as in your divers letters of the same. And we lack nothing: our husband is ever the longer the better to us, as

---

[43] Ellis's Historical Letters. No given date.

known God; who right high and mighty Prince, our dearest and best beloved brother, have you in governance,

Given under our signet, at our Palace of Linlithgow, the 9th day of April.

Your loving sister

Margaret.'[44]

James also wrote to Henry in the flattering terms common to royal correspondents of the time. He commiserated with him for having lost his own admiral, Sir Edward Howard, son of the earl, with whom he had struck up such a friendship at the time of his wedding to Margaret.

The war between Henry and Louis had begun with a naval battle in Conquet Bay, a harbour of Brest, in which Henry's admiral was killed.

'Surely, dear brother,' wrote James to Henry on 23 May, 'we think there is more loss to you of your late admiral who deceased, to his great honour and laud, than the advantage that might have been to you of winning all the French galleys and their equipage. The loss is great to Christendom of that said umquhile valiant knight, and other noblemen on both sides apparently perished.

Pray you dearest brother, to take our writings in gude part... for verily we are sorry, and also our dearest fellow (wife) for this loss, through acquaintance of his fader, the Earl of Surrey, who conveyed our dearest fellow the Queen to us.'

Despite these flattering assertions, hypocritical as Henry, that most astute of sovereigns, certainly knew them to be, Doctor West had hardly returned to England before another demand for Margaret's legacy was made, this time under the threat of war, the one thing, above all other, that Henry did not want. If King Louis had used bribery to make James go to war with England so that Henry would withdraw from France, now Henry would do likewise, offering totally unfeasible inducements, to make certain he kept the peace.

---

[44] Ellis's Historical Letters, 1st series, vol.1.

'My Lord ambassador desires to have of me silver-work, golden work, rings, chains, precious stones, and other the abuilzements pertaining to a prince, left in legacy by my eldest brother Arthur, to my eldest sister Margaret, Queen of Scotland. I grant thereto she shall be well answered of the same, and the double thereof.

And if the King of Scotland will promise faithfully to keep his word by me, I shall incontinent, with the consent of my nobles, make him Duke of York and Governor of England to my home-coming – for heirs of England must come either of him or me, and I have none as yet lawfully; but I hear that Margaret my sister hath a pretty boy, likely to grow a man of estimation. I pray God to bless him, and keep him from his enemies, and give me the grace to see him in honour when he cometh of age, that I may entertain him according to my honour and duty.'[45]

---

[45] From a folio in British Museum.

CHAPTER 21

'I TRUST NOT THE SCOTS'

Still James waited, undecided as to whether to take the final step of formally declaring war on England. Impatiently he waited for King Louis' ambassador Jehan de la Motte, known to be on his way to Scotland with despatches from the French king.

De la Motte finally arrived in Scotland at the beginning of May. On the 19[th,] he presented James with instructions from Louis, dictated on 5 March. He was pleased, so he said, to hear of the proposed Scottish invasion of England at midsummer, but refused to send guns, ammunition and other supplies until the Scottish fleet lay off the coast of France. These must include the great ship, described to him by de la Motte.

Shortly afterwards James Ogilvy, who had gone with Bishop Forman to France in February, returned with King Louis' answer to the letter James had sent with his ambassadors. Louis now told him, that as soon as the Scottish ships arrived in a French port, they would be fully equipped with both arms and provisions, and that the promised fifty thousand francs would be delivered to Forman or anyone else James might care to send. The ships would then be sent back from France, together with seven French galleys, to serve the king of Scots. But then, emphatically, he demanded that James should invade England as soon as King Henry embarked for France.

It soon became known that the French army, which had tried to conquer Milan, had suffered a catastrophic defeat by the Swiss before the town of Navara on 6 June. This meant that King Louis was more than ever desperate for help from his allies in Scotland, where preparations for war continued at an ever more pressing pace. In the second week of June, no less than fifty carts trundled down from Edinburgh to Leith taking guns from the arsenal at the Castle to the port. Then in the third week, riders were sent to every port of Scotland to enlist sailors to man the warships that were being prepared to go to sea.

King Henry himself embarked on 30 June. Before leaving he made Queen Catherine Regent while the veteran soldier, the Earl of Surrey, was to be his Lieutenant of the North. Henry's parting words to Surrey who had come to Dover for final instructions, were 'My Lord, I trust not the Scots, therefore I pray you not to be negligent.'

The news reached Scotland at the beginning of July. King Henry had left England, sailing for the French coast, on 30th June. James waited no longer before launching his campaign.

At once he gave orders that his two great ships, the *Margaret* and the even larger *Great Michael*, which always sailed together, must leave for France. Also, protected by the cannons of the great flagship, went a fleet of smaller vessels under the command of the king's cousin, James Hamilton, the Earl of Arran and his most loyal northern noble, Alexander Gordon, Earl of Huntly.

On board one of them – it must have been the *Great Michael* – was the Lord Lyon who, in full regalia, finding King Henry in his camp at Thérouanne, declared war on Henry on the part of the sovereign of Scotland, King James.[46]

The Earl of Surrey, beginning his march from the south of England to the north on 22 July, reached Pontefract by 1 August. From there he summoned the leaders of the county levies to join him, while sending the artillery of his army to Newcastle.

Meanwhile, at Linlithgow, the tension between James and Margaret grew. No longer the young girl she had been at the

---

[46] Lesley, History of Scotland p.89.

time of coming to Scotland, she was now a woman of twenty with a strong mind of her own. Resentful, as she must have been over James's mistresses, she felt herself mortally insulted as the queen of France, who in her own right was the Duchess of Brittany, chose to make James her knight errant by sending him a valuable ring. With it came 'ane love letter,' plainly written on the dictate of King Louis to invoke James's participation in his cause, but causing great jealousy to his queen.

Relations between the royal couple had not been good for some time. Margaret was every inch a Tudor, the Princess Royal of England, who felt herself insulted were her rank not properly observed. Her intense resentment over her imagined relationship between her husband and the queen of France, a woman beset with illness, who was in fact old enough to be her mother, seems to have provoked furious recriminations with James, whose planned attack on her own country of England was already a source of difference between them both.

It was at this point that Margaret is known to have formed a liaison with Archibald, Earl of Angus, a man a great deal older than herself, who was known to have been an enemy of the king. James had shamelessly seduced Angus's mistress, Janet, daughter of Lord Kennedy, whom he had installed, together with the three children she had borne him, at Darnaway Castle in Morayshire on the south side of the Moray Firth. James's frequent pilgrimages to the shrine of St Duthac at Tain, on the north shore, included, inevitably, a sojourn at Darnaway, placed so conveniently on the route. But his seduction of the fair Janet was something that her erstwhile lover found impossible to tolerate or forget.

Archibald, 5th Earl of Angus, chief of the family of the 'Red Douglases,' still commonly known as 'Bell the Cat' was one of the most powerful men in Scotland, overlord of much of the south of Scotland, including Dumfries and Galloway in the south-west. Now, in his late sixties, he retained the powerful presence that, as a young man, had made him so greatly feared. Born in 1449 in Tantallon Castle, that great fortress of the family in East Lothian, standing on a cliff top overlooking the Bass Rock, he had succeeded his father at the age of only fourteen. Then, twenty years later, when in his early thirties, he had famously earned his nickname of 'Bell the Cat,'when, as leader of the conspirators against the low born, supposedly homosexual favourites of James III, he had offered to enact the fable of the 'Mice in Council' by undertaking the dangerous task of arresting and then hanging them all over the old bridge at Lauder.

Striking his colours to the mast as an anglophile, Archibald Angus had joined Alexander, the Duke of Albany, brother of James III, in a league against him with Edward IV of England. Signing the convention at Westminster, on 11 February 1483, both nobles had acknowledged the over lordship of Scotland of the English king.

However, pardoned a month later, the two recalcitrant lords had returned to Scotland for a brief period of amity with James III. But Angus had quarrelled with him again before, in 1488, he had allied himself with the rebels, headed by the king's son, to fight against the king at Sauchieburn in the battle in which, at the hand of an unknown priest, he was stabbed to death.

The Earl of Angus, appointed one of the guardians of James IV, had been nonetheless affronted by the wardenship of the marches being granted to Lord Home. Secretly he had then made a treaty with Margaret's father, Henry VII, in which he had pledged himself to obey the king's instructions in regard to his custody of James. At that time he had even agreed to hand over Hermitage Castle in exchange for promised English estates.

In October 1493, Angus had returned to favour to the point where he had become chancellor of Scotland for a period of about five years, until, after a quarrel with James, being held briefly as a prisoner in Dumbarton Castle.

But, pardoned, Angus had returned to court, where, he had had the perspicacity to take advantage of the lonely and clearly resentful, young queen. Their meetings, arranged with such secrecy, as to leave even the prying eyes of the courtiers unaware of them happening, were held in quiet rooms most probably when James was away. Margaret turned to the old earl, seeing him as a father figure who had once been her own father's friend.

To him she poured out her troubles, her fury at her husband's infidelity and the way he still treated her as the child, which, on her first arrival in Scotland, she had been. Most passionately she fumed at this latest supposed involvement with Louis XII's ageing queen. Archibald Angus listened and sympathised, agreeing that she was mistreated and urging her to enlist the aid of her royal brother into bringing her erring husband to his senses. Most urgently did he abjure her into making him abandon the war with England, a project beyond all common reason as anyone with normal perception could ascertain.

That the old Earl had a grandson, a particularly handsome young man, may not at this point have been an issue as far as Margaret was concerned. However, it is known, that by this time, if not before, she was at least in some sort of communication with the faction of one of the most influential families in Scotland who, if not in active opposition to her husband, were at least to a large extent, rivals to his ruling power.

Meanwhile, through the short nights of mid-summer, furnaces roared in Edinburgh Castle as blacksmiths wrought on anvils, forging yet more guns. In the harbours of Newhaven and Leith, riding lights shone in the rigging of the ships lying at anchor, while men laboured to hoist the masts and caulk the seams in readiness for the order to put to sea.

The call to battle came on 24 July when those in command of the levies, raised on the summons of the king, were summoned to meet in the Border town of Ellem in Berwickshire.[47] Then, on the next day, *the Great Michael,* followed by the *Margaret* and four smaller ships of war, sailed down the Firth of Forth, passing the Isle of May, on the first stage of their long voyage to France.

Relations between them still appear to have been strained, but, at the beginning of August, James went with Margaret and their son, now sixteen months old, to her favourite palace of Linlithgow. Margaret, at odds with James, if to some extent exasperated by his obduracy, still seems to have been fond of him, this being a very major reason why she still continued to beg him not to risk his life in what she believed could only be a senseless war. Moreover, much as she disliked the thought of his fighting her brother, she had even less enthusiasm for what to her seemed his illogical dream of a crusade.

---

[47] C.T.S., vol. iv. pp,416-7.

CHAPTER 21

PORTENT OF DISASTER

Margaret was ready to go to any lengths to prevent James from waging war against her brother in what she could foresee must be ruinous results. James she knew was superstitious, like most men, particularly Scotsmen, of his time. Gambling on this last chance of making him see sense, she arranged a supernatural warning.

The king was sitting in his stall in St Michael's Church, standing just before the gateway into Linlithgow Palace, where Evensong was drawing to a close, when a strange man pushed his way through the assembled lords and knights of the congregation to bow before him. The man with bright yellow hair, and wearing a long blue robe, with a great staff in his hand, seemed the image of St Michael stepping out from the painted wall.

Speaking to the king in a deep sepulchral voice, he told him 'Sir King, my mother has sent me to thee, desiring thee not to pass at this time where thou art proposed, for if thou does thou will not fare well in thy journey... further she bade thee not to mell with no woman.'

James simply stared at him, too astonished to speak, before, in the words of Robert Lindsay of Pitscottie, quoting from Sir David Lindsay who had seen it happen, 'the man wanischit away... as he had bene ane blink of the sone or and quhipe of the whirle wind.'[48]

The blue robed figure is supposed to have been seen by someone, slipping across the courtyard and into the Palace by a side door. But other ghostly warnings were more difficult to explain.

---

[48] Pitscottie vol.i.pp.258-9.

Night and day without ceasing, cannon pulled by teams of oxen rumbled from Edinburgh Castle down the Royal Mile. It was midnight, when, by the light of flaming torches, men were still hauling down the newly cast cannon, called the Seven Sisters, when they clearly heard an unearthly voice echoing from the Mercat Cross. Calling itself Platcock, assumed by them to be a fiend, it summoned 'certain earls, lords, barons, and certain gentlemen and sundry burgesses, calling each one by name, to appear before his master in forty days, wheresoever he might be.'

One of those named, a man called Richard Lawson, (later to be provost of Edinburgh) who had just stepped off his balcony, clearly heard his own name. Petrified, he called for his servant to bring him his purse before throwing a crown over the balcony crying 'I for my part appeal from your summons and judgement, and betake me to the mercy of God.'[49]

Afterwards it was noted that amongst those whose names were called out by the so-called fiend, Richard Lawson, who appears to have been a friend of Queen Margaret's, was the only one amongst them who returned to Edinburgh unscathed.

But nothing could deter the king from going to the Boroughmoor (now Colinton) where, under ancient oak trees, all his earls, lords, barons and burgesses were assembled and all manner of their men between sixty and sixteen, spiritual, temporal, burgh and land, Islesmen and others, which amount to the number of a hundred thousand, not reckoning carriage-men, and artillery-men who had the charge of fifty sort of cannons. [50]

Lindsay of Pitscottie continues to tell that, while 'James IV was not at this time on very good terms with his Queen,' the king probably guessed that Margaret was behind some of the spectral phenomena forecasting doom to the enterprise, which

---

[49] Ibid.
[50] Ibid, Dalyell's edition. vol.i. p.267.

obsessed his mind. Pitscottie, as he was always known in Scotland, taking his name as then was common from that of his land, then refers to what was obviously a source of both gossip and scandal in the court at that time. People were whispering behind their hands that the queen was known to be consorting with the Earl of Angus.

Their liaison, it would seem, was not an illicit romance, but sprang from a common cause of resentment concerning the king's paramours. Pitscottie merely states that' Margaret had, moreover, excited her husband's displeasure by connecting herself with the Douglas party, ever inimical to the Scottish crown. The old Earl of Angus, 'Bell the Cat,' had incensed James by joining in the remonstrances of his Queen, made against his war with England.'[51] Thus Queen Margaret's name was identified with the Douglas faction even before the death of her first husband. 'It is true that the infidelities of the King made Angus and the Queen make common cause together. The old Earl was jealous of his gay countess, Janet Kennedy, who was likewise a cause of some displeasure to Margaret.'

Yet despite their differences and the quarrels that had torn them so very far apart, James and Margaret seem to have, at least to some extent, become reconciled on the eve of his going to war. Together, as dusk dimmed the castle, late on that August night, they went by the light of a lantern to some secret part of Linlithgow Palace where, perhaps after lifting a floor board to reveal a cavity beneath, or in a garret at the top of one of the turrets, reached by a dusty, seldom used stair, he showed her the casket, which, when he opened it, in the light of the lantern, shimmered with glittering gold. This was the treasure, sent by King Louis of France, he told her. No one must know of its hiding place other than herself.

Trusting her honesty, she afterwards said that he had shown her the hiding place of the eighteen thousand golden crowns

---

[51] *History of House of Douglas* by Hume of Godscroft. p233.

that King Louis (who had promised fifty thousand) had at last sent him from France and some other things of value including jewels. Also he left written instructions that, in the event of his own death, unless she remarried, she should become both regent of Scotland and custodian of their infant son.

Thus it would seem, that with anxiety for his safety, uppermost in her mind, Margaret said goodbye to James at Linlithgow before, from the great courtyard of the castle, she saw him, wearing a steel breastplate below the doublet which concealed the belt of penance still encircling his waist, mount the charger which a groom was holding, and with a concourse of mounted men behind him, ride away to war.

Slowly and carefully, as by now she must have guessed that she was pregnant, she climbed the spiral stair of the castle, her skirts dragging over the stone steps, to the top of a turret at the south-east end of the palace. From there, in the eerie turret, still called Queen Margaret's Bower, where the slit of a window gave a clear view across the loch below, she watched as the party of horsemen, the royal banner of crimson and gold, flying above their heads, headed south-east for Edinburgh. Seeing them go, her throat constricted with terror as the certainty of forthcoming disaster took possession of her mind.

CHAPTER 22

THE FLOWERS OF THE FOREST

On 17 August the artillery began to be moved from Edinburgh Castle. In all there were seventeen cannon, 'as goodly guns as have been seen in any realm'[52]. They were drawn by no less than four hundred oxen and attended by a gang of forty men, together with a crane, powder carts and pack horses carrying gunstones.

The king, having returned from the north, where he had gone to make one of his habitual pilgrimages to the shrine of St Duthac in Ross-shire, left Edinburgh two days later with the army of men who had gathered on the Burgh Muir.

On 22 August the Scottish army crossed the River Tweed to advance over the Border into England. King James first laid siege to Norham Castle, which surrendered after a week on the 29th.[53] He then led his army up the right bank of the River Till, and took the castle of Ford.

It was there that he lingered fatally, dallying with the beautiful Elizabeth, Lady Heron whose husband, conveniently, was a prisoner in Edinburgh Castle, so the story goes. It is certainly true that he made a bargain with her, promising not to destroy the castle if she, in return, arranged for the freedom of two prisoners held in England, Lord Johnstone and Alexander Home. Many are the reasons put forward for James's apparently inexplicable delay. It has been suggested that Lady Heron was a spy for Lord Surrey and had used her powers of seduction to make James stay with her at Ford Castle, wasting time for fourteen days. More factually,

---

[52] Nicholson. R. The Edinburgh History of Scotland. Vol.2. p.600.

[53] *Letters of King Henry VIII,* Vol.1 pt. ii. Nos.2270,229.2283.

however, it would seem that there were other, more valid reasons for doing so. It was harvest time and many of his enlisted soldiers were deserting, eager to get back to ensuring that the crops, on which life depended, were saved. Also the pestilence, as the plague was called, at that time rampant in Edinburgh, carried by some of the men on the march south, was now spreading its deadly infection through the ranks of the Scottish army.

Another cause for concern was the guns. It had been unseasonably wet for late summer so that carts, when heavily loaded, frequently sank into the ground. On 29 August James sent the treasurer to Edinburgh to find both more oxen to pull them through the rough and boggy ground and replacement wheels for the gun carriages, which were constantly breaking or buckling under the weight of iron cannon pulled along deeply rutted roads. [54]

Certainly, on leaving Ford, James broke his word to Lady Heron by having her castle destroyed, an indication that the rumour of his infatuation with her may have been either exaggerated or untrue.

One thing that cannot be doubted is that the Earl of Surrey's liking for James had turned to hatred and distrust. When, ten years ago, he had escorted Margaret to Edinburgh to be married to him, as had been so much remarked upon, the two had been constant companions, friends hardly separated as they had made merry, drinking, feasting and jousting in the lists. But now relations between them were hostile over James's affiliation to King Louis of France. To Surrey, James was a traitor to King Henry to whom he had said on his departure .'I shall do my duty that your grace may find me diligent and to fulfil your will shall be my gladness. May I see him or I die that is the cause of my abiding behind [in England]

---

[54] C.T.S. vol. iv. p. 522.

and if ever he and I meet, I shall do that in me lieth to make him as sorry.' [55]

Surrey, in command of the English army, was at Pontefract when, on 25 August, he heard that James, leading his force had crossed the Tweed. He at once sent out a summons to the sheriffs of surrounding areas to call out their men before advancing upon York. From there, in weather, unusually atrocious for the time of year, he pushed on to Newcastle to be joined by Lord Dacre and other landlords with their enlisted men.

Surrey with about twenty thousand men under his command, was facing a hostile army slightly larger than his own. But, now a man of seventy, he was one of the most experienced generals in Europe, whereas James had never fought a battle in his life.

Knowing the Scottish king as he did, as one who could not resist a challenge, Surrey sent the Rougecroix Pursuivant to tell him that he would be ready to do battle with him on Friday 9 September at the latest. He had judged his man correctly. The ruse worked as he had planned. On 6 September, by which time he had reached Bolton in north-west England, Surrey had his reply. The Islay Herald appeared to tell him that James would wait for him till noon on Friday 9th.[56]Having received this message, Surrey moved on to Wooler Haugh on the left bank of the River Till, a tributary, running north through a narrow valley, to join the Tweed.

Some six miles ahead, at the eastern end of a ridge of the Cheviot Hills, rose the height known as Flodden Hill where, so his scouts informed him, the Scottish army waited to attack.

Surrey then knew at once, that to outwit James, he must entice him to come down from a nearly impregnable position onto the stretch of flat ground called Milfield to the south-east of Flodden Hill. Accordingly, on the morning of 8 September,

[55] *Hall's Chronicle*, Ed. By Sir H Ellis, London 1899. pp.555-6.
[56] Ibid. p.558.

he ordered his men to cross from the left, to the right bank, of the river Till. Outposts at the Scottish camp saw them moving, but James and his commanders believed that Surrey's intention was to go north into Scotland, to raid the area known as the Merse, in Berwickshire, as a ruse to draw them back across the Border to defend their own country. Surrey's trick had worked. No one in the Scottish camp realized, that the wily old earl's real intention was to lure James from his safe position, by cutting off his line of retreat.

But Surrey could only do this by re-crossing the Till.

He encamped that night at the side of Barmoor Wood, about four miles to the north-east of Flodden Hill. Then next morning, at five o'clock, just as it was getting light, he ordered his men to cross the Till at the ford called Heron's Mill, before, shortly afterwards, his son Admiral Thomas Howard, led his division across the Twizel Bridge. The combined forces then wheeled round to the left to head for a height, only a mile and a half east of Flodden, called Branxton Hill.

It was only when, on seeing this happen, from his vantage point on Flodden Hill, that James realized the strategy of Surrey's move. The English general, who had once been his friend, had outflanked him. Not only was he now blocking off his retreat back to Scotland but plainly he intended to take Branxton Hill, a position as unassailable as his own.

Suddenly aware of the danger, James ordered an immediate advance. The trumpets blew and teams of men and oxen strained at ropes, to haul the guns from their emplacements down the south side of Flodden Hill, and across the swampy ground below to take up a new position above Branxton Church on the northern side of Branxton Hill. So great was the hurry that the camp fires were left smouldering, forming a great cloud of smoke to drift over the hillside smarting, and in some cases temporarily blinding the eyes of men stumbling as they marched.

Quickly they were arranged in a great square and diamond shaped formations. The division on the extreme left was commanded by Lord Home and the Earl of Huntly. Next was that led by the earls of Montrose, Crawford and Errol. On the right, the division was commanded by the king himself, while on the extreme right the men of the Highlands and the Western Isles were led by the earls of Lennox and Argyll. A fifth division, under the Earl of Bothwell, was placed in reserve immediately behind that led by the king. With James, together with the nobles and knights of his household, was his natural son and namesake, the young archbishop of St Andrews.

As was usual at the start of a battle, the horses of the mounted men were led to the rear. Amongst them was James's own charger, for now the words of the Spanish ambassador de Ayala, who had said that James was a bad commander as he would always lead the fight, must have been remembered. Those nearest to him begged him, as a general, to direct the battle rather than take part, telling him that his own life, was worth a hundred thousand others. But James did not heed them even if their voices reached his ears. This was his moment of glory. This, as if it could be against the infidel, was his crusade. King James would fight and die amongst his men.

At once the Scottish cannon began to fire, but, aimed by inexperienced gunners, the cannonballs missed their mark passing harmlessly over the heads of the advancing English to fall harmlessly in their rear. The English guns, manned by German gunners were more accurate. The king's own division came under fire and seeing his men fall, James realized he had no alternative other than to advance. Again the trumpets sounded as the spearmen led the way towards the enemy.

Lord Home, leading the first charge, then withdrew his men, an action which would later be seen as deliberate treachery to the king. Nonetheless, at first James seemed to be winning as the enemy fell back before what looked like an advancing wall of death, formed by the Scottish long pointed spears. But then the English footmen charged forward with the shorter, but more deadly halberds. The Scots fought on, the Highlanders, yelling in the charge, throwing off their shoes to get a better grip on slippery ground. The king fought frantically, killing five men before his spear shattered in his hands. He was within a spear's length of Surrey, when he fell, pierced by an arrow and wounded by a spear.

So too died most of the Scottish nobility, the earls of Crawford, Errol, Montrose and Argyll amongst them, lying slaughtered on the field.

Night brought a merciful shroud of darkness over the carnage on the lower slope and the foot of Branxton Hill. Amongst the piles of the bodies, discovered only the next day, was that of King James. Lord Dacre, who knew him well, identified the corpse before, when it was taken to Berwick, its identity was confirmed by Sir John Forman, the king's Sergeant Porter and Sir William Scott, a member of the Council.[57]

Finally, conveyed by his enemies down to England, James is currently believed to be buried somewhere in Richmond Park.

But soon after the battle the stories began. James had been seen in Kelso on the night following the battle. He had been treacherously murdered by one of the Homes, so the rumour ran. He had escaped and was on his way to Jerusalem to lead his great ambition, that of leading a crusade.

Meanwhile, alone in the turret of Linlithgow Palace, Margaret sat waiting, looking out over the loch for the first sign of the royal banner to tell her that James was coming home.

---

[57] *Letters of Henry VIII,* vol.1.pt.2. No 2913. Lord Dacre to the Council.

PART 2

CHAPTER 1

THE MOURNING CORONATION

The Palace of Linlithgow was like a morgue. A cloud of sadness enveloped the whole great building as servants talked in whispers and shuffled along with bowed heads. High in the turret rising above the battlements, Margaret at last rose to her feet and turned from the window, accepting that James would now never return. The great house seemed empty without him and the men who were his closest friends. All were dead. Never would she hear their laughter or the thud of their feet on the stairs. Now all she wanted was to escape the building and its memories. She must take the road and go…

Accordingly she gave orders for her litter to be made ready, and for some of her best gowns and cloaks to be packed in readiness for little James's coronation which must, almost immediately, take place. Thankfully she left Linlithgow and, with a trail of carts holding her possessions following behind her, she headed north for Perth.

There, once ensconced in the Royal residence attached to the Dominican Priory, where the first King James had been murdered now eighty years ago, she at once wrote to her brother Henry, begging him to remain at peace with Scotland and not to oppress her 'little King' his nephew who was very small and tender being only one year and five months old. She then told him that she was pregnant with her husband's posthumous child.

Henry replied telling her 'that if the Scots wanted peace they should have it; if war they should have it; as for her husband, he had fallen by his own indiscreet rashness, and foolish kindness to France, but he regretted his death as a relative.'[58]

From Perth, Margaret moved to Stirling where, on 21 September, only twenty days since the death of his father, the little prince was crowned in the Chapel Royal of Stirling Castle. Old Bishop Elphinstone of Aberdeen, named by King James as a guardian of his infant son, held the crown over the head of little James in a ceremony, remembered largely for its pathos, as so many wept for all that had been lost. Mostly they remembered the boy's father, who in the words of the Scottish historian George Buchanan, was 'dear to all men living and mightily lamented by his people at his death.'

Following the coronation the Parliament, which convened at Stirling, confirmed Margaret's position as chief guardian of the king, provided that she did not remarry. The Lord Chancellor, James Beaton, Archbishop of Glasgow, together with her late husband's cousin, the Earl of Arran, his most loyal friend the Earl of Huntly, and rather surprisingly the man with whom her name had been linked, old 'Bell the Cat,' Archibald Earl of Angus, were deputed to assist her. Thus at the end of September 1513, following the battle which at first sight would seem to have destroyed any form of relationship, the whole of Britain, both north and south was ruled by the Tudor brother and sister Henry VIII, King of England and Queen Margaret of Scotland.

But there was opposition. In the month of the new king's coronation, September 1513, the Earl of Arran and Lord Fleming, who albeit the suspected murderer of James IV's mistress Margaret Drummond, held the office of Lord Chamberlain, sailed with the Scottish fleet to France. When they learned of the catastrophe of Flodden they supported, or suggested, a proposal that the office of governor of Scotland

---

[58] Strickland. A. p. 95.

should go to John, Duke of Albany, first cousin of the late King James.

Logically Arran himself, grandson of the elder daughter of King James II, should have held this office. But Arran, with great estates of his own, did not want the extra responsibility of running the country.

Albany was the only son of the second marriage of his father, Alexander, Stewart, 1st Duke of Albany, who, having quarrelled with his brother James III, had fled to France where, his first marriage annulled, he had married the great French heiress, Anne de la Tour d'Auverne. Reconciled to his brother, he had then returned to Scotland, only to quarrel with him again, this time declaring his children to be illegitimate and himself the rightful heir to the crown. Imprisoned for treachery in Edinburgh Castle, he had escaped with the help of a page, by climbing from a window down a rope. The page had fallen, breaking his leg as the rope broke, sending him crashing to the ground, but Albany had then carried the boy to safety over his back, before again contriving to escape to France. There he had been killed, jousting with the king's brother, the Duke d'Orléans, leaving his son John fatherless as a very small child.

Recognized as his father's heir, despite there being children of a previous marriage, the young Duke of Albany had grown up entirely in France, becoming in every respect a Frenchman, handsome, charming and imbued with all of the sophistication of the French court. On the death of Louis XII in 1515, his successor, Francis I urged this second Duke of Albany to accept the proffered government of Scotland. But, unwilling to leave his wife who was ill, he deferred the decision, sending his friend Antony d'Arcy, the Sieur de Bastie back to Scotland with Arran to command the castle of Dunbar in his name. De Bastie already knew Scotland. He had been one of the knights who, during the celebrations following King James's wedding to Margaret, had jousted with the king whose favouritism he had won. Thus de Bastie came to Scotland to be made Warden of the Marches from the bastion of Dunbar.

In Scotland Margaret soon had her critics. Accused of purloining the French money, which James had showed her on that fateful night before he rode off for Flodden, she was believed to be spending it on herself. The bishop of Aberdeen, addressing the parliament at Stirling, lamented the poverty of the royal exchequer. Great claims, he said were being made by the queen for her jointure and for the education of the young king, therefore, he too suggested that John Duke of Albany, as the first cousin of the late King James, should be asked to come from France, to help the widowed Margaret, who was only twenty-two and inexperienced, both in government and in managing the country's finances.

Henry VIII, when told of this intention was horrified. Writing to Margaret, he tried to bully her into doing everything in her power to prevent it happening. The last thing that he wanted being more interference in Scotland from France. Margaret herself seems to have played little part in politics, living quietly at Stirling Castle, before, on 30 April of the following year of 1514, she gave birth to another boy, who baptised Alexander, became the Duke of Ross.

Shortly after this happening, the now widowed Louis XII– whose wife Anne of Brittany had been a cause of such jealousy to Margaret– made a proposition to marry Margaret himself. Henry VIII, even more upset by this news, quickly put a spoke in the wheel by suggesting his own and Margaret's younger sister Mary, reputedly one of the most beautiful young women in England, as a bride for the now ageing French king.

Margaret herself, in the meantime, had fallen desperately and dangerously in love, not with a man much older, as was King Louis, into whose eager wrinkled arms her poor young sister was thrust, but with a man five years younger than herself who, although a widower himself, was only nineteen.

Archibald, 6th Earl of Angus, was the grandson of the 5th earl, so famously nicknamed 'Bell the Cat,' the man with whom, during her much rumoured altercations with King James, Margaret had formed what can best be termed as a liaison. Seen in retrospect her reasons for doing seem obvious. Angus was the head of the all-powerful faction in Scotland adhering to England. Therefore, he seemed a natural ally against the pervading influence of the French, so much in favour with the husband, with whom, during the latter years of their marriage, she had been so bitterly at odds. Logically, it would seem, that in defiance of her husband, Margaret may have sought what amounted to fatherly advice.

Yet, be that as it may, it is not beyond possibility, that the wily old Earl saw a way to manipulate the young and lonely woman, neglected by her husband for the mistresses with whom he so flagrantly consorted, by throwing his handsome grandson in her path.

Angus had lost two sons at the Battle of Flodden as well as two hundred Douglas men. Heartbroken he had retired to his castle of Tantallon, in East Lothian, where during the winter, as gales from the North Sea blasted the stone walls, he had died. However, his eldest son George (killed at Flodden) who had married Elizabeth, the surviving daughter of Lord Drummond of Stobhall, had left a son Archibald, handsome and red-haired as most of his family, who now, on the death of his grandfather, succeeded him as the 6th earl. This was the man with whom Margaret, spontaneously as it would seem, fell passionately in love.

As the grandson of old Angus, the young Archibald may well have been about the court but it is known that it was his maternal grandfather, Lord Drummond of Stobhall, who introduced him to the parliament of September 1514.

Lord Drummond was the man whose daughter Margaret, the long term mistress and supposed secret wife of James IV, had been poisoned with two of her sisters to make certain that the king did not renege on his politically important marriage to Margaret. As the Lord-Justiciary of Scotland, Drummond was one of the most important officers of the crown. A man of great ambition, unscrupulous as most of his kind, he may have regarded the infatuation of the queen, for whose import as a wife for the late King James his daughters had so cruelly died, as a just act of revenge. Be that as it may, Drummond also chose to disregard the fact that his grandson, Archibald, Earl of Angus, headstrong as he is known to have been, already had a mistress in the form of Janet Stewart, daughter of the laird of Traquair.

If Margaret was aware of these connotations involved in her association with the young Lord Angus, she wilfully ignored them. In doing so she was at the same time influenced by Lord Drummond who pointed out that, with the powerful influence of the Douglas family behind her, she could refute the intentions of the pro French faction in the government which wished to bring the Duke of Albany from France to undermine, if not supplant, her own rule. This, to her mind, gave her a sound reason for remarrying Archibald Angus in defiance of her late husband's will.

Margaret married Angus on 6 August 1514 in a private ceremony in Kinnoul Church. Arranged by Lord Drummond, the clergyman officiating was his nephew Walter Drummond, the dean of Dunblane. Two weeks later, on the 18th, the Council deposed her from the regency, ruling that, in accordance with the late king's will, by marrying again she had lost her right to be guardian of the young king. Lord Home, as spokesman, voiced their opinions.

'We have shown heretofore our willingness to honour the Queen, contrary to the ancient custom of this kingdom, we suffered and obeyed her authority the whiles she herself kept her right by keeping her widowhood. Now she has quit it by marrying, why should we not chuse another to succeed in the place she has voluntarily left? Our old laws do not permit that a woman should govern in the most peaceable times, far less now when such evils do threaten as can scarcely be resisted by the wisest and most sufficient men.'

While most of the counsellors agreed with him, one of them then spoke up, saying that the point that principally annoyed them was that the Earl of Douglas, as head of the house of Douglas, was already great: the queen marrying him had made him greater still... but now he was her husband, would make him far too great for the peace and safety of Scotland. The Council concluded by solemnly deposing the queen from the sovereignty of Scotland as Regent. Moreover, the Lord Lyon, king-at-arms, was formally ordered to signify to Lord Angus 'that he must forthwith appear before the Lords of the Council to answer for his boldness in marrying her without their assent and recommendation.'

Then, following their almost unanimous decision to demote Queen Margaret from the regency, the members of the Council sent an urgent message to the Duke of Albany to leave France and come to Scotland with all possible speed.

Margaret and her two little boys were then living in the stronghold of Stirling Castle of which Lord Drummond was the keeper and he, together with the Douglases, supported her in defying the Council's authority. Thus, in November, not one but two separate parliaments were convened, one in Stirling, the other in Edinburgh.

Foremost amongst the items discussed at both conventions was the primacy of St Andrews, left vacant by the death of King James's illegitimate son James Stewart at the battle of Flodden. The choice of the much respected Bishop Elphinstone to replace him had been unchallenged, but Elphinstone died in October 1514. Margaret, supported by her brother King Henry, then demanded that Gavin Douglas, the bishop of Dunkeld, be appointed to the see. The Bishop seized St Andrews Castle but was driven out after a siege by John Hepburn, the prior, who had been elected to the archbishopric by the chapter. Margaret, perhaps to console Gavin Douglas, gave him the prayer book which her father Henry VII had given her at the time of their emotional parting at Collyweston, before she left for Scotland. On the first leaf of the book now in the Harleian Library, is inscribed.

'This book was given by Henry 7 of England to his daughter Margaret, Queen of Scotland (mother to the Lady Margaret Douglas) who also gave the same to the Archbishop of St Andrews.'

The Bishop, who was a poet, returned the compliment with verses extolling her beauty entitled *The Palace of Honour*.

'Amidst them, borne within a golden chair,
O'er-fret with pearls and colours most precair,
That drawn was by hackneys all milk white,
Was est a queen as lily sweetly fair,
In purple robe hemmed with gold ilk-where.

With gemmed clasps closed in al perfite,
A diadem most pleasantly polite,
Sate on the tresses of her golden hair,
And in her hand a sceptre of delight,

So next her rode in granate-violet,
Twelve damsels like ane on their estate,
Which seemed of her counsele mos secrete;
And next then was a lusty rout, God wot!
Lords, ladies and full mony a fair prelate,
Both born of low estate and high degree,
Forth with their queen they all by-passed me,
At easy pace, they riding forth the gate,
And I alone abode within the tree.'

CHAPTER 2

A NATION DIVIDED

The Council, having decided to depose the queen as qegent, the Lord Lyon, Sir William Comyn, was deputed to inform her of this decision and also to tell her that the Lord Angus 'must forthwith appear before the Lords of the Council to answer for his boldness in marrying her without their assent and recommendation.' The Lord Lyon, in full regalia, then set off for Stirling Castle where he began badly by asking to be admitted, not to presence of the sovereign, but to 'My lady Queen, the mother of his Grace our King.' Despite this gaffe he was then received by Margaret in her presence chamber where, on one side of her chair of state, stood her new husband Angus and on the other, the austere figure of Lord Drummond.

Margaret listened to the Lord Lyon's denouncement of her rank as regent in silence but then, as the officer approached her new husband to tell him that he was summoned before the national council, Lord Drummond stepped forward and gave him 'a thundering box' on the ear!

Margaret, in a letter to her brother, passed off the incident, telling him that Lord Drummond, had only 'shaked his sleeve at a herald and gave him on the breast with his hand because of his rudeness in saying that 'he came in message from the Lords to my Lady the King's mother,' but the Council, furious at such an affront of their envoy, despatched Sir William Comyn immediately to France to ask the Duke of Albany, as fourth in line to the throne following the two little princes and the Earl of Arran, to come to rule Scotland as regent with all possible speed.

Meanwhile, in Scotland, Archibald Angus continued to throw his weight about. Foremost amongst his enemies was the Lord Chancellor, Archbishop Beaton, who had publicly voiced his disapproval of their marriage. Angus confronted him, at Perth and tore the Great Seal of Scotland out of his hands. Then scandal upon scandal, it was rumoured that Margaret, besotted with her young husband, had given him some, if not all of the gold sent from France, entrusted to her by James on that night of his leaving for Flodden. On the strength of this, the Scottish Council, made it a convenient excuse to refuse to pay her the rents of her dower lands.

Margaret, at Stirling Castle, frightened by what was happening and furious at her loss of income on which she was so largely dependent, wrote of her wrongs to her brother, thanking him for his promised support in 'his loving letters which had arrived at her castle of Stirling on November 22, that she had showed to the lords of her party (plainly Angus and his relations) to their great consolation.'

'My party adversary continues in their malice, and proceeds in their Parliament, usurping the King's authority as I and my lords were of no reputation, reputing us as rebels… I beseech that you would make haste with your army both sea and land, especial on the chamberlain (Lord Fleming). On that other side the Prior of St Andrews (Hepburn) with the power of my counter party, (the Parliament) has laid siege to the castle of St Andrews, which I would your navy would revenge, for it stands on the sea-side, free against Berwick by north. I have sent my husband, Lord Angus, to break the siege, if he may this 23rd day of November. I am at great expenses, every day a thousand in wages, and my money is nigh hand wasted; if you send not soon other succours in men and money I shall be super-expended, which were to my dishonour, for I can get no answer to my rents, as I showed you before. All the hope that my party-adversaries have is in the Duke of Albany's coming, which I beseech you to hinder in any way; for if he happens to come before your army, I doubt that some of my party will incline him for dead. There is some of the lords of my party who dread that your army shall do them scathe, and that their lands shall be destroyed by the fury of the army, wherefore I would that you wrote to them that their lands and goods shall not be hurt, and that they shall be recompensed double and treble. The King, my son, and his little brother, prospers well, and are right life-like children thanks be to Almighty God. It is told me that the lord adversaries are purposed to siege me in this castle of Stirling. I would therefore that Lord Chamberlain Fleming be held waking in the meantime with the Borderers, I trow I shall defend me well enough from the others till the coming of the army, I pray you give credit to Master Adam Wilkinson in other things as it is written by him, and thank him for his good service, and the peril he was in for my sake in the ship that was broken.'[59]

The shipwreck that she refers to, was that of the vessel carrying the Lord Lyon to France to explain the wrongs done to him, and to ask the Duke of Albany to come to Scotland.

'God was of my party, seeing that he letted the Lord Lyon's message and furthered mine,' she added triumphantly, in her letter to her brother before telling him that, if her letters were only signed Margaret R and no more, they were mere state papers either forged or forced from her. She ends with a plea for support. 'Brother, all the welfare of me and my children rest in your hands, which I pray Jesu to help and keep eternally to his pleasure.

Your loving sister
Margaret R'.[60]

Margaret left Stirling to spend the rest of the winter at Perth where she began planning to escape to England with her two little boys. Both her brother King Henry and his chief advisor Cardinal Wolsey, seem to have urged her to do this, but, claiming that she was spied on by agents of her enemies in the government, she told her brother:

---

[59] Cott. MS Cal. Bi.fol.164.
[60] Ibid.

'but it is impossible to be performed by any manner of fashion that I, or my husband, or his uncle Gavin, can devise. Considering what watch and spies there is daily where I am, I dare disclose my counsel to none but God! An I were such a woman that I might go with my bairn on mine arm, I trow I should not be long from you, whose presence I desire more than any man.' Then once again emphasising her poverty, she told him that:

'I trust dear brother, to defend me from mine enemies, if I had sufficient for expenses till the coming of our help; but I am so super-expended that I doubt but poverty shall cause me to consent to some of their minds, which I shall never do against your counsel while I have a groat to spend. Wherefore I pray you to send me some money, for it is not for your honour that I or my children should want.' [61]

Such was the strength of the opposition to Margaret and Angus that, by the beginning of 1515, the men in power in Scotland were the Earl of Arran, the archbishop of Glasgow, James Beaton and Lord Home, the latter of whom detested Queen Margaret knowing that she and all those close to her, suspected him of treachery at Flodden. Soon, however, they would have to abide by the ruling of the regent they themselves had summoned from France.

John, Duke of Albany landed at Dumbarton on 18 May 1515, arriving with a convoy of eight ships loaded with stores and his escort of men-at-arms. There to meet him was Lord Home at the head of a party of his famous March-riders to the number of ten thousand mounted men. Albany already knew, from the ambassador de Bastie, that Home was suspected of treason at the battle of Flodden to the extent that he might have been responsible for the king's death. Home strode down to the landing place resplendent in what is described as 'Kendal

---

[61] Cott. MS. B. iii. f.278. Queen Margaret to Henry VIII, January 23. Perth.

green velvet' only to meet a cool reception when Albany made a quotation in Latin implying that such a train of followers was not necessary for a mere subject, and that such a flamboyant dress was unbecoming to such a small man. Incensed by Albany's undisguised contempt for him, Home instantly decided to support Queen Margaret's claim to the regency against him. It was not an auspicious beginning to the acquaintanceship of two men destined to influence the future of an already divided land.

Margaret, for her part, although inwardly seething with anger, put on the best show of hiding her feelings, of which she was capable, by descending from Edinburgh Castle to meet the new regent and (according to Bishop Lesley) 'do him all possible honour.'[62] No doubt she did so because, like many other women, with his good looks and charming manners, learnt at the French court, she found him a most attractive man. So much did she apparently like him that rumour went round that she wanted to marry him something, which, under the circumstances, with both his wife and her husband alive, was blatantly impossible. Nevertheless, as later would become obvious, she does seem to have become enamoured of him at this time, doubtless to the fury of the young husband with whom she had made such a precipitate marriage less than a year before.

Margaret's unconcealed liking for Albany must have been a cause of annoyance to Angus, even if, for no personal feeling of jealousy, it resulted in his family's fall from power. At the Parliament, which assembled in Edinburgh in July, when Albany as the new regent, was invested with the sword and sceptre of state, Lord Drummond, Angus's grandfather, for so rudely assaulting the Lord Lyon, was not only arrested and imprisoned in Blackness Castle on the Forth, but had all his lands and possessions forfeited to the crown. Worse than this, Angus's uncle, Bishop Gavin Douglas, was also held captive

---

[62] Lesley. p.102.

for attempting to seize the primacy of St Andrews from John Hepburn, the prior. Suddenly frightened by this unexpected proof of the power of the new ruler, something plainly beyond anything that she herself had expected, Margaret wrote to the Scottish ambassador in London, 'that the Duke of Albany had made fair and pleasant semblance to her at his first coming, but now, by the advice of his council, was meditating to take her tender children from her keeping.'[63]

Ever the drama queen, she continues, 'I went down from Edinburgh Castle sore weeping to Holyrood, where the Regent lodged, entreating him to let them out, as they were the principal members of the council, but grace I got nan' [from] this Albany who has done nothing but vex and trouble (her and her friends.) 'All her party had deserted her', she wrote, 'except the Earl of Angus and Lord Home.'

Volatile as Margaret's relationships are known to have been, this one exceeds them all. Lord Home had been her greatest enemy, believed by some to have engineered the death of her husband on Flodden Field, but now, almost overnight, apparently her closest and most trusted friend. Meanwhile, thanks to a petition raised by the Parliament, in which Margaret joined, Lord Drummond was pardoned and restored to his lands and goods.

Uncertain now as to what Albany intended, Margaret was still in Edinburgh Castle, when at the end of July, the Parliament, sitting at the Tolbooth, chose eight peers, out of whom Albany was to select four, and of the four Margaret could pick three to be guardians of her two little boys. What then happened was described in a letter to Lord Dacre from Doctor Magnus, the English priest, who was both Margaret's confessor and the resident minister in Edinburgh for English affairs.

The four lords chosen went in solemn procession from the Tolbooth up to the gate of Edinburgh Castle. Behind them

---

[63] Cott. MS. Calig B, vi.f.115.-British Museum.

came a great concourse of citizens all agog to see what would happen. As the gates were opened, the excited crowd outside saw the queen standing within the entrance, holding the three-year-old little king's hand. Behind, a nurse carried his brother, the fifteen month old Duke of Ross, while close to her, forming a semi-circle, stood her husband, the Earl of Angus, and members of her household staff. Immediately, on sight of them, the crowd burst into cries of joy and applause, and it was only when this abated, enough to make herself heard, that Margaret shouted clearly to the lords:

'Stand! Declare the cause of your coming before you draw nearer to your sovereign.'

The four Scottish peers, somewhat cowed by this reception, explained 'that they were deputed by the Parliament, then sitting, to demand and receive their infant King and his brother,' at which Margaret shouted 'Drop the portcullis' at which the massive iron structure crashed down before her, shutting out the lords and the crowd. From behind it, Margaret spoke to the lords, who pressed forward to hear her voice:

'This castle of Edinburgh is part of my infeoffment. By the late King, my husband, I was made sole governess of it, nor to any mortal shall yield the command. But, I require out of respect to the Parliament and the nation, six days to consider their mandate. For my charge is infinite in import, and alas my councillors be few'!

She then turned and led away her son, the little King James V, with her husband and attendants following in her train. At sight of them disappearing, the crowd again began to cheer and the four lords, thwarted in their purpose, are nonetheless claimed by Doctor Magnus to have been much impressed, both with her beauty and her spirit.

CHAPTER 3

THE FLIGHT INTO ENGLAND

The same could not be said of Angus who, again according to Lord Dacre, had a notarial instrument drawn up, properly witnessed and sent to the regent, in which he declared that he had told the queen that she should surrender her children to a named authority. Lord Dacre's opinion of Angus is summed up in his saying that he was 'childish young,' a characteristic which, as Agnes Strickland points out, may have descended to Darnley, the grandson who, at the same age of nineteen was to find himself consort of the reigning queen of Scotland. Margaret herself, having asked for six days to reach her decision, finally made a formal offer to Parliament 'that, if James V and his brother were left in her care, she would maintain them on her dowry, and that she would submit that they should be committed to the custody of the Earl Marischel, of Lord Home, by then Lord Chamberlain, of Sir Robert Lauder of Bass and of her husband Lord Angus'.[64]

As she had guessed, her offer being rejected, she moved for greater safety to Stirling Castle, and it was at this point that Angus deserted her to go to his own lands or, as seems equally probable, to his mistress Janet Stewart at Traquair near Peebles in Berwickshire. Margaret, furious with him as she must have been, left to protect two small children and pregnant with his child, did reach the secure fortress of Stirling before, on 4 August, Albany appeared outside the walls of the town with a force of reputedly seven thousand men. Told they were approaching, she despatched a letter to Lord Dacre to tell him, that when they reached Stirling, she intended to make the little

---

[64] Cott.MS. Calig. B. ii.p.281. Aug. 1515. Lord Dacre's narrative to the Council of England.

king stand on the battlements wearing the crown, so that Albany's supporters, who included some local lairds, would be forced to realize that they had taken up arms against their sovereign.[65]

In the event however, this never happened, dramatic as it would have been. Albany brought not only soldiers but the great cannon, Mons Meg, lugged across from Edinburgh Castle, at sight of which, with the muzzle aimed at the walls, Margaret hastily surrendered.

Once again she staged a spectacular scene, standing at the gates of the castle, hand in hand with little James, to whom she gave the heavy iron keys, which he, walking forward unsteadily alone, presented to the kneeling figure of the regent who at once took him in his arms. Again we have it on the word of Lord Dacre that, once in possession of the castle, he treated Margaret with great kindness, letting her see her children whenever she pleased, although forbidding her to take them from Stirling Castle, which, he had learned from some secret intelligence, supposedly with the co-operation of Lord Home, had been her plan.

From Stirling, marooned as she now was with her children, Margaret wrote again to Lord Dacre telling him that:

'I perceive that ye are not sykerly (certainly) informed of what state I stand in, for ye trow (trust) that I may pass wherever I will wish. It is not true, but this bearer can show you the truth of all, and what my mind is, and how I am constrained to do against my will. And I pray you give him credence as ye would do myself, for it is o'er long to write – for I have great trust in this man,

And send me your utter mind and answer in all thing, and God keep you.

Written with my hand this Monday.

Your friend,

Margaret R.'

---

[65] *Letters and Papers of Henry VIII,* Vol.II.pt.I No. 783. Lord Dacre to English Privy Council, 4 August 1515.

She then, on 20 August, wrote another letter to her brother Henry, specifically in the knowledge that it would, as she had previously warned him might happen, be seen by the Scottish Council. In it she praised the arrangements made by Albany while, at the same time telling him that she would shortly 'be taking to her chamber' for the birth of her expected child by Angus.

'Brother, I purpose by the grace of God to take my chamber, and lie in my Palace of Linlithgow, within this twelve days, for I have not past eight weeks to my time, at the which, I pray Jesu to send me good speed and happy deliverance, and to have you, dear brother, eternally in his keeping.'[66]

Margaret had herself carried from Stirling to Linlithgow in a litter. Once there she withdrew into her lying-in chamber, a room hung with tapestry and with all the windows shut although it was August, where she pretended to be very ill. Word being sent to Archibald Angus he promptly joined her, prompted it seems by Lord Home.

The next night she crept down the stairs, heavily cloaked and into the courtyard where, in the shadow cast by the building, she found men and horses waiting as her husband had arranged. There was no question now of a litter. Angus said it would move so slowly that they would certainly be caught. Instead, heavily pregnant as she was, she had to ride pillion behind him as, with the horses' hoofs muffled by rags, they rode out of the courtyard into the night.

The regent had guessed correctly that she was planning her escape with Lord Home. Margaret and Angus and the few attendants they had taken with them, had gone barely three miles from Linlithgow when Lord Home appeared with an escort of horsemen, 'hardy well-striking fellows' as she described them to her brother, with the little Lord Chamberlain

---

[66] Cott. MS.

himself at their head. Protected by them they rode to Tantallon, the great fortress of the 'Red Douglases', as Angus's branch of the family were known, standing on cliffs just south of North Berwick looking out over the Firth of Forth, the Isle of May in the distance and beyond it the wide North Sea.

Once within the castle Lord Home explained his plan. He was going to do some 'roughing' as he called it, on some of the royal property now in the hands of the Duke of Albany as regent, which would divert his attention from Stirling Castle. Once he was known to have left it, Home would use his position as Lord Chamberlain to gain access to Margaret's two little boys, after which he would join her at his castle of Blackater and they would all escape into her brother's kingdom.[67]

However Albany, wise to Lord Home's tactics, was not taken in. Furious at his destruction of royal property, he made him an outlaw so that Home joined Margaret and Angus at Tantallon Castle where they waited, expecting an invitation from King Henry, until 23 September.

Instead, one of Angus's scouts came in with a rumour that Albany was approaching with a large force of men to lay siege to Tantallon. With that they were away. Margaret did not even have time to pack her jewel box before Angus had her out of the castle and onto a pillion behind his saddle.

They rode, first through the fertile lands of the Firth, where men and women, harvesting corn and hay in the fields, stopped their work to watch them ride by. Then it was up the slopes of the Lammermuirs, the great sheep rearing area of Scotland, where the grass in late September was just beginning to die back, losing its summer growth. Beyond lay the Border Country, intersected by the great River Tweed, land of the Douglases and Homes.

---

[67] Lesley, p. 103.

Here they felt safer, but Margaret was now ill. The long ride had tired her and somehow, perhaps when the horse stumbled, she had wrenched her hip. Carried into the Nunnery, attached to the Priory of Coldstream, she was cared for by the prioress, who, to her delight, proved to be none other than the aunt of her own faithful controller of her household, Robert, or as she always called him, Robin Barton. Also to her bedside came old Lady Home, a diminutive lady of much the same stature as her son, who brought her comforts such as wine and sweetmeats and offered consoling advice.

Then at last came the invitation from Henry, brought by a rider together with the safe conducts that they needed to get into England. Margaret was still far from well and in pain from the torn muscles in her hip, but the mere thought of England was enough to make her determined to proceed.

She left, as it proved just in time, before Albany sent a Frenchman, a man called Monsieur de Barody, to arrest poor old Lady Home. Forced to ride a high stepping nag which jolted every one of the arthritic bones in her body, she was taken to Dunbar Castle, where, thrust into a dungeon, in that freezing rock-bound castle above the North Sea, she was given only bread and water.

'I verily believe, considering her feebleness of body, that the Duke of Albany's Frenchman means to be the death of old Lady Home' wrote Margaret later. But fortunately the old lady was saved when Albany exchanged her for the Lord Lyon, taken prisoner at Berwick, on his way to deliver letters to Henry VIII.

Meanwhile, carried in a litter between horses at head and tail, with Angus now riding beside her, armed as were all of his men, Margaret was taken down the most direct route to the south over tracks across the Cheviot Hills. Inevitably the jolting of the litter increased the pain in her hip but, when they were still nearly forty miles from Morpeth Castle, a new pain, which she recognized as the onset of childbirth, wracked the length of her body.

She could not possibly travel farther. There was only one thing for it. She had to be taken to Harbottle Castle, a garrison of the frontier, which stood conveniently nearby. Fortunately Lord Dacre himself was there. War having broken out recently between Scotland and England meant that cattle raiding, always endemic on both sides of the Border, was now, when the beasts were fat with summer grazing, a most lucrative pursuit. Lord Dacre, as Warden of the Marches, had made Harbottle his headquarters in an effort to maintain order in these most lawless of lands.

But plainly he hated the Scots. Not one of Margaret's Scottish attendants was allowed to enter the castle. She found herself in a building not much better than a barn. Wind blew through cracks in the rough stone walls and water, when it was raining, dripped through holes in the roof. There she lay in her agony on a soldier's rough pallet bed until, three days after arriving, late on the evening of 7 October, she gave birth to a baby girl.

Surprisingly, in view of the circumstances of her birth, the child appeared to be healthy. But Lord Dacre was taking no chances. A child unless christened was believed to be without a soul, so he saw to it that the little red-haired baby, named after her mother, was baptised the very next day when, as promised prior to her birth, a knight stood proxy for Cardinal Wolsey as her godfather.

Three days later Margaret, although still very weak, managed to dictate a letter to Albany saying that 'she had been forced for fear and danger of her life to depart from Scotland to the realm of England...

'so it is that, by the Grace of Almighty God, I am now delivered and have a Christian soul, being a young lady.'[68]

---

[68] Cott. MS. Calig. B. vi.

She continued to exhort him, in God's name, that he should suffer her, as his honour, and right and good justice require, to have the whole rule and governance of Scotland, and of her tender children as their tutrix, according to the will of the late king of Scotland, her spouse. The letter, dated October 10 1515, written by a secretary, was not signed by Margaret, too ill at that time even to lift a pen.

Half conscious, lying in that remote Border fortress, she was barely aware of the threat of bands of marauding raiders roaming the district who seized on any loot, be it animals or possessions, that they could find. Sentries kept watch continually, ever on the alert for moving figures particularly on nights when clouds drifted over the moon, listening for muffled hoof-beats and the rattle of moving stones.

'Glad would I have been', wrote Lord Dacre in the dispatch he sent to King Henry announcing the baby's birth,

'to have advertised your Highness of the Queen's safe deliverance, but our causes here was intricate, with so much cumber and business that we could not ascertain your Highness of the same till this time, unless we should have sent up a post purposely for the said Queen's deliverance, which we thought not greatly requisite.'[69]

But it was not only the raiders who they had reason to fear. Hardly was Margaret's letter despatched with a courier, before another outrider appeared with a warning that Albany, with supposedly forty thousand men, was advancing to lay siege to Harbottle. This proved to be false. Albany was in fact in conflict with Lord Home, described as 'a man unpolisht, stubbornly stout, hazardous, mighty in riches and power and consequently proud.'[70] Albany placed him in ward under the jurisdiction of his cousin Lord Arran. However Arran then not only helped Home to escape, but joined him in an attempt to overthrow the regent's power.

---

[69] Ibid. Lord Dacre's letter.
[70] Bingham, C, James V King of Scots p.37.

Together, with the earls of Glencairn, Eglinton and Lennox, they arrived at Harbottle, to be permitted in this instance, by Lord Dacre, to have entrance into his castle. Here, together with Angus, they signed a pledge to free both the little king of Scotland and his brother Alexander, Duke of Ross, from the control of Albany, from whom they would take the regnant power to restore it to the queen.

Albany, in the meanwhile, had marched west from Edinburgh to take Arran's lands of Hamilton, thus ending his attempt at rebellion. Subsequently, Arran himself was pardoned as were Home and his brother William, on condition of their accepting the regent's rule.

Shortly afterwards Margaret received two answers to her letter from Albany, one officially from himself and the Council, begging her to return and promising that if she did so, she would have not only the rents from her dower lands returned to her, but control of her children on condition of her sworn promise not to take them out of the country. The contents of the second letter, written in his own fine hand, are unknown, but Albany was later to tell her brother King Henry, that she had turned all proposals down.

Because of her great weakness, Margaret could not leave Harbottle until the beginning of November, when, again in a litter, she was carried the forty odd miles to Morpeth Castle, Lord Dacre's Northumberland seat. The journey, in her perilous state of health, must have been exhausting, and the days at that time of year being short they must have stayed at least one, if not more nights in wayside inns, in one of which she may have become infected with the typhoid fever, so soon to bring her close to death.

At last, in the distance, they saw the grey stone walls of Morpeth Castle, on a hill above the River Wansbeck, rising clear against the sky. Entering through the magnificent gatehouse, which, with some alteration, stands to this day, she found herself in the luxury of which, in the rigours of

Harbottle, she can only have dreamed. Fires heated the rooms where tapestries kept draughts from the walls. Upstairs in the bed-chambers, where feather filled mattresses lay on the curtained four-poster beds, servants carried water heated in the kitchens to fill hip baths, while downstairs, in the great hall, silver gleamed on the table reflecting the light of candles and rush-lights burning in brackets on the walls.

Then, to add to her contentment, Margaret found that her brother had sent her presents, lengths of velvet and the expensive cloth of gold. Delighted by the soft touch, as she smoothed the material with her fingers, she asked Lady Dacre to summon local seamstresses to cut out and sew dresses to her own design. They would replace the travel worn garments which were all that were left of the clothes she had seized to take with her on that hectic departure from Tantallon, as it seemed such an age ago. These were not the only gifts carried by a courier from England for, in addition, most touchingly, Queen Catherine, once again pregnant herself, had sent a layette of baby clothes for the little red-haired Margaret Douglas, now some six weeks old.

This happy interlude ended tragically, however, when news came from Scotland that Alexander, Duke of Ross, the younger of her two little boys had died. Margaret, hysterical in her sorrow, immediately accused Albany of poisoning him. But, as historians then and now have pointed out, Albany, who is known to have shown both great care and affection towards both children, would have had to kill both boys to take possession of the throne, whereas James, the elder, was known to be perfectly well. Therefore it must be taken, that Alexander died from natural causes, as happened so frequently at the time.

Overcome with misery over the loss of her child, Margaret succumbed to the typhus fever with which she may have been infected somewhere on the road. Weakened by childbirth, she was again so ill that her life was despaired of, or so a contemporary claimed.

It was at this, of all moments, that something happened which then, as now seems almost impossible to believe. On the very day when Margaret's attendants thought she was dying, Angus left her.

He claimed, to those willing to listen, that he had problems on his own estates to attend to, but few amongst them doubted that it was his mistress across the Border in Dumfriesshire who was claiming his prior attention.

Nonetheless, Margaret, with the robust constitution of the Tudors, survived her illness, recovering to the point where, after four months of staying with Lord and Lady Dacre, who must have found her a trying guest, she was strong enough to continue her long postponed journey to her brother's court. Doctor Magnus, her confessor, who seems also to have become her friend, wrote to King Henry saying that 'he should write comfortable letters to his sister and send for her, because she has daily messengers coming out of Scotland so that she is troubled in her mind, and put to study, to imagine and cast what answer to make to them.'[71]

---

[71] Lesley p. 105.

CHAPTER 4

KING HENRY'S COURT

It was not until the beginning of April, when the roads were clear of snow and ice bound ruts melted by the sun, that Sir Thomas Parr, with an escort of armed men, appeared at Morpeth Castle. He had ridden from London, bringing a present for Queen Margaret from her sister-in-law Queen Catherine, of her favourite white palfrey carrying a specially cushioned pillion for Margaret to sit on during the long journey to London. This may have been the same white palfrey on which, during Henry's absence in France, Catherine, while herself pregnant, had ridden at the head of Surrey's army for the first part of its march to Scotland to defeat King James on Flodden Field. Kindness it certainly was on the part of Queen Catherine, who, from the time of their first meeting, when she had come from Spain, lonely and frightened to marry Prince Arthur, had made a friend of his sister Margaret four years younger than herself. But Margaret, at sight of it, cannot but have remembered those two other white ponies which, having carried her up to Scotland, had died so horribly in the fire at Dalkeith Castle on the night following her first meeting with her own future husband King James.

Also in the party came Sir William Blackwell, Henry's clerk of the spicery, bringing silver vessels, probably small pots and kettles that could easily be heated on an open fire, for Margaret's use on her journey.

She was ready to go, farewells had been said and Margaret mounted on Queen Catherine's pillion, when it was discovered that Angus, who had promised to ride beside her, had not returned from Scotland as he had sworn to do. Immediately a hunt for him was organized, but then, perhaps from a frightened servant to whom he had disclosed his plans, it was discovered that he had indeed come back from Scotland to Morpeth, but had ridden away again during the night to return, as Margaret must have guessed, to Janet Stewart at Traquair.

Furious, feeling herself betrayed, she left without him, but as she rode south through Northumberland, in the sunshine of early spring, she was much mollified by the extent of the welcome that she met in every village and town. True there was no longer the ecstatic greeting of twelve years ago, when she had come to Scotland as a bride, but leading citizens and churchmen rode out to meet her and people cheered, the men raising their bonnets, the women curtseying, and children clapping their hands, as, easily recognisable on the white palfrey, she rode past.

Resting at Stony Stratford, while still some fifty miles from London, she wrote to her brother the first of many letters that indicate her double dealing in affairs of Scottish importance of which she was keeping him informed.

'Dearest Brother

As heartily as I can, I recommend me unto you, and let you wit that yesternight I came hither, so being comforted by you in my journey in many and sundry wises (way), that, loving be to our Lord God, I am in right good heal (health) and as joyous as my said journey toward you as any woman may be incoming to her brother, as I have great cause, and am most desirous now to come to your presence, and to have sight of your person, in who, next God, is my only trust and confidence.

Advertising you, dearest brother, (that) I have received this day a letter from my son's ambassadors now in London, which letter I send you herein enclosed, and have addressed unto them mine answer severally in two sundry letters, (copy whereof I send unto you) that, upon notice had of the same, I may like you to command whether of the said letters it seems best at your pleasure shall be delivered.

And the Holy Trinity have you, my dearest Brother, in tuition and governance. At Stony Stratford the 27 day of April.

Your loving Suster
Margaret.'[72]

Two days later she reached Enfield where she stayed in the royal palace occupied by Sir William Lovel, the Lord Treasurer. Here she rested until, on 3 May, she rode on to Tottenham Cross, then the main entry into London from the north. Approaching the venue, to her great joy, she recognized the royal standard flying over the heads of a party of gaily dressed courtiers and ladies, their velvet cloaks brilliant to the eye, with a larger figure riding in front of them which could only be Henry coming to meet her, conspicuous on a great charger, leading a welcome party of lords and ladies of his realm.

Henry leapt off his horse to kiss her before looking round to demand immediately, 'Where is my Lord Angus?' Then told what has happened he slapped his leg, saying contemptuously, 'Done like a Scot!" Then, his eye falling on the litter in which Margaret's baby daughter sat with her nurse, he seized the child from her arms, and holding her above his head, called her his little Marget, a nickname that clung throughout his life.

Margaret and her brother spent some of the day at a house belonging to a Mr Compton on Tottenham Hill, before, in the afternoon, they set off again for London, she still riding the white palfrey, behind the stout figure of Sir Thomas Parr as, all the way from Scotland, she had done. That night she spent at Baynard's Castle, a structure of Norman origin, rebuilt by her grandfather, Henry VII after its destruction by King John, on land reclaimed from the Thames, between the present day Blackfriars Station and St Pauls.

Although said to be one of the most beautiful and comfortable houses of its day, Margaret stayed only for the night. Eager to see, not only her brother again, but his wife and others of her family, she was ready the next morning, standing

---

[72] Cott. MS, Calig. B.i.fol.25. Letters, first series, Vol.i. p.129.

on the wharf below the palace, to embark on the barge Henry had sent for her, his standard flying at the helm. Thus on that day of early May, she travelled in state down the Thames to land at Greenwich Palace, and the reunion that awaited her with the sister and sister-in-law whom she had not seen for twelve long years. Both were now new mothers, Catherine having given birth to a living daughter called Mary in February, and Mary to a son in March.

Both had changed considerably in the time since she had seen them last. Catherine was older and stouter from the many pregnancies she had endured whereas Mary, last seen as a little girl of seven, had now achieved the beauty for which she was so justly famed. Sent by her brother to marry the ageing Louis XII of France, Henry had promised her, on her departure, that should she become a widow, she could then marry whomsoever she chose.

Subsequently, the French king had died, reputedly from his efforts on the marriage bed, leaving Henry to keep to his word so that Mary had married Charles Brandon, the Earl of Suffolk, with whom she had been in love for years. Mary, still known as the French queen, a title she would retain, was at Greenwich to meet the sister who had come with her own little red-haired daughter, now just eight months old.

Never had it seemed, after Margaret's arrival, had there been a merrier month of May. Her brother proclaimed a grand tournament in her honour when he entered the lists with his brother-in-law Charles Suffolk, both gorgeously dressed, their tabards embroidered with golden honeysuckles, their visors closed as 'they ran volant against all comers' while watchers applauded from the stands. Henry's lance crashed against that of an enormous man called Sir William Kingston, who fell, together with his horse, to loud cries from the spectators. It was only when, after darkness had ended the tournament, that Henry went to Queen Catherine's chamber where, as he removed his helmet, his wife and both his sisters recognized him as the hero of the hour. The whole party then sat down to a banquet in honour of the queen of Scots.

The family reunion, arising from Margaret's visit to England, was commemorated on the order of her brother, by an artist who, in the frontispiece of one of the king' s music books, still in the Harleian Museum, depicted the arms of England. Beneath them are shown the rose and the pomegranate, symbols of Henry and Catherine of Aragon, with opposite the daisy called a marguerite and the marigold, badge of the queen of France. The date, clearly inscribed, is 1516.

But Henry, that most devious of monarchs, never did anything for nothing. Soon he was questioning his sister regarding the situation in Scotland, asking for every detail of the doings of the Scottish Council, the strength of the Scottish army and in particular the ordnance, the number of cannons and their size, also the details of ships, which at any time could put to sea. A letter from Lord Dacre to Cardinal Wolsey, describing a scheme to dislodge the regent Albany, gives the first indication that Margaret, in her transactions with her brother, was actually acting as a spy.

As it was throughout the summer, Margaret persisted in intrigues against Albany. Lord Dacre, in correspondence with Cardinal Wolsey, mentions the queen's involvement in a scheme of his own, evidently in collusion with Angus to dispose of the regent. That Albany intended to visit the English court himself, is revealed by a letter from Margaret to Cardinal Wolsey in August 1516.

'My Lord Cardinal, I am gladder of the tidings of the King's Grace telled me of the Duke of Albany, that he will come hither, which I beseech God may be true, but I dread it be not.

My Lord, I think [it] right long till I speak with you, for next to the King's Grace my next trust is in you, and you may do me most good of any. And I pray you, my Lord as soon as anybody comes out of Scotland, that you will send me word, for I think long till I hear these tidings. No more, but God have you in his keeping.

Your friend

Margaret R.'[73]

Margaret was proved to be right in assuming that the regent would not come to England in person, to confront her brother, who was known to be hostile to anyone with French connections as had Albany. Another reason for him staying in Scotland, however, must have been that a new conspiracy against him by Lord Home was revealed by the interception of treasonable letters.[74]

The regent, however preoccupied otherwise, did allow the Master of Graystock College, on the authority of Lord Dacre, to cross the Border into Scotland, and in the presence of the English Herald Clarencieux, to collect Margaret's plate and jewels which had been taken from Tantallon Castle by the regent's men.[75]

An inventory in the Chapter House at Westminster lists so many articles that one wonders, if in sending them to her, Albany was hoping that she might remain in England for ever, never disrupting his status by returning to Scotland again.

When she opened the casket, or wooden box, that was their receptacle, as the glittering gold and jewels of glorious colours caught her eye, she found that they were just as she had left them, on that hectic morning, when with Angus shouting to her to hurry, she had left Tantallon to ride behind him, so uncomfortably due to her pregnancy, on a pillion as they fled away from the castle towards his own Border lands.

In addition to many chevrons (ornaments of fret or zigzag work) one with a bird of gold with seventy-one pearls, another

---

[73] Cott. MS, Vesp. F. iii, fol.36. August 1516.

[74] *Historical Letters and Papers of Henry VIII.* Ed. Sir Henry Ellis, Vol. ii, pt. 1.1531, 1, t. 1

[75] Cott. MS Vesp. F. iii, fol.36.

with leaves of gold with three rubies and eighteen pearls, there were chains of gold, ornamented with pearls and other jewels. There were also gold collars, one decorated with red and white roses, sleeves (then separate items) of cloth of gold, the king of France's great diamond, set upon a red hat of silk, a ruby on a black hat set with pearls, and many other hats. There were also lengths of material, satin, taffeta, velvet and inevitably cloth of gold, and finally fur trimmings, delivered, for some mysterious reason, by the bishop of Galloway.

The duplicate of this long list, kept in the Public Records of Scotland, entitled 'Inventory of jewels and baggis (bagues=French for rings) being in the coffer taken furth Tantallan, delivered to the Commissioners of the Queen's Grace now being in England, September 25 1516', gives further proof of this transaction, 'the great diamond, given by the King of France, worth eight hundred crowns of gold, and worn on a red hat,' being again specifically mentioned.

Another item of great interest was the coffer, which held her trinkets, or smaller jewels. Subsequently to be given to Lord Forester by Margaret's grand-daughter Mary of Queen of Scots, it was thought to have come from Tantallon because, made of black oak and silver, it was intricately carved all over with the crowned hearts of Douglas and the daisies called marguerites, surmounted by regal crowns with the initial M entwined.

The Scottish inventory also includes Margaret's chapel furniture, delivered to her priest, William Husband, one of her commissioners and to John Sympson, his assistant, who gave their receipt to the Scottish Lords of the Council, by the hands of the master of St Anthony's, 'for a book belonging to Queen Margaret, a vestment of cloth of gold, a vestment of green velvet, altar cloths and cushions of gold cloth and velvet, two cruets of silver and a silver sacring bell as well as books and other items, including half a lining of ermine for a night-gown, apparently only available after the return of the bishop of Caithness, were sent later on 11 October 1516.'

It was during the late autumn that news reached England that Albany had imprisoned both Lord Home and his brother. Home, who as Lord Chancellor, had held high office in James IV's government, had been chagrined by Albany's refusal to restore him to the position to which he felt himself entitled by birth. But Home had many enemies, John Hepburn, the prior of St Andrews 'a man of subtle mind, malicious, crafty and undued with courtly elegance' amongst them, who somehow discovered that Home was in contact with someone in Henry's government, most probably Wolsey, and reported it to Albany with whom he kept constantly in touch. Albany had Home arrested, and with his brother, put on trial at which James Earl of Moray, an illegitimate son of James IV, appeared to accuse Home of having murdered his father the king, after Flodden. This charge was dropped for lack of evidence, but both Home and his brother, convicted of high treason, were executed in the second week of October 1516.

Albany appeared triumphant. All opposition against him in Scotland finally quelled. In November he further strengthened his position by persuading the Estates, as the Parliament was called, to name him the 'Second Person', in other words heir presumptive to the Scottish throne.

Henry had written to the Scottish Parliament in support of Margaret's letter to Albany asking that she be restored to her position as head of state in Scotland. His demand, however, that Albany should resign the regency and return to France, had been met with a firm refusal.

It was just before Advent 1516 when Henry, by that time himself living at Westminster Palace, had the old house, below Charing Cross, known as Scotland Yard, prepared for his sister Margaret. The building was so called because in the past it had been used as a residence for Scottish visitors. Believed to have been given by the Saxon King Edgar to Kenneth III of Scotland when he came to do homage for his kingdom of

Scotland, the entrance known as the guard room was later used as a barracks for the Scottish Guard of Queen Anne. It was also used for Scottish visitors of which Margaret now was one.

Margaret herself was by now preoccupied in extracting money from her brother to pay for the Christmas and New Year presents, always distributed to friends, relations and staff. To fail to comply with the custom would greatly lessen her prestige.

'I am sorry to put the King to so great charge and cost as I do' she wrote to Cardinal Wolsey, 'howbeit I have been so in times past, I shall not be so in times to come. Nevertheless I think I should be like his suster, to his honour and mine. Now, my Lord, you know Christmas-tide is near and part of things I will need for me and my servants, and I trust to get part of money out of Scotland, for you see they owe me much, and say they will cause me to be paid. And they do, I have as great wrong as is possible, but my trust is the King my brother will see me have reason. Therefore, I pray you, my Lord, let me borrow as much as two hundred pounds English. And I shall give you a writing of mine own hand, to cause my Lord Dacre to take off as much of mine of the first that is gotten. Now I shall trouble you for no more money, for I trust to get mine own, and I shall do the best I can with it. I pray you heartily, my Lord, to put me off no longer for the time is short.'[76]

When it appeared that no money was forthcoming, Margaret, in desperation wrote again to Wolsey.

'My Lord Cardinal

I commend me to you, and I would fain have spoken with you, but ye were gone ere I could come to you, and therefore I must write you my mind.

My Lord, I beseech you to show your good mind to me as ye have done ever, but specially now, for now is the time.

'I pray you heartily to get me some money against New Year Day, for ye now well that I must give part of rewards and

---

[76] Ibid Calig. B.ii.fol.283.

other needful things, both for the King, my brother's honour and mine'.

The outcome of these appeals is unknown, but is on record that when the royal family celebrated what is described as 'The feast of Kings' at Greenwich Palace, a grand pageant was performed in Margaret's honour. A contemporary chronicler has left a rather charming description of how, when the queen of Scotland and her sister Mary were seated in state with their brother and sister, King Henry and Queen Catherine, in the hall at Greenwich, there was wheeled in a *garden-artificial,* called the Garden of Esperance, railed in with gold pales, a tower at each corner, and the banks set with *flowers artificial* of silk and gold, the leaves cut out in green satin. A pillar of antique work in gold rose in the midst of the garden, set with pearls and precious stones, beneath a gilded arch or rainbow stood a bush of red and white roses, worked in satin, representing the royal brother and his two sister Queens Margaret and Mary, and near it was a plant of pomegranates in honour of Queen Catherine, being her device. Twelve knights and their lady partners sat in the garden and in its towers, and they all came down and danced an elegant ballet before Queen Margaret and the rest of the royal company.[77]

Christmas came and went, and there was still no sign of Margaret's possessions from Scotland. It transpired that her herald, a man named Ross, had been arrested by the northern wardens because his passport was out of order. Eventually he did appear with all her treasures intact, but this did not stop her from continuing to pester Wolsey because 'I am loth to speak to the King my brother in it, because I trust you will do it for me.'

The royal family are known to have been at Greenwich Palace in early May when word came from Scotland, perhaps brought by the herald Ross, that Albany had asked the Scottish

---

[77] Hollinshed,black letter, Vol.xi.p.339.

parliament for permission to make a visit to France on account of his wife's failing health.

Margaret, when told of this, immediately began to visualise the possibility of regaining the regency. With her brother's influence behind her she believed she could rule Scotland in the name of her son, King James. In this she was much encouraged by Henry, who saw Margaret's acquisition of the regency as a means of ultimately achieving his own control of the neighbouring country he aimed to subdue. Perhaps it is even fair to suggest, that behind his enthusiasm to forward his sister's ambition, lay the anterior motive, sublimating her constant demands for money by sending her back where she belonged. Safe be it to say that King Henry, seeing Albany's departure as a chance to reinstate his sister in Scotland to his own advantage, arranged the day when she would leave.

Margaret had been staying with Henry and Catherine both at Windsor Castle and at Richmond, when a strike of the London apprentices against free trade interrupted the farewell festivities. They had however, returned to Greenwich when on 9 May, the Lord Mayor with his body of civil servants, all dressed in deepest mourning, came down the Thames by barge to beg for leniency to the boys. It is also known that it was on this occasion that Margaret, together with her sister Mary and her sister-in-law Queen Catherine, went down on her knees to Henry to beg him to show mercy to the young insurgents. That Henry yielded to their supplications is proved by his granting the apprentices a public pardon when sitting on the king's bench in Westminster Hall on 19 May 1517.

Margaret, in the meantime, not daunted by Wolsey's remonstrance that London was far too dangerous for a woman like herself to visit, had returned to Baynard's Castle. Never one to lack courage, she told him that she had business to attend to concerning her return to Scotland in a letter headed May 1517,

'My Lord Cardinal

I commend me to you as heartily as I can, and wit ye, my lord, that I have spoken with James-a Borrow, and he hath shown to me that ye and the Lords of Council would not that I should come to Baynard's castle today.

My lord, I will do as ye think best, but I pray ye, my lord, as heartily as I can gif there be no trouble today, to let me come tomorrow. I trust to God there should be no like trouble but that I may come tomorrow, for an it be well this night, I trust to God the worst be past.'[78]

This is the last episode recorded of Margaret's activities during the year she spent in England at her brother's court. By this time she was already on the road. On the 18 May she left London, loaded with presents of jewels, plate, tapestry, money and horses –certainly much richer than when she had arrived– all her charges coming and going, paid for by Henry so the English Exchequer records - when, together with her little daughter, Lady Margaret Douglas, she began her journey back to Scotland.

---

[78] Cott. MS Calig, Bi. fol.251.

Lady Margaret Beaufort, Countess of Richmond, mother of King Henry VII, © *Bridgeman Images*

James IV, © *Bridgeman Images*

Linlithgow Palace

Edinburgh Castle

Catherine of Aragon, © Bridgeman Images

Henry VIII, King of England, © Bridgeman Images

Holbein px.

MARGARET TUDOR.

SISTER TO KING HEN. 8TH

OB. 1541.

Margaret Tudor, sister of King Henry VIII, by Holbein, © Bridgeman Images

*Archibald Douglas, 6th Earl of Angus, second husband of Margaret Tudor,
Queen of Scotland, © Bridgeman Images*

James V of Scotland and his second wife Marie de Guise, © Bridgeman Images

CHAPTER 5

'I WILL NEVER ABIDE HERE IN SCOTLAND'

Margaret, on her return journey to Scotland, did not receive the adulation in the towns and villages she passed through which she plainly considered her due. In fact, on nearing York, the Earl of Northumberland, he who had so gladly escorted her into the city on her first entrance on his curvetting horse, declared, in answer to King Henry's summons to do honour to his sister, that 'his lady was in no condition to mount on horseback [but] he himself would meet the Queen without the gates of York, seeing he was not ordered through the city, where the expenses would be great, he would escort her to Newborough.' Lord Hastings and Sir Richard Sacheveral did appear to meet Margaret, but for some mysterious reason were fined in the Star-Chamber for bringing their retainers in their liveries as they had done before.[79]

From York, where presumably she stayed again in the archbishop's Palace, she wrote to Henry revealing what had happened to the much disputed money sent by Louis XII to further the cause of her late husband, King James's long dreamed-of crusade.

'Your Grace knoweth, it is concluded between your Council that I shall have all that I have right to, pertaining to me, with one clause in it – that is, I giving again what I have pertaining to my son.

'The King my husband, ere he went to the field, gave me a letter of his hand, commanding to be delivered to me 18,000 crowns of weight that the French King did send, which was without the Council of Scotland's consent. Also they (the

---

[79] Strickland.p.148.

Council) may claim any other things that I have which the King my husband gave me, which were wrong. And I spent most part of it ere I came to your Grace, for I was not answered of my living, since the field (Flodden) to hold my house with. Therefore I beseech your Grace to command my Lord Dacre to see a sure way for me and Master Magnus ere we go in. Now that the Duke goeth away I set not much by the remnant that is behind, for I know them and their conditions. The fear they have of your Grace will make them glad to please me. '[80]

Then, preoccupied with her money, she adds, in a postscript, that Albany had sent his pursuivant to ask that the truce, at that time existing between England and Scotland, should continue to St Andrew's Day, on 30 November.

From York Margaret went on to Morpeth Castle, where Lord Dacre once more found himself forced to entertain her as a guest. Albany's departure had been delayed. He had asked Cardinal Wolsey for a safe conduct through England to allow him to sail from Southampton to save the long voyage from Scotland, but this had been refused. Therefore, he was waiting for a suitable ship in which to depart from Leith. Margaret, therefore, stayed at Morpeth Castle, unwilling to cross the Border into Scotland, until word came that he had sailed.

It was only when Albany finally left for France, on 7 June 1517, that, together with her small daughter, she moved on to Berwick to be re-united with the child's father Archibald Angus.

Their meeting was far from convivial. Margaret had found out about Angus's liaison with Janet Stewart and according to Hall, the chronicler, 'gave him anything but a kind reception.'[81] Then it was on to Edinburgh when, as she crossed the Border she left the country of her birth to which, unknown to her at the time, she was never to return.

---

[80] Cott. MS Calig. B. vi.
[81] Hall & Hollinshed Chronicles. Vol.ii.p.844.

Margaret, on reaching Edinburgh, immediately met with a rebuff. Demanding to see her son she was told by Lord Erskine, at that time his personal guardian, that he had removed him to Craigmillar Castle, on the outskirts of Edinburgh, because of fears that she, or one of the people who had come with her from England, might be infected with the dreaded sweating sickness, known to be rampant over the Border. Furious, but unable to come up with a good argument against Lord Erskine's apparently sensible precautions, Margaret was allowed to visit James, now a little boy of five, at Craigmillar, where to her great sadness, she found that he hardly knew her, all his affection being centred on Sir David Lindsay, who to him had become a surrogate father. But soon however, she was going so frequently that Erskine, believing she meant to kidnap him and take him to England, had him removed from Craigmillar to the greater security of Edinburgh Castle where, to her utter surprise and dismay, she was not allowed to see him.

It soon became plain to Margaret that, in her hopes of regaining the Regency, she had been sadly disillusioned. Albany had made himself not only dominant, but respected in Scotland to the extent that his absence was only regarded as an adjournment of his rule. To make matters worse, she was quarrelling bitterly with Angus, who was taking the rents of the lands, given to her as part of her marriage settlement, for himself.

Disillusioned, and disappointed at losing all that she had hoped for on her return to Scotland, she poured out her woes in a letter to Wolsey.

'My Lord Cardinal

In my most hartly wise I recommend me to you and would be glad to hear from you.

Pleaseth you to wit that I am come to Edinburgh, and hath been very well received, saving the sight of my son, the King, which I think right strange, and this (the carrier of the letter) will show you my mind, to whom I pray you give credence. My good lord, next the King my brother, my special trust is in you and you may do me the most good and gif so this realm keep not to the King my brother and you, this promise, I must needs call for help to his Grace and you. For I trust to rule me so that the King and you shall be content, for I will do nothing but I will axe counsel of my Lord Dakers, and I pray you my Lord command him that he send often to see how I do and am entreated. But and ever the Duke (Albany) come into Scotland again, here is no biding for me, and that this bearer can show you. No more but God have you in his keeping.

Written the 26th day of June with my hand.

Margaret R.'

Then writing to Henry himself, she complained about Scotland, telling him 'that she will never abide therin,' grumbling about the iniquities of both the Scottish Government and the husband who she calls a thief.

'If it please your Grace to wit how the King your nephew does, he is in good health, thanks be to God. As touching myself, an it please your Grace to wit how I am done to since my departing from you, it has been very evil.' She then goes so far as to suggest, that in lieu of the Scottish Government refusing to give her the rents of her lands that he 'may of reason cause the ships of Scotland to be taken' and the cargoes of them given to her. ' 'Dearest brother, the King, your Grace will not let me be overborne, and I wot well ye will never get any good of Scotland by fairness. Nor, I shall never, with my will, abide here with them that I know loves me not, which is proven daily, howbeit, do to me as your Grace will, for all my weal is in your hands. Also please you to wit that I am sore troubled with my lord of Angus, since my last coming to Scotland and every day more and more, so that we have not been together this half year. Please your Grace to remember that at my coming now into Scotland my Lord Dacre and Master Magnus made a writing between me and my Lord Angus for the security of me, that he might not have it in his power to put away nothing of my conjunct feofment (marriage jointure) without my will, which he has not kept...The Bishop of Dunkeld, his father's brother, and others of his kinsmen caused the Earl of Angus to deal right sharply with me, to cause him to make this bond he made to me, which I would not do.'[82]

Tiresome and covetous as she certainly was, the intensity of Margaret's misery at this moment, when, on returning to Scotland she had been deprived of everything she had imagined and in part led to expect, springs poignantly to the mind. In the flush of her first love for Angus, she had given him the rents of her Forest of Ettrick worth four thousand a year. Now, when, at the instigation of his uncle, the bishop of Dunkeld, he would not return them, she accused him of robbery. Deceived, as she believed, and deserted by her husband, deprived of the money owed to her by the Government and above all, not allowed to even see her child, she must have felt that she had little to live for. But Margaret was not a Tudor for nothing. Anger and a sense of injustice spurred her on to tell her brother that the messenger who carried her letter could describe much more the evil that Angus had done to her. She intended to divorce him and return to England:

'And I am so minded to part with him, for I wit he loves me not, as he showeth to me daily, wherefore I beseech your Grace, when it comes to that point (she means divorce) as I trust it shall, you will be a kind prince to me, for I shall never marry but where you bid me, nor never part from your Grace, for I will never, with my will, abide here in Scotland. And so send me your pleasure, and what your Grace will do for me, for all my hope and trust is in your Grace. I durst not send by land to your Grace for such causes, as I shall cause you to understand, and I beseech your Grace to write to me your mind

---

[82] Cott. MS. Calig. B. i.

by this bearer, and God preserve you. At Edinburgh, your humble cyster,

Margaret.'

From this letter in which she says she 'durst not send by land' it seems that she must have devised a way of sending letters by ship, perhaps in the hand of some sea-captain whom she could trust. Because of his known hatred of the French, she did not enlighten her brother on the arrangements made by Albany with King Francis of which by then, in substance, if not in detail, she must have been aware.

Albany, on his arrival in France in June 1517, had, almost immediately negotiated a treaty with King Francis I, which was very favourable to Scotland. Francis had two daughters, the eldest of whom, Princess Louise, was already promised as a bride for the son of King Charles of Spain. In August 1517 Albany reached an agreement with Francis that his second daughter, Princess Charlotte, should marry King James, or if this for any reason failed, the next daughter born to the queen of France. In addition to this there was also an agreement reached of a renewed alliance between Scotland and France. Much involved in diplomacy, he seems to have remained in ignorance of the terrible fate of the man he had left behind in Scotland to act as deputy during his absence in France.

In May, before leaving Scotland, Albany had given a commission of regency to the archbishops of St Andrews and Glasgow, the earls of Angus, Huntly, Arran and Argyll, the Sieur de la Bastie, his special agent, being made president of the Regency during his absence. Argyll was left in charge of the West Highlands and Isles, Huntly for the rest of the Highlands, comprising the north-east, and De la Bastie for the Lothians and the area of Border country known as the Merse.

Negotiations were still in progress, for what would later be known as the Treaty of Rouen, affecting the marriage of James to a French princess, when word came from Scotland of the murder of the Sieur de la Bastie, under circumstances which were horrific even by the standards of the time.

Antoine d'Arces, Sieur de la Bastie, renowned as a contestant in the lists, had first come to Scotland to take part in the tournaments organized by James IV. Famous for his valour, he was also so handsome, wearing his hair long in the fashion of the previous reign, that the Scots nicknamed him 'Sir de la Beauty.' Lured from Dunbar Castle by a rumour of trouble in the Borders, he was attacked by a party of the Homes. Riding for his life, he might have escaped had his horse not taken him into a swamp. Trapped there, his enemies surrounded and killed him, finally cutting off his head. It was Home of Wedderburn, who tying the head to his saddle-bow by its long hair, carried it in triumph to the Berwickshire town of Duns, where, holding it on the end of his spear, he claimed he had won vengeance for Albany's execution of Lord Home.

The crime, which horrified people both in Scotland and in France, went largely unpunished because of Arran's connection with the Homes. Subsequently the Council of Regency split into factions, one headed by Arran, head of the house of Hamilton, and the other by Angus, backed as he was through his acrimonious marriage to Margaret, by the influence of her brother the English king. Thus, through the old animosity between two of the most powerful families in the country, Scotland became politically divided, by parties known ultimately as the English and the French.

The rivalry between them developed into the incident known as Cleanse the Causeway in the High Street of Edinburgh when, on 30 April 1520, a party of the Hamiltons, led by Sir Patrick Hamilton of Kincavel, a half-brother of Arran's, and Sir James Hamilton of Finnart, Arran's bastard son, picked a fight with Archibald Angus. The people of Edinburgh scuttled like terrified rabbits into the tenement houses rising on either side of the street. Bolting doors and windows behind them, they listened to the clash of weapons and the screams of fury and pain as the two sides set on each other and the street became slippery with blood. The Douglases won the day, killing seventy of the Hamiltons, Sir Patrick being amongst them. Later Wolsey was to hear that Angus himself had killed him, striking him down with either a sword or a dagger with his own hand.

But Arran and his natural son James of Finnart, escaped down a narrow alley. Then spying a horse pulling a cart in front of them, they took it out of the shafts, and clambering, one behind the other onto its back, rode it, splashing through the shallows of the Nor Loch (now Princes Street Gardens) to reach safety on the far side.

Arran had been provost of Edinburgh but, following this slaughter, the Scottish Government decreed, that neither a Hamilton nor a Douglas would be allowed to hold that post.

Margaret, in the meantime was taking steps to get her divorce. The fact of his having been previously, what is described as 'troth-plighted', to his mistress Janet Stewart, being in her estimation a good enough reason to negate her own marriage to the man she now detested as much as she had formerly loved. Queen Catherine, in England, was scandalized by the behaviour of the woman she had first known as a girl and to whom she had shown such kindness throughout their subsequent acquaintance. In the autumn of 1519 she had sent one of her own priests, Father Bonaventura, to remonstrate with Margaret, who was then at Perth. On the good Father returning, saying that she had totally ignored both him and his advice, King Henry, to whom his sister's estranged husband Archibald Angus had now become a source of great use, had sent another churchman, a man called Henry Chadworth, a very stern friar of the rigid order of Observants, to tell Margaret that 'her ideas of divorce were wicked delusions, inspired by the father of evil, whose malice alone could prompt her to blame her husband, Lord Angus, or unnaturally to stigmatize the daughter she had by him'[83] Chadworth, on Henry's instructions, 'thundered terrible denunciations against the heinousness of Margaret's intended divorce,' but only succeeded in making her more determined than ever to stand firm, ignoring the protests of her brother, hypocritical as they were soon proved to be.

Meanwhile, seething with rage, she wrote to the man she had formerly repudiated, now, 'her dear kinsman Albany', begging him to return and deal with the husband who was treating her so cruelly, and likewise the people of Scotland whom she openly despised. 'I had liever be dead than live my life in Scotland' she wrote to Lord Dacre, in a long catalogue of her woes.

'I stand in a sore case', she wrote to him from Stirling Castle, 'an I get not the King my brother's help, and my Lord Cardinal's, for such jewels as his Grace gave me, at my departing, I must put away for money. I have discharged all my servants, because I had naught to give them, scarcely finding meat for the day to sustain myself, and for that I is indebted to my faithful controller, Robin Barton, for very sustenance. Lord Dacre intercedes that I may return to live in England, for the Lords of the Scottish privy-council prohibit me from seeing my son, Let no peace be kept within the realms. His Grace promised me, at my departing that Scotland should never have peace from England without I was well done by, which is not done, for I was never so evil, wherefore I beseech his Grace to remedy it hastily, for all my hope and comfort is in him. And wit you, my Lord, this realm stood never as I doth now, nor never like to have so much evil rule in it, for every Lord prideth who may be the greatest party, and have most friends, and they think to get the King, my son, into their hands, and then they will rule as they will, for there is

---

[83] Pinkerton, John, The History of Scotland from the Accessions of the House of Stewart to that of Queen Mary, (2 cols 1797) vol. ii. p.174.

many against the chancellor (Archbishop James Beaton) and think to put him down from his authority, and I am the most beholden to him of any here. And thus I see no good for my son nor me.'

Finally she asks Lord Dacre to buy from her 'two cups of gold,' which her brother had given her as a parting present and likewise some gold chains, as he had better have them than anyone else, for they must be sold, but she is embarrassed by having her poverty made public. [84]

Unfortunately Lord Dacre somehow got wind of her correspondence with Albany, telling her that it was treachery to deal with the leader of the party who disputed her brother's interests. Margaret, her double dealing revealed, then had to admit that she had written to the king of France, but defended herself by saying that she had done so for the sake of her son.

'For the furthering of the Duke of Albany's coming into Scotland, my Lord there was a letter written into France to the King of France from me, by the special desire of the Duke of Albany and the Lords, which I might not deny, for they said it was for the veal (weal) of the King my son, and his realm... For an I should refuse to have written when I was desired, the Duke of Albany and the Lords would have thought I had stopped his coming, and therethrough I might get evil, and thus I trust my Lord, that the King's Grace, my brother, and my Lord Cardinal (Wolsey) will remember as I stand in this realm. And in the last writing I had from the King, my brother, he commanded me I should do nothing that the Lords might have occasion to complain of me, which I trust I have done. And suppose it be evil to me, it is dishonour to the King's Grace, my brother, as well as to me, but the unkindness I find doth me more evil nor any thing in the varld, for I see well what point that ever it stand me on, I will get no help but fair words.

---

[84] Cott. MS, Calig. B. i.

My Lord, ye must pardon that I write so sharp, for it touches me near, and God kype you. At Edinburgh the fourteenth day of July,

Your friend,

Margaret R.'[85]

[85] Ibid. B. ii. fol. 195.

CHAPTER 6

DAMNABLE ABUSING OF OUR SISTER.

In the autumn of 1521 the king of France, Francis 1, sent Albany back to Scotland. The reason was largely diplomatic. The alliance made between the kings of France and England at the Field of the Cloth of Gold had collapsed. Henry VIII had made an agreement with the Holy Roman Emperor Charles V, that they should make a joint attack on France, and now Francis wanted Albany to attack England from Scotland to distract Henry from invading France.

Albany landed at the Garveloch, in Dunbartonshire, on 29 November 1521, bringing with him a small fleet of ships. From there he rode to Linlithgow to be received with open arms by Queen Margaret, or as one chronicler put it, 'with the utmost distinction and respect.' Together they rode in state into Edinburgh, where Margaret ordered the keys of the castle to be given to the regent in token of his sovereign power. The English resident in Rome, where Albany was on good terms with the Medici Pope Leo X, his sister having married the Pontiff's nephew, reported to Cardinal Wolsey that 'The Queen of Scots sueth her husband, the Earl of Anguish, in cause of divorce and dissolution of matrimony. Her case is committed to the root, and the Duke of Albany promotes the same.'[86]

Whether, at this time, Margaret knew that she was being manipulated as a political bargaining counter, remains open to speculation. She certainly made a *volte face* as far as Albany was concerned, but she may have seen her undisguised infatuation as a means of getting even with Angus, whom she now so openly detested.

---

[86] Ibid. Calig. B.ii,fol.195- Lett er to Wolsey, October 1521.

In England however, King Henry was doing everything possible to prevent his sister's divorce from the man he had literally schooled in his court to be his greatest protagonist in Scotland. Cardinal Wolsey, Henry's all powerful minister, announced to him that he had done all that he could to encourage all Scots rebels, so that they might continue to harass Albany's ruling. Not only had he written to his orator in the papal Court of Rome 'to impeach and hinder the suit made in that court for a divorce between her (Queen Margaret) and her husband, the Earl of Angus, but also caused the Pope's orator here to write in the most effectual manner to his holiness for stopping the same, by means whereof the said divorce shall not proceed, when the Pope shall be informed that this divorce is to be procured only for marriage, to be made between Queen Margaret and the Duke of Albany, whereby the destruction of the young King of Scots shall ensue.'[87]

What was really happening in Scotland in the relationship between Albany and Margaret? Rumours were already abundant that she was planning to marry him, regardless of the fact that his wife, although ailing, was still alive. Albany was certainly a most handsome and charismatic man, so unlike many of those uncouth lords of Scotland, with his manners of the French court. In retrospect it would seem that, while he was perfectly happy to have an affair with Margaret, thereby traducing her to his will, he had no intention whatever of leaving his French wife, Anne de la Tour Auvergne, who, apart from everything else, was one of the greatest and richest heiresses in France.

Margaret, volatile in her emotions as she proved herself to be, was now plainly just as enamoured of Albany as she had been of Angus, whom she had married, with what some thought undue haste, less than a year after King James's death. Lord Dacre, who, as Margaret's constant correspondent, must

---

[87] *State Papers*, published by Commissioners, 1830. Part i.p.91.

have known more about it than most, was plainly horrified, writing to Wolsey that:

'There is marvellous great intelligence between Queen Margaret and the Duke of Albany, as well all the day as mich of the night. In manner they care not who knows it. And if I durst say it – for fear of displeasure of my Sovereign – they are over tender, whereof, if your Grace examine the Bishop of Dunkeld of his conscience, I trust he will show you the truth.' He added that Queen Margaret had offered Angus her forest of Ettrick, worth two thousand marks yearly, to consent to her divorce. Her conduct with Albany was scandalous.[88]

Angus, meanwhile, on Albany's arrival, took refuge in a church on the Borders before riding down to London to King Henry's court. Protesting with great vehemence against Margaret's demand for a divorce, it is thought that he took their daughter with him, the little red-haired Margaret Douglas, now five years old. Margaret certainly complained that the child had been torn from her, but she does not seem to have done much or anything to try to retrieve her and later would own, when willing her possessions, that she had given her nothing during her lifetime.

Margaret, much more pre-occupied it seems with her love affairs than with care of her child, then caused another scandal by riding alone with Sir James Hamilton of Finnart, from Edinburgh Castle to the Palace of Linlithgow at dead of night.

This is the first mention of James Hamilton in connection with Margaret's name. As the illegitimate son of James Hamilton, 1st Earl of Arran, he was therefore a second cousin of the young King James, over whose life he was soon to hold a significant, if decadent influence. Born c. 1495, Hamilton was in his middle twenties when, on that dark night, with his hand ever close to the pommel of his sword, he rode beside

---

[88] Ibid, Cal.B.vi. 205. Dec 1521.

Margaret for the twenty odd miles between Edinburgh and Linlithgow.

As a child James Hamilton had been taken into the king's household where, as is proved by the Exchequer Rolls, he was given boots and shoes.[89] Granted the lands of Finnart in 1507, when he was only twelve, and knighted four years later by James IV, although still always known as the Bastard of Arran, he had been formally legitimised in 1512. In the following year, in the event of his father not having male children, which did afterwards occur, he had been named as his heir. Sent then as a courier to France, he had returned with letters from Francis I to King James and forthwith sent back again with explanations of the king's dealings with the murderers of the Sieur de la Bastie (Albany's lieutenant and Warden of the Merse and Lothian) who had been trapped in a bog, and killed by the Homes in 1517, while Albany himself was in France.

It was while he was in that country that, just as James would do later, Hamilton had become captivated by the ideas of the Renaissance architecture that was just coming in vogue. Clever as he undoubtedly was, he must have learnt the rudiments of construction to the point where he was able to draw out the designs and graphs, decipherable to Scottish artisans, which would soon enable James to complete the work in Stirling Castle, initially commenced by Robert Cochrane in the days of the king's grandfather, and partly completed by his father before his untimely death.

Responding to a letter from Lord Dacre, in which he reprimanded her for her foolish behaviour in laying herself open to slander by riding alone with Hamilton at night, Margaret laid the blame on Angus saying that:

'gif he had desired my company or my lord, he would have himself more kindly than he has done, For now, of late, when

---

[89] Accounts of Lord High Treasurer of Scotland, Vol.4. 53,82,99,233.

I came to Edinburgh to him, he took my houses without my consent, and withheld my living from me, which he should not do of reason. Methinks my lord, you ought not to deem this reasonable if you may be my friend as I trust you be.'

Then, refuting his accusations concerning Albany, she told him that 'his assistance was somewhat more than fair words.' Had it not been for him giving money both to her and her son, the King, she would have to have sold, or pawned, both her cupboard of plate and her jewels.

'My Lord Dacre, you should not give so lightly credit to evil tales of me as you do, when you know the truth, suppose you bear great favour to my lord of Angus, as I see you do... Also you say I came out of Edinburgh in the night, but that was not so, for all the Lords (of the Council) knew of my coming away, and I saw no good to bide there. And where you say I am ruled by advice that will never do me good nor honour, my lord, I did never dishonour myself nor them that I come of. Methinks you should not give credence to that of me, both for my brother's sake, and the King my father, (whose soul God pardon) and I have done better for your cause than my lord of Angus hath done, or any of his. But I know well, when the Bishop of Dunkeld hath been with you lately, which has caused you to write so sharply.'

Having blamed her former friend, her husband's uncle, Gavin Douglas, the bishop of Dunkeld, whom she knew had been visiting him, for slandering her name, writing from Stirling on 11 March 1522, she assured Lord Dacre.

'As to Sir James Hamilton, I could not hinder him from riding on the way, but he conveyed me not. It was the other lords that brought me from Edinburgh to Linlithgow as is known. My Lord you also write sharply to me in your last article, saying that I do dishonour to myself in abiding away from my Lord Angus, and that I follow them that will be my destruction, and cannot stand in the pleasure of the King's Grace, my brother, and that I may not look for any favours from the King my brother's hand, for it is thought that I am sore abused under colour of fair promises, which will bring me to the displeasure of God, and my dishonour and undoing at length. My lord, these is sore words…That evil and false folk make such a report of me… And I may think it strange that my lord Angus can make the King, my brother, so displeased at me without any fault. Wherefore it is no marvel supposing others be unkind, considering that I took my lord of Angus against all Scotland's will, whereby I lost the keeping of my son, and my house in Stirling, and my rule of the realm, which I had by right. You may think it strange that my Lord of Angus can make the King, my brother, so displeased at me without any fault. And all this for his sake who has now shown himself to me as unkindly as possible, which all the realm knows, holds my living from me as far as he may, and above all things, he spoke open dishonour of me, which is no token of love and I did neither displeasure nor dishonour him as well as is well known.' She continues to rail against Angus before writing. 'Thus I must do the best I may to get friends, since his Grace, that I trusted most in, puts me by without a fault, which I shall never make to his Grace, as I shall write at length to him by a servant of mine.' [90]

Write she did to Henry, who was so astounded by her allegations that he summoned his Council to see the correspondence that had passed between Wolsey, Lord Dacre and others, describing Margaret's infidelities and the hostile attitude of Albany's government to England. Unwilling to believe what was being said of her, he sternly ordered Wolsey to produce Margaret's correspondence with him, and on reading of the wrongs she claimed that had been done to her, retired wrathfully to contemplate in private.

The gist of Margaret's fury was directed, not so much at Angus, but at his uncle Gavin who, as she explained to her brother, was not only 'the cause of all the trouble and dissension in this realm', but had 'made evil report of her, both

---

[90] Cott. MS, Calig. B.vi.f.232.

in Scotland and England, falsely... I helped him to get the benefice of Dunkeld, I sal now help him to lose the same... I trust your Grace will make him na help, na favour him.[91]

Gavin Douglas, now a man of forty-eight and suffering from poor health, did manage to reach London after a journey of ten days. The main purpose of his visit was to remind the king that as Albany had exceeded his agreed time of absence from Scotland, the legality of his Regency could now be contested. Questioned by Henry, he blamed all that was wrong in Scotland on the queen's infatuation with the regent. He must have mentioned the current rumour that she meant to marry him, for Henry, at last convinced of the truth of what he had told him, in an open letter to the Scottish Council, accused Albany of :

'contriving and heinously proposing the divorce of the Queen our sister, from her lawful husband Angus, and purposing to contract marriage with her himself, whereby not only the person of our nephew is in great danger of being destroyed, but also our sister, Queen Margaret, is on the eve of ruin, to our great dishonour and displeasure.' He then advised the Council to dismiss the regent 'lest, they should dishonour the Queen my sister, and provoke us to do you all the harm and damage we can.' [92]

The bishop was still in London when he heard, to his utter disgust, that his nephew had made some sort of reconciliation with Albany and returned to Edinburgh.

'Yon witless fool is running on his own mischief by the continual persuasion of wily, subtle men, showing to him, I doubt not, many feigned letters and wonderful terrors, and that the Duke of Albany should marry the Queen', he wrote on 31 January 1522.[93]

---

[91] *Letters of Henry VIII*, Ed. Sir Henry Ellis. 3rd series, Vol.ii. p.289.

[92] Ibid Vol. i. P.267.

[93] Ibid. p.229.

This was the last thing that he wrote before, just a few days later, he died of the plague. He is buried in the church of the Savoy where a monumental plaque still records his death and internment.

John, Duke of Albany, renowned for his outbursts of temper, reputedly when angry, threw his bonnet in the fire. His rages, however, were nothing compared to those of Henry VIII, who made no attempt to conceal his fury over the Scottish regent's alleged liaison with his sister. In return to Albany's politely worded letters, he sent a ferocious reply, accusing him of 'dishonourable and damnable abusing of our sister, inciting her to be divorced from her lawful husband, the Earl of Angus, with what corrupt intent, God knoweth'. Refusing to grant Albany a renewal of the truce, which would expire in the following February, he sent his herald Clarencieux to tell him that 'he would use every possible means to get him out of Scotland.'[94]

Albany told Clarencieux, when he attended Parliament, that 'The King of England need not misdoubt he would attempt anything should derogate from the honour of his sister, that compliments of mere courtesy in France might be surmised sometimes by English ladies to be solicitations and suits of love.'[95] He told him that he had shown mercy to Angus 'not for his own deserts, but out of respect for the Queen 'whom he ever honoured as his sovereign's moder.'[96] In fact, if legend can be believed, the regent had drugged both Angus and his brother George so that they were carried unconscious to be put aboard a ship at Leith and therewith taken off to France. This may be pure fallacy, but it is known that Henry was so angry over the banishment of the man who he now

---

[94] Ibid. Letter from Henry VIII, to John Duke of Albany. Ed. J.C. Halliwell

[95] Bingham. p.44.

[96] Lesley, p.118.

regarded as his agent in Scotland, that he made every Scotsman in England wear a white cross on his back.[97]

War broke out between Scotland and England but Margaret nonetheless was happy. Angus was gone, banished out of the country to France, where, as far as she was concerned, he could forever remain. He had lost his power in Scotland and with it the support of her brother King Henry. Soon she would get her divorce. Albany's wife was known to be dying; she would almost certainly be dead by the time the Pope sanctioned the divorce. Then she would marry him, the one man she truly loved. Her moment of triumph was near. Little could she have guessed, or even imagined at that time when it seemed she had succeeded beyond her remotest dreams, that the tide of her fortune was carrying her over the lip of the waterfall, down to the depths of despair.

It was in the autumn of 1522 that Margaret began to feel ill, and in November the malignant disease became smallpox of which she nearly died. She did recover, however, but her looks had gone. The portrait by Holbein in the National Portrait Gallery, painted it is believed after her illness, shows her wearing one of the high pointed head-dresses, so fashionable at the time, and with a pronounced squint or what looks like a growth over her right eye. Confined to Stirling Castle, from where the Privy Council instructed that the young Prince James be removed to Dalkeith Palace to escape infection, Margaret, because of her illness, was not involved in public life.

Pathetically, in a letter to Wolsey, written from Stirling on 26 December, she told him:

'And his Grace and you my Lord, must needs have me excused that I wrote not to his Grace and to you with mine own hand at this time, for because my hands and all my body be so full of the small pox that I neither write nor sit, nor scantly

---

[97] Ibid. p,191.

speak, and hereafter when I may I shall write with my own hand, at length, as please God, who preserve you ever more in prosperity.'[98]

---

[98] State Papers, Vol. iv. Queen Margaret to Wolsey, December 26,1522.

214

CHAPTER 7

'AS TOUCHING THE KING MY SON'

Prince James's removal from Stirling Castle to the palace of Dalkeith, seems to have been well timed. Now aged eleven, his mother overindulged him, telling the Earl of Surrey in a letter that:

'Of his age, my Lord, I trow there is not a wiser child, nor a better hearted, nor that dare take on him as far as he may, he wants nothing but help to bear him forth in his good quarrel. And I assure you, upon mine honour, that he loves not the Governor, the Duke of Albany, nor no Frenchman, and that the King, my brother, will find, an his Grace will help him, and as to his coming forth at freedom, he will bide no longer in then Monday come eight days, without he be beholden perforce by the Lords, and he saith plainly "that no good Scottishman will hold him in one house against his will." Whereof the Frenchmen that are here are right sore displeased, and maketh all the ways they can to stop it, by money giving and other fair promises.'[99]

In praising him thus, his mother did not add that, once given his head, James was becoming a young tyrant. He struck one of his gentlemen, who was resisting what Margaret termed 'his educational restraint,' through his arm with his dagger, and he threatened a porter with his weapon 'because the man would not open the gates of Stirling Castle at his order.' Margaret had a wild plan that she with her son would escape to England, but could not find enough money to do so.

'I have nothing now to uphold my honest expenses, without I lay my cupboard of plate in pledge, which is not to the King my brother's honour.' She wrote to Surrey (son of the man

---

[99]*Ibid.* Vol. iv. p.4. Margaret to Surrey.

who had escorted her to Scotland, now, since his victory at Flodden, the Duke of Norfolk) who, in return, suggested that she should come to 'her house at Boncle' (a confusing statement as Boncle Castle belonged to Angus, but in his absence she must have had the use of it) under the pretence of mediating for the poor miserable people of the Borders who were ruined by the burning of their corn. He told her to bring all her plate and jewels and then 'I, with good power, will suddenly come and fetch your Grace, stuff, plate and jewels away, otherwise I can none devise, and whereas your Grace sent for a token a pair of beads to Lord Maxwell, trusting he would have suffered you to pass through his country into this realm, it was thought by me and my Lord Dacre not meet to be done.' He then wrote immediately to Wolsey that 'the Queen of Scots had altered her good mind to run away into England, by the reason of the gifts given her by the French'.[100]

Surrey was probably referring to presents brought to Margaret by Albany on his return from France. He did not impart to the cardinal that one reason for his doing so had been reports that had reached him of her son being out of control.

Margaret's supplications to her brother for money were at that time peremptorily refused. Nonetheless, with Angus out of the country, she now had the full income from her Ettrick Forest, and Albany had granted her some of the money he had brought from France. It was just at this moment, when, secure at last in her financial position, her future prospects seemed good, that her world seemed to collapse about her as she discovered, it seems from English spies, that Albany was having an affair. Of the woman herself little is known, except that she was a sister of Lord Fleming, the man supposed to have been responsible for the poisoning of Lord Drummond's daughters. Margaret was convulsed with rage, the more so because she believed that Albany no longer loved her on account of the ravages done by smallpox to her looks.

---

[100] Ibid.

Dishonest and duplicitous as she undoubtedly was, Margaret, at this stage in her life, does deserve some sympathy, if only for the dire situation in which she found herself placed. It now seemed barely possible that it was only three months ago since the world had seemed to be at her feet. Albany's wife was dying. There would seem to be nothing to stop her from marrying him. Angus, who she never wished to see again, was safely in France. A future, glorious in its possibilities, had lain, so it seemed before her.

Now it had vanished, the vision, apparently so marvellous, had disappeared, as if overnight.

Facing reality, in all reluctance, her true situation became clear as she realized that all she had envisaged had been a cruel and tantalising dream. Her first husband was dead, her second had deserted her, her son had been taken away from her, and now the man, who if not in truth her lover, she had thought to be a supportive friend, had left her for another woman, unscathed by the scabs of smallpox, which had ruined her own once much admired skin.

She may have felt some satisfaction at Albany's humiliation, when, as the Scottish army reached Carlisle, the commanders, informed by scouts of action being prepared against them and with memories of Flodden in their minds, refused to cross the Border. Nonetheless, it was partly thanks to Margaret's intercession that Lord Dacre offered a temporary truce, which Albany thankfully accepted.

Margaret's suspicions, long voiced to her brother that her letters were intercepted, seems in this case to have been true. Albany must have realized, or at least suspected what she was up to, for very soon he passed an interdict forbidding her access to her son in Stirling Castle. Margaret, incensed, wrote at once to her brother, in this instance sending the letter by a man she could trust.

'You shall wit that I am by force put away from the King, as in part you may see by other letters which this bearer will

217

show you. Give credence to him, and answer for it, so great need. In all haste.

Written ye wit whom

To the Right High and Mighty Prince my dearest brother the King. October 1522.'[101]

Early in the following year, King Henry sent a large English army to support Lord Dacre in the event of a Scottish invasion over the Border. Faced with the threat of a wholesale attack on Scotland, Albany returned to France with the purpose of raising military support. Meanwhile the Earl of Surrey in command of the English force, discovered that the prioress of Coldstream, had been sending all sorts of information concerning the numbers of his men and guns, to the Scottish Council. By now the prioress (successor to old Lady Home) was an aunt of Robin Barton, Queen Margaret's controller, who begged her for help. Margaret, remembering how she had been saved at Coldstream Priory, in the hour of her greatest distress, when, heavily pregnant, she had been escaping to England, immediately wrote to Surrey telling him that she knew he had come to the borders,

'forenent Scotland and there is a good friend and servant of mine, which was nearest to your bounds of England, and is prioress of a poor body of sisters, called Coldstream, and it appears to be in great trouble on both sides… I pray you, for my sake, that her place may be untroubled, and be brought in no straight by Englishmen… I believe she has the King my brother's protection to show, therefor you will show more kindly to her.'[102]

In November, seizing on the chance of the regent's renewed absence, Henry offered a five year truce to Scotland and the hand of his daughter Mary for the young King James V, on condition that Albany was dismissed as regent. But the

---

[101] Cott. MS. Calig.B.i.p.117.

[102] *State Papers*. Vol. iv. note written in March or April 1523.

Scottish Government, having through Albany renewed the French alliance, and accepted the suggestion of a French princess for James, refused the offer. Henry, fulminating with rage, in June of the following year of 1523, ordered the burning of Kelso in reprisal, and on 24 September, an English army, under the command of the Earl of Surrey, made a disastrous raid on Jedburgh.

A strange story of witchcraft involves the English forces, which on the night of the battle, were encamped around the town. What may have been a prank of Border horse-boys was taken to be a spirit which terrified the horses into breaking their tethers and stampeding into the camp. English soldiers, mistaking them for Scottish cavalry, shot at them with arrows and guns so that some galloped headlong over a precipice and others into the burning town, where Scottish women led them away, some of them 'right evil burnt,' according to Lord Surrey, reporting that eight hundred horses were lost in all, adding that he 'dare not write the wonders Lord Dacre and all his company do say they saw that night of sprites and fearful sights; and universally all their company say plainly that the devil was that night among them six times.' [103]

On the same day, Albany returned from France, this time bringing with him an army, four thousand strong, with both arms and ammunition, sent by King Francis I.
On reaching Edinburgh he received a letter from Margaret, raging at being told that she could not have access to her son. She quickly fired off another missive to Albany, the words somewhat incoherent in her fury.

'You, my Lord, and the rest of the Lords, has ordained that I shall not abide with my son, but whiles come and see him, and if this be reasonable or honourable, I report me to the deed,

---

[103] Donaldson Gordon, *Edinburgh History of Scotland*. Vol.3. p.21.

and I believe in God, that hereafter I shall have cause to bethink you of the good and true part I have kept to you.'[104]

Somehow she must have come to terms with Albany, he, with his infinite charm winning her round, for just over a month later, on 10 November, she wrote, it seems at his request, what was this time a public letter asking for a truce for Scotland:

'gif I might bring the same to good point, considering the great trouble that is like to be, and hath been between the realms, and I being so tender on both sides, bethink of reason there should none be so well heard of as I.'[105]

It was thanks to her compliance over this letter that Albany did allow her, not only to see her son, but to spend a week with him in November in Stirling Castle. From there she wrote another letter to Surrey, telling him:

'And as touching the King my son, thanked be God he is in good health, and I am with him in Stirling, and think not to be far from him in any danger that may come, if that I be not put from him by force: I beseech God if but that you could see him, so that nobody knew of you but I, and then I trust you would be right well contented with him.

And also, wit you, my Lord Surrey, the Governor Albany is in Edinburgh, and I saw him not since he came from the unhonest journey, but he thinks no shame of it, for he makes it his excuse that the Lords would not pass into England with him, and says they would have sold him in England, and therefore he hath begun the Parliament this Tuesday.'[106]

The members of the church, burgh and nobility, who comprised the Scottish Estates were already complaining of the cost of Albany's household. Now to add to it, came the exorbitant price of maintaining four thousand French soldiers,

---

[104] *State Papers* Vol. iv. p.56.

[105] ibid.

[106] Ibid.

a number of arquebusiers [musketeers] and over five hundred horses, a serious drain on the economy of a country with few natural supplies of wealth.

Margaret, aware that she had been defeated in her own duplicitous game of seduction, now again hated as once she had loved. At what can only be described as the nadir of her fortunes, she may perhaps be at least partly forgiven for taking, what in anyone's estimation, must be termed vicious vengeance against the charming regent by whom she now felt betrayed.

Sending a messenger galloping to Berwick, she immediately reported Albany's arrival to the Earl of Surrey, warning him of an imminent invasion.

'My Lord, if England ever made them strong against Scotland, make them now right strong... And therefore I warn you to look upon your weal and honour, for you will be rightly sharply assayed. But to show you the truth whether the Duke of Albany will pass to the Borders or to the west, I promise you, as yet there is none that knows, for the Duke will show his mind to no Scottish man... Now I will advertise you what he hath brought with him and this I promise you is the truth. First, he hath eight and twenty cannons, and four double cannons that are far greater than any that was brought to Norham at the field. [Flodden.] Also he has great pavasies going upon wheels with the artillery, to shoot and to break the hosts asunder, and of these he hath many, and every one of them has two sharp swords before them, that none may touch them. They have besides this, great number of small artillery of all sorts, and much powder, and all with them that pertains to it, and twelve ships with victuals and wine. And of these they have sent four of their ships, with wine and flour and four great cannons, to the west Border. I promise you my Lord they trust to win Berwick with other places. Wherefore I pray you, my Lord, to cause the King's Grace to look well to this matter... for an they win any advantage now, my son and I are undone, he (Albany) will be so high in his mind... I can do no more for my part, but advertise you of all the things that I know, and that I shall not fail.'[107]

The cost of maintaining the French soldiers is said to be the reason why Albany decided to attack at once. But, unfortunately for him, the weather immediately deteriorated, rain making the roads almost impassable particularly for transporting the heavy guns sent by the king of France. Albany, undeterred, however, ordered the religious houses on their route to provide oxen to pull the cannons loaded onto flat carts.

Then, once again, as they reached the Border, the commanders of his army began to waver, as reluctant to proceed into England as they had been in the previous year. He managed to persuade them to cross the Tweed and to attack Wark Castle. But the fortress, forewarned of what was coming, was both heavily defended and well supplied enough to withstand even the cannon balls thundering against its walls. Meanwhile the deluge continued. The Tweed threatened to burst its banks, and when word came of Surrey approaching with a large army, Albany decided that, while the river was still passable, to withdraw.

His army marched back to Edinburgh through a snowstorm, and the regent asked Surrey for a truce, to which the English general agreed. The French soldiers were not allowed to stay in Scotland for the winter, the cost of keeping them being too great. On reaching Edinburgh, Albany was met by Margaret at the Gatehouse to Holyrood Palace when, so Pinkerton writes, 'great professions of kindness were exchanged on both sides.' Inevitably rumours of an illicit relationship between them were circulated; Lord Dacre, in particular, spreading scandal with his pen.

In retrospect the extraordinary convolutions of their relationship is difficult to discern. To Surrey she complained of Albany's parsimony.

---

[107] *State Paper Commission,* printed 1836, vol. iv.p.110.

'Wherefore I pray you my Lord, to do so to me that I need not to set by the displeasure of the Duke of Albany, or else I must be content to follow his pleasure, whether it be against my son or not...And you well know, my Lord, that my living that I may live upon is here, and he may do with it what he pleases. And how I have been treated since my last coming out of England is well known, and have lived, not like a princess, but a sober woman, and fain perform to take any money the Duke of Albany would give me, as I have written before and gotten no answer.'[108]

Vindictive in her fury, to the point where it suggests an unbalanced mind, she wrote to Surrey, asking him first to help her to return to England.

'devise the best way for me, and the King my son, as my trust is in you,' she told him 'be not blinded no more with the Duke of Albany's falsehood, and make no truce while this be remedied, for no sending without I send you a token.'

Then, because she now suspected that the prioress of Coldstream, whom she had formerly asked Surrey to protect, had been acting as a double agent, giving her letters to Surrey, she urged him:

'And haste me your counsel, I pray you, and cause the Prioress of Coldstream to send surely the answer to this bill... For there is none that may so well and surely as she may convey letters betwixt, and if she fails to do it, that you will cause her place to be burnt. And this I pray you fail not to do and God keep you.'[109]

Then, plainly obsessed with jealousy over the woman for whom Albany had abandoned her, she concluded:

'And God send you grace to help my son out of his enemies' hands, which he will be daily in, now when these persons be put to him. For the Lord Fleming, for evil will that

---

[108] Ibid.

[109] The letter is dated Stirling, on St Catherine's Eve, being November 24 1523.

he had to his wife, caused to poison three sisters, one of them his wife, and this is known of truth in Scotland. An if this (man) be good to put to the King my son, God knoweth! And another thing I know perfectly, that he would have my son dead. The Governor Albany and the Earl of Murray like such, for the Governor hath his (Fleming's) sister now to his paramour.'[110]

Margaret, embittered as she was in the knowledge that, with her looks ruined by smallpox, she had lost the man she longed for, did have some small consolation when her brother Henry, for the information she had sent him, rewarded her with the gift of a diamond. In return she sent him, what she termed a token, in the form of a ring which he must have recognized, having given it to her himself before!

At this point, still with her son at Stirling Castle, she wrote to Albany saying that the Council was threatening to order her to leave. Albany arrived to settle the matter on 9 December. After a private meeting, at which she told him she was going to show him up before the Lords, she carried out her threat at a meeting of the Privy Council the next day. There, in a long speech she denounced them for refusing her free access to her son and as she wrote to Surrey, 'I discharged me of many sharp words that were too long to write.'

The Duke of Albany then bluntly informed the Council 'that if they would not stand to what they had agreed on (namely Margaret's access to her son) the responsibility must rest on them. Then, on the next morning, of the 11th, alone with Margaret and James, he produced a list of the people allowed to be with him, and asked him to be content, at which Margaret snorted, 'I have shown my mind before him and the Lords, and therefore I can say no more.'

In fact she had been warned that Albany had summoned eight hundred of his French auxiliaries to take the king from her to 'some abiding place on the west coast of Scotland',

[110] Ibid.

should she make a fuss, 'Wherefore, to eschew more evil, I thought for that time, I would not contrary them as to the Lords that should be about him.' At a meeting of the Privy Council, which took place immediately afterwards, she agreed to abide by what had been arranged, promising to be 'ane good Scotswoman' but, once the session had ended, she stormed out of the Council to instruct a lawyer to draw up a legal document in which she revoked all that she had said.

Meanwhile, before Albany left the chamber, he told the assembled Lords that 'his ships were ready, and he desired their consent to pass to France without returning more.'

This brought an outcry. They begged him to stay at least until the following spring, to which he reluctantly agreed. His wife is believed to have died in the following January of 1424, so he did not return in time to see her alive.

Margaret's hopes were renewed. She spent the winter agitating about her longed-for divorce, waiting for the ultimate sanction from Pope Adrian VI to end her marriage to Angus, and, it would appear, still clinging forlornly to the hope that Albany might marry her. It may have been in desperation to make him jealous, that she began an affair with one of the best looking men in the palace guard, but if that was so, it failed to achieve its aim. Albany, born and bred in France, put loyalty to that country first, and King Francis had summoned him with urgency.

Lord Dacre informed Wolsey, 'I am apprised by my secret espial out of Scotland, that the Lords continued together all Witsun week in Edinburgh, and were sitting in the Tolbooth in council. The Duke entreated the Queen to hold the young King in the Castle of Sriveling (Stirling)... abjuring her not to confederate with her brother Henry VIII; To which desires the Queen denied him in part, saying "if he rode away, she must needs do the best she could for herself."'. The Duke then expressed his desire to the assembled Lords that 'Queen

Margaret should be obeyed in all her rights.' To which the Lords replied that 'All the pleasure and service they might do should be at her commandment.'[111]

Once having attended the bidding of the Lords of the Council, assembled in the Tolbooth to bid him a formal farewell, Albany rode the same night to Linlithgow and from there on to Stirling where he stayed for two days, while he privately said goodbye to Margaret and the young king, now a boy of twelve years old. From Stirling he rode west to Dumbarton from where, on a fair wind, 'he sailed out of sight forthwith,' as the spy informed Lord Dacre.

Like most of the Scots, Dacre's anonymous informant did not realize that Albany, in his association with Queen Margaret, had skilfully contrived to oppose the influence of her brother, King Henry of England. But he did persist in informing the Warden of the Borders of the Queen's ongoing infatuation with the now departed Regent.

The Earl of Surrey, however, knew better. Thomas Howard, who would shortly succeed his father, now an ailing man of eighty-one, as the 3rd Duke of Norfolk, was in tune with what was taking place. His spies in Scotland had told him that Margaret, for all her apparent fondness for Albany, had a new man in her life.

He was referring to Harry Stewart, the palace guard with whom Margaret is thought to have begun a flirtation, in a vain attempt to recapture the affections of Albany by inciting his jealousy. The second son of Lord Avondale (who himself was a great nephew of the 4th Earl of Douglas for whom the title was created), Harry was an exceptionally good-looking young man with whom Margaret, in defiance of Albany's rejection, regardless of public opinion, just as before with Angus, had precipitately fallen in love.

---

[111] Cott. MS.B.xi.f.246.

CHAPTER 8

THE CONTRARY WINDS OF POWER

So Albany was gone, leaving Margaret to become regent once again. She was supported by the Earl of Arran, still second in line to the throne. A clever man, but easily influenced, Arran was soon persuaded by Margaret that the regency of Albany (at that time still expected to return) and the king's minority should both come to an end. James should be brought to Edinburgh to be invested with the symbols of sovereignty after which, while he was the nominal ruler of Scotland, his mother and Arran would hold the real power.

A fortnight after Albany's departure, Margaret made a pilgrimage to the shrine of St Ninian, on the south west tip of Galloway, as in the past her husband, King James, so frequently had done. There she met, what is described as 'a convention of the lords of her faction', who promised to agree to her decision to give her son regal power. She returned to Edinburgh, satisfied with the arrangement, only to be told that her estranged husband Angus had returned from exile in France, to be welcomed by her brother Henry as a member of his court. With him was their daughter Margaret Douglas, now a girl of nine, tall for her age and with the hair that marked her as a 'Red Douglas' distinctive of her father's family. Her mother, however, showed little maternal affection for this daughter she had not seen since she was three.

Instead, her mind was convulsed with fury, obliterating all reasonable thought, as she realized that her brother, plainly now regarding her as a spent force, was intending to use Angus, the husband she detested, but to whom she was still married, as a means of obtaining the power in Scotland at which, oblivious of the position in which she now found herself placed, he so consistently aimed. Astounded at the treachery of the brother, whose own marital difficulties were now commonly known, and who showed so little sympathy for hers, her sense of injustice further inflamed by some sort of illness, she dictated a letter to him, dated 14 July.

'As to my part, your Grace shall find no fault, but I am a whaman (woman) and may do little but friends.

'Also dearest brother, I have seen your writing touching my Lord of Angus, which, as your Grace writes, is in your realm, and that ye propose to send him here shortly, and that ye find him right wise, and hath ruled him well, and that he hath desired that a peace may be between these two realms, and that he will do his labour and diligence to the same, with many other good words of him, praying me to have him in my favour, and that he is well minded of me, and beareth me great love and favour. Dearest brother, as to my Lord Angus and me, when your Grace desireth me to take him into my favour, as yet he hath not shown, since his departing out of Scotland, that he desireth my good will and favour, neither by writing nor word. But now he has desired your Grace to write for him to me, knowing well that there is nothing I will do so mickle for as for your Grace. But I trust, dearest brother the King, that your Grace will not desire me to do nothing that may be hurt to me your sister, nor that may be occasion to hold me from the King my son.

I beseech your Grace pardon me of my evil hand, for I am something not well disposed and therefore I have caused my hand to be copied, in adventure your Grace could not read my evil hand, and God preserve you.'

This done she added a postscript, which, like the rest of the letter, was dictated to a secretary,

'Dearest brother, please your Grace touching my Lord of Angus coming here, I would beseech your Grace to be well avised in the same, as I have written of before, and touching my part if he put hand to my gonrouffe (jointure) I will not be contended therewith, for I have but right sober thing (income) to find myself with, and have shown your Grace that divers times, and got but little remedy. Wherefore, now, am I to be troubled with the Earl of Angus, it is your Grace that doth it, and then I will be constrained to look for other help, for I will not let him trouble me in my living, as he hath done in times past.

(Signed)Your humble sister
Margaret.'[112]

Margaret's threat 'to look for other help' was of course construed to mean the return of Albany. But things had gone badly in France. Francis I, taken prisoner by the forces of the Emperor Charles V at the battle of Pavia in 1425, was held captive in Madrid and Albany, left to command what was left of the French army, was fighting a form of guerrilla warfare almost to the gates of Rome. Margaret sent letters, begging him to come back to Scotland, but, even if they reached him, it seems he made no reply.

It was on 26 July 1524, that James was brought from Stirling to Edinburgh Castle to be invested by Arran with the crown, sceptre and sword of state. Then, on 1 August, in the upper chamber of the Tolbooth, he attended a meeting of the Privy Council, at which the officers of state having resigned to him, most were immediately reappointed. Most significantly, the regency of Albany was abrogated to the great anger of James Beaton, now the archbishop of St Andrews, the primus of Scotland, who objected on the grounds that the regency had been settled on Albany until King James reached the age of eighteen. Beaton, the chancellor, supported by five other bishops and the earls of Argyll, Lennox and Moray, refused to affix the Great Seal to the document restoring the queen to regnant power from which, on her marriage to Angus, she had been deposed.

Margaret, incensed at what she termed his disobedience, sent her new favourite, and as was rumoured paramour, to deal

---

[112] State Papers, Vol.iv. p.81.

with the archbishop who fled, but was pursued by Stewart, who tore both the Great Seal of Scotland, the Privy Seal and the Signet and Quarter Seal from his hands. Beaton and Andrew Forman, the bishop of Moray, were then imprisoned in a show of force, which subdued the rebellious earls and clerics into submission.

The archbishop of St Andrews, James Beaton, was the next to fall foul of Margaret's wrath, for objecting to her plans for allowing her son to rule. Likewise Lord Dacre, no lover of petticoat rule, was completely exasperated by her behaviour. Margaret, however, got her own back by telling her brother of how his Lord Warden had insulted her.

'Also I complain to the King my brother of what my Lord Dacre

'does and says to my hurt, for he says to Scottish folk 'that he marvels that they will let any woman have authority, and especially me. Quilk words should come of others, not of Englishmen. For, the more honour I get, England will have the more; and such words as these will do me mickle ill. Therefore I desire remedy to be found in that behalf.'[113]

King Henry had, by that time, given her enough money, paid in monthly instalments, to raise a guard of two hundred mercenary soldiers to be stationed in Stirling Castle to protect the king. Thus, with James secure in her keeping, Margaret had achieved the absolute power in Scotland for which she had so persistently aimed.[114]

The foreign policy of the new Council was made clear when, on 5 August, King James signed a letter to his 'derrest and rich inteirlye weilbelufit uncle, the king of Inglande' telling him that he had ended the authority of Albany 'under quhais governans oure realme an liefes hes bene richtevill

---

[113] *State Papers*. Vol.iv. p.118. Letter of Queen Margaret to the English Council. At Edinburgh. August 31 1524.

[114] *State Papers,* Vol, iv, p.148. Norfolk to Wolsey, September 1524.

dem'nyt'[115] Then, early in September, arrangements were made for an embassy to go to England to conclude a truce.[116]

Writing to the Duke of Norfolk, now more than ever in King Henry's confidence as the uncle of his new love, Anne Boleyn, Queen Catherine's lady-in-waiting, Margaret reminded him about the monthly instalment of money to pay the soldiers guarding her son, King James, which had not been paid.

'I sent Patrick Sinclair to you, my Lord, touching the money that the King's Grace my brother ordered to the King for my son for two hundred men to be about his person, which money he hath not gotten. Wherefore I desire perfitley to know if this money shall be furnished or not, and thereupon I send this bearer to know what we will trust to. Whereof, my Lord, I pray let me be advertised...

'Let this said money be sent with this bearer, to keep the two hundred men about the King my son, these men to be chosen as I think best for the surety of the King my son, and not to be chosen by other men's advises... And as to the money that his Grace has given to furnish the two hundred men, I assure you, my Lord, it hath done great good to the King my son, and hath hindered much evil to be done, and it is not a month since it began. And thus, my Lord, I trust you will send the money by this bearer, and shall order it to be well ordered to the weal and surety of the King my son.'

Then, adding a postscript, she wrote, 'Touching my Lord of Angus, I pray you to keep promise with me, for I trust the King's Grace, my brother, will not fail in that he hath promised me, but, as yet, I hear the Earl of Angus is not yet past the hope of the court, whereof I marvel.[117]

---

[115] Ibid. Henry VIII. Vol.iv.pp.95-6.

[116] Donaldson. G. The Edinburgh History of Scotland. Vol.3. p.38.

[117] Cott. MS, Calig. B. vi. Fol.402.

Margaret and Arran believed themselves victorious. Arran, using the excuse that they were both descendants of the Beauforts, wrote to Henry praising the appearance and capability of governing of his nephew, the young King James, before presuming to tell him that, 'if he suffered the Earl of Angus to re-enter Scotland, it sall not only be hurtable and annoy the Queen's Grace, but break the peace between the realms of Scotland and England.'[118]

Queen Margaret then sent Norfolk a hawk, with the promise of another, in the hopes of winning him over to her side in the tussle with her brother over the threatened return of Angus, 'her great dishonouring,' as she called it, 'Gif it be the King's Grace's pleasure to send in the Earl of Angus, yet he cannot cause me to favour him, or to let him be in my company.'

Norfolk, however, gave her no thanks, either for the hawk or the letter. Writing to Wolsey, he merely observed, 'that Queen Margaret was marvellous wilful against the Earl of Anguish, and that she talked of throwing him into prison if he tried to come into Scotland.' [119] Wolsey in reply, merely told Norfolk, not to detain Angus, 'but to speed him across the Border.'

King Henry, who had brought the Earl of Angus back from France, for the express reason of sending him to Scotland to be reconciled to his sister and establish his own dominance in the country of which she was queen, was not to be thwarted. The Duke of Norfolk, urged him to 'send home directly the Earl of Anguish' as he called him, and also to send Doctor Magnus, Archdeacon of the East Riding of Yorkshire, back to Scotland, who, as her confessor, might reason with the queen. Writing to Wolsey, he described the assault on Archbishop Beaton, who, Magnus had at once ordered Harry Stewart to

---

[118] *State Papers,* Vol. iv. pp.157-8. Arran to Henry VIII, October 3, 1524.

[119] Ibid. p.181. Wolsey to Norfolk, October 10. 1524.

release, together with Andrew Forman, the bishop of Moray. He then added the scandalous information that now, above everything, Margaret had made her new favourite the Lord Treasurer of Scotland.

'Henry Stewart, presuming on Queen Margaret's favour, and his command as lieutenant of the royal life-guard, filled the court with his swaggering and bawling', so Magnus described to Wolsey. He had quarrelled savagely with Margaret's private secretary, Patrick Sinclair, but she had taken his part, 'giving 'right sharp words to Patrick Sinclair because he had not brought her a letter from the Duke of Norfolk.' She had then sent one of her messengers, whom she called Jemmy Dog, to complain to Norfolk who sent Jemmy back with a reply, that had he not sent Patrick Sinclair to tell her on no account to let the young king leave Edinburgh, she would totally have lost all authority, adding that in future she need not expect any more advice from him.[120]

On the day of the state reception of the English ambassadors, Archbishop Beaton and Bishop Forman said high mass before both Margaret and her son. Then, when letters from King Henry were presented to them 'the trumpets blew up and did sound right merrily.' But even as this was happening, Doctor Magnus knew that Angus had crossed the Border and was in Scotland. Margaret, he guessed was bound to hear of it soon, so he thought it better to pacify her by giving her the gifts, which her brother had sent both to her and her son, without any further delay. Fine presents they were too. James had a coat of cloth of gold, which fitted him perfectly, and to go with it, a sword.

Margaret was delighted, so Magnus seized on the chance of suggesting a private conversation, in the course of which he put forward King Henry's suggestion of the hand of his daughter Mary as a bride for King James. 'Her Grace, Queen Margaret, was right joyous thereof', Magnus reported to

---

[120] Ibid. pp.126, 148,155.

Wolsey, but then came a violent knocking at the door, and a messenger shouting that he must speak to her Grace immediately on a matter of life and death. Watching her closely, for he knew what was coming, he saw her face change as the man told of Angus's arrival. 'She turned to me full of wrath and disclosed the same. I confessed that it was so, showing that it was not possible to be contrary.'[121]

This then was the moment when Margaret realized that her brother King Henry, Machiavelli of manipulators, ignoring all her pleas, had sent Angus to Scotland. Leaving London in the first week of October, he reached Brancepath on the 16th, before crossing the Border to his own castle of Boncle, from where, on 1 November, he sent a personal letter to Margaret, still at that time, his wife.

Thanks, it is believed, to Harry Stewart, she refused to read it in front of him, and returned it, unopened, to Angus. However, secretly she is thought to have steamed open the seal and read the letter before sealing it up again. Whatever the truth of this, a copy, which Angus sent to the Duke of Norfolk, survives. Doctor Magnus, who saw it, thought it 'singularly well composed.'

'Madame

In my most humble and lowly manner I commend my service to your Grace.

It will please your Grace to know that I have been with the King your brother, the which is one of the most christened Princes and his Grace hath entreated me so marvellous well, that he hath addetted me to do his Grace service and honour, so far as lyse in my power – mine allegiance accepted to the King's Grace, my master (King James) and your Grace, and shall do the same as any other in all the realm of Scotland, if your Grace will accept it. For there is no manner of thing that may be well for the King's Grace, my sovereign, nor to your

---

[121] *State Papers,* Vol. iv. p. 213 – Magnus to Wolsey.

Grace's honour and pleasure, but I shall be glad to fulfil the same.

Madame, if there be any of my unfriends that, in my absence, have made sinister information of me to your Grace, I would beseech your Grace so that ye would stand so good and gracious lady unto me, that ye would be content that I may speak with your Grace, and if I have offended your Grace in any manner of way, I shall reform it at the sight and pleasure of your said Grace.

Beseeching your Grace that ye will advertise me of your mind in writing, as that I shall be ready to fulfil the same, As knoweth God, who preserve your Grace eternally.

At Boncle, the first day of November, by the hand of your humble servant,

Angus.'[122]

It was at this point that Margaret, blaming her brother for harbouring Angus, sent him an insolent letter, carried by a courier called Appleby, which has not survived, but Cardinal Wolsey, on seeing it, told Norfolk that:

'her insolent behaviour, causeth the King's highness to think that she is not only the most ingrate and unkind sister that ever was, to whom his Grace, neither in her tender youth nor since, hath given any cause.'

To make matters worse, the bishop of Dunkeld, had heard of a plot to assassinate King Henry of which Margaret, if she even knew of it, failed to send warning. Henry, however, was convinced that she had done so deliberately, in revenge for his sending Angus back to Scotland, and was apoplectic with rage.

'There has been no matter', wrote Wolsey to Norfolk, 'which, in my life, I have seen his Grace take more unkindly, or that more hath moved his royal and princely courage to think of the extreme high ingratitude, and unnatural dealing in any person, than her most strange answer given to Appleby,

---

[122] Cott. MS. B. vi.p.372. *State Papers, Vol. iv.* P.217, note.

and the continued delay which the said Queen Margaret hath used in opening and disclosing a matter, as it is said, much to the danger of the King's live (life) and person, so to satisfy her own malice, she would be contented to conceal, and not suffer to be discovered that thing which she might endanger her own brother's life, and consequently, either to destroy her brother, her son and herself, for revenging her own rancour and malice'. Concluding, he says spitefully, that he hopes that Margaret hereafter may not have cause to be sorry that she had ever been born.[123]

Margaret may well have been innocent of all that Wolsey implied. Proof does not exist of her conniving at her brother's death. Nonetheless Henry and his minister believing it, immediately stopped paying the monthly instalments of money for the two hundred mercenaries, who formed the young King James's special guard. Norfolk plainly doubted her involvement in the conspiracy, of which the bishop of Dunkeld had warned. Writing to Wolsey he told him that:

'Pleasanter letters must be written to her, or the truce will be run out, and when the war is renewed, of which she will be glad, the mischief done by the English borderers will all fall on the demesnes of her enemies.' Plainly in touch with someone at the Scottish court, he adds that he 'perceives the unsteadiness of the Queen's demeanour, and that he knows her love for young Harry Stewart is so much, that he can turn all as he list, and it shall be well done that master Magnus, as a priest, gives her wholesome counsel for her honour in this world, and the weal of her soul in that to come, and be plain with her, as is his first instructions, and unless he sees some likelihood that she follows the mind of the Lord Cardinal, to be round with her, not sparing to tell her, that all the realm doth marvellously speak thereof, as I doubt not they daily do.'[124]

---

[123] *State Papers*. Vol. iv. p.220. Wolsey to Norfolk.
[124] Ibid. p.226. Norfolk to Wolsey. November 5, 1524.

Margaret, however, impetuous as when she had fallen in love with Angus, now disregarded all warnings as she plunged into a new affair. She refused to listen to the wise counsels of her confessor, Master Magnus, warning her that her passion for young Stewart could only lead to disaster and the ruination of her name.

All the old councillors had told Norfolk 'that since the Queen had had the mercenary guard, she had not heeded the advice of the wise men of the realm, thinking that, with the strength of the said armed men, she would force everybody to follow her mind, which ye shall see will be as Harry Stewart will have it, and that shall be nought for us.' To Wolsey he poured scorn on Margaret's chief minister, the Earl of Arran, saying that he daily wore the French king's order of St Michael on his breast and that 'whoever have him best, is no more sure of him than he that hath an eel by the tail'[125]

Dismissive as she had been of her husband Angus, Doctor Robert Magnus, Archdeacon of the West Riding of Yorkshire, sent specifically to Scotland by Henry to try to reason with Margaret, had met with nothing but rude rejection. Not only had she refused to listen to him, but had subjected both him and his fellow envoy, Roger Radcliffe– who had come with a piece of gold-tissue from her brother– to insult when, having sent for them, she took them into her chamber where a party of ten to twelve Edinburgh housewives, yelling at the top of their voices, accused them, as representatives of the English government of capturing their husbands, who were the crew of a merchant ship taken prisoner at Sandwich.

Margaret then, plainly relenting, took them that afternoon to see her son riding and running with a spear, among his lords and servants on the sands and the links above the sea at Leith. Magnus was much impressed by the boy, not yet thirteen, who, he reported to King Henry, greatly resembled himself.

---

[125] Ibid. Norfolk to Wolsey. P.226. November 5. 1524.

He did not tell the king how those lords and servants were leading the young king astray. The guards, which he paid for on a monthly basis, being it would seem, the most profligate amongst them. Sir David Lindsay, of the Mount, devoted carer of James's childhood, now a pensioner, wrote satirically of what was taking place in a poem headed The Complaint.

'Sir, some would say,'an' like your majesty
Shall we now go to your liberty,
Thou shalt by no man be subjected,
Nor in the school no more corrected.
We think them very natural fools,
That learn o'ermeikle in the schools.
Sir you must learn to turn a spear,
And bear you like a man of war.
For we shall put such men about you,
That all the world and more shall doubt you,
Then on his Grace they put a guard
Which hastily got their reward.
They did solace his majesty,
Some caused him revel at the racket,
Some haled him to the harley-hacket,
And some, to show their courtly courses,
Would ride to Leith and run their horses,
To swiftly gallop o'er the sands
They neither spared spurs nor wands,
Casting gambades width bends and backs
For wanntoness some broke their necks.
There was no play but cards and dice,
And vilest flattery bore its price,
Methought it was a piteous thing
To see that fair young tender King,
Of whom these gallants felt no awe
Playing with them at 'pluck the draw.'
They became rich, I can be sure,
But aye my Prince remained poor.
There was not one of that ill garrison

But learned him some evil lesson.
Some want to crack, and some to flatter,
Some played the fool, and some did chatter.
Said one,'De'il stick me with a knife,
But Sir, I know a maid in Fife,
One of the loveliest fairest lassies,
For which, by Mary! There she passes.'
'Hold thy tongue, brother,' said another,
'I know a fairer than that other!
Sir when ye please to Lithgow pass,
There ye shall see a buxom lass!'
Now pribble, prabble, hey, trow low!'
Cried the third man,' thou dost but mow
When his Grace comes to Stirling,
There he shall see a day's darling.'

The next day, the ambassadors were again summoned to the queen's presence, this time thankfully without the Edinburgh sailor's wives, but to discuss the cause of their complaints, namely piracy at sea. Arriving in Margaret's presence chamber they found the Earl of Arran and the sea captain known as Hob-a-Barton, the Controller, standing beside her chair. Magnus then showed a letter from King Henry to Arran, upon which that nobleman took such a fit of the sulks that he stalked out of the room, refusing Margaret's orders to return.

The meeting then dissolved into an argument between Margaret and Doctor Magnus over whether Angus should attend the Parliament about to assemble in the Tolbooth, Magnus insisting that he should, Margaret that he should not.

The Douglases, encouraged by the return of Angus, had already been causing trouble. The Douglas Lord of Drommellar had killed Lord Fleming, a known supporter of Albany, in the doorway of St Giles's Church in Edinburgh. Margaret, who hated Fleming, calling him the poisoner of the Drummond sisters in several of her letters, agreed to the imprisonment of his son, but trouble between the Douglases, incited by the return of Angus and the queen's supporters headed by Arran, continued to increase.

Now it was Angus, who learning of his wife's refusal to let him attend the forthcoming Parliament, took decisive action himself. With a party of some of his own men, he scaled the Edinburgh town wall in darkness before opening the nearest gate to a larger force, headed by the earls of Lennox and Glencairn. Once within the city he rode to the Mercat Cross where his herald proclaimed his so-called peaceable intentions.

As the noise caused by much shouting was heard down at Holyrood, Margaret, courageous in an emergency, whatever her other faults, acted decisively. Immediately she ordered two small cannons, which stood at the front of the palace to be loaded and, at any sign of Angus and his followers, to be fired. Doctor Magnus and Roger Radcliffe, ostensibly as Henry's representatives Angus's partisans, requested an audience, but were promptly told by Margaret not to meddle in Scottish affairs. She then ordered the cannons to be fired, whereupon an old woman, a priest and two sailors, unlucky enough to be standing near, were killed.

At four o'clock in the afternoon, King James ordered Angus and Lennox to leave Edinburgh, which instruction they obeyed going only as far as the Douglas castle, the Palace of Dalkeith. Then as it grew dark, Margaret had all her jewels carried before her in a casket, as, together with her son, the young king, she walked from Holyrood Palace up the Royal Mile to Edinburgh Castle, most secure bastion of the realm. Escorting them was Harry Stewart and the rest of the Palace Guard, holding the flaming torches blazing above their heads. The men gave much needed protection, as in the many alleyways, dividing towering tenement houses of five storeys or more, lurked thieves and the vagrants of the city, ready to leap out on anyone climbing the steep cobbled walkway unless defended by swords.

All this was reported by Doctor Magnus to Cardinal Wolsey, to whom the queen wrote a personal letter:

'Therefore my Lord, I pray you consider how I am done to, and how daily the Earl of Anguish set to take me from the King, my son, wherefore I marvel what pleasure it may be for the King's Grace, my brother, to hold me in daily trouble. In your hands, God willing, I sal never come to any evil. And should I leave this realm, when any other princes understand how I am done to they will have pity on me. I can no more.'[126]

Angus, by this time, within the strong walls of Tantallon, also wrote to Wolsey, pouring out his bitterness, telling him:

'Ye are deceived by the Queen, the greatest ennomyse (enemy) I have in Scotland. Therefore please your Grace, to give no credence whatever you hear report of me. For Harry Stewart, and the Earl of Cassillis are cousin-german.'

The ambassador Doctor Magnus, already ticked off by Margaret for trying to interfere in Scottish affairs, wrote to Wolsey telling him;

'Your Grace knoweth what a haught letter the Queen wrote when she heard the Earl of Angus would enter Scotland, therefore it is not to be thought but when the Earl was come indeed, that her Grace should be some deal further moved.'[127]

Wolsey tried to pour oil on the very troubled waters by suggesting that Margaret should be given two hundred pounds and Arran one hundred pounds, an idea angrily refuted by Magnus who gave Margaret £one hundred and Arran nothing. The Duke of Norfolk, furious that they should receive anything at all, expressed his wrath to Wolsey:

'I think none worthy to bear any blame but only the Queen, who is so blended with the folly that I have often written to your Grace, that to have her ungodly appetite followed she careth not what she doeth. And yet for all her evil dealing, I greatly doubt not that all will come well to pass, in despite of those who would be to the contrary.'[128]

---

[126] *State Papers*, Vol.iv,p.264 – Margaret to Wolsey.

[127] Ibid. p.276. Magnus to Wolsey. November 27.

[128] Ibid. p.272. Norfolk to Wolsey.

CHAPTER 9

'WE WILL PULL YOU IN TWO PIECES RATHER THAN PART WITH YOU'

Margaret and James were in Edinburgh Castle when, on the night of Epiphany, 6 January 1525, the building was battered by a gale. The battlements of David's Tower were blown down and a room in Margaret's lodging set on fire, most likely from burning soot. The bishop of Galloway's house came crashing about his ears as he was actually saying mass, giving him such a fright that he fled from the queen's court and returned to his own see.[129]

People prophesied disaster, but Margaret, disregarding the gale as a natural phenomenon, continued to defy her brother with his offer of the hand of his daughter Princess Mary for her son, by bargaining with King Francis's mother, Louise of Savoy (acting as regent while he was embroiled in the war with the Emperor Charles) for the hand of the king's youngest daughter Madeleine, from whom (Louise of Savoy) according to her own word, she extracted thirty thousand crowns. Triumphantly, she told Doctor Magnus that 'It were long before I have had so much from England', a taunt he must have passed on to Henry VIII.

Margaret herself was still trying to get her divorce, and it was with this knowledge in mind that Sir James Hamilton of Finnart, described by the ambassador Magnus as 'a right proper gentleman, and one that has the greatest rule with the Earl of Arran,' contrived a meeting between the Earl of Lennox and others of her husband's friends. Having assured them that she would not oppose Angus's assumption of political power in return for his agreement to their divorce,

---

[129] Lesley. p.130.

Hamilton also said that she had promised to give him part of her dower lands worth an annual £one thousand. The upshot of this was that Margaret made a formal reconciliation with her husband in March 1525.

On 6 March Angus attended the council over which, having formed a triumvirate with Lennox and Argyll, he quickly contrived to gain control. His achievement in doing so is symptomatic of the charismatic power of this chief of the Red Douglases, to which Margaret herself had once succumbed. Now at thirty, Angus was no longer 'the witless young fool' his uncle Gavin Douglas had once called him, but a powerful man of physical and mental strength, his energy, enhanced with personal charm, now focussed into achieving the ruling power in Scotland, which with the backing of the English king – ruthless as himself, his counterpart in every sense – appeared to be within his grasp. But now, as he tried to mediate with Margaret, Henry's sister, the woman who had once lost both the power of her regency and control of her son, to marry him, he found her implacable in her defiance to comply with him in any way.

It was only after much argument, that Margaret agreed to come down from Edinburgh Castle to Holyrood to open Parliament. Eventually she did so on the understanding, as Magnus reported to Wolsey, that Angus would not interfere with her in any way until the following Whitsun by which time she hoped her divorce would be through.

This being agreed, Margaret and James came in state, magnificent in royal robes, the Earl of Angus carrying the crown before them and the Earl of Arran the sceptre. They opened the Parliament but during the proceedings, Harry Stewart made himself so obnoxious to the lords by his assiduous attention to the queen, that they ordered him to go to Stirling where, with his brothers, he waited for a message from Margaret to tell him what he was to do.

From Edinburgh, Margaret, with James, moved to the royal residence in the Blackfriars Benedictine Monastery at Perth. Here Doctor Magnus appeared, bringing letters from her brother King Henry which, after reading a line or two, reduced her, first to fury and then as he described, to 'excessive weeping. ' Margaret, shouting through her sobs, accused Henry of sending the Earl of Anguish to torment her, and declared that she would send no more ambassadors to England. She then told Magnus to bring her no more letters from Henry, 'for if she did read any more, she was right sure it would be her death.'

In July it was arranged that King James should remain in the custody of each of the four leading nobles, namely, Angus, Arran, Lennox and Argyll each of whom would be responsible for him for a quarter of the year. Then, on 3 August, the estates declared that Margaret would lose her authority within twenty days unless she would resume co-operation with the lords.

Inevitably her absence sparked off rumours that she had made a secret marriage with Harry Stewart and was about to have his child. Her whereabouts are unrecorded but she was probably at Stirling Castle when she heard, that in November 1425, when the time had come for Angus to hand over custody of James to the next in the rota of the four lords, he refused to do so. Margaret and Arran accused Angus of treason for 'invassalling his Prince to his attendance', to which accusation Angus did not deign to reply, but his brother George Douglas, ever an evil influence, forced James to write to his mother that 'with none more cheerfully, willingly and contentedly could he live and spend his time with the Earl of Angus.'

This was far from the truth. James was held a prisoner, although Angus was by then trying the age old strategy, so often used by dissident parents, in attempting by spoiling, to win him to his side. In this case Angus, as James's step-father, did his best to turn him into a libertine, encouraging him in debauchery with wine and women, hoping in this way, by giving him hitherto forbidden distractions, to make him forsake his mother in happily enjoying the distractions available to a young man. That James did indulge in such activities is believed to have been the reason for his later love of low life, but nonetheless, carouse with him as he might, James's detestation of Angus was not in the least subdued.

The letter, written at the dictation of George Douglas, evil amanuensis of his brother, as both Margaret and Arran guessed, was written under constraint. Then James contrived to smuggle out another letter telling them the truth and begging them to free him from Angus and 'if it could not otherways be done to accomplish it by force of arms,' if they had any pity.'[130]

Margaret did not wait. Despite it being January, the coldest month of the year, she rode south towards Edinburgh with a force, hastily gathered, of six hundred men, commanded by the Earl of Moray. She expected Arran, now at odds with Angus, to meet her. But instead it was Angus who confronted her near Linlithgow with, not only a large army, but the young King James in tow. This was a clever move, putting Moray in risk of treachery should he oppose his sovereign. Accordingly, he at once went over to Angus, as did those under his command, before in one party, they all marched back to Edinburgh.

Angus now entrenched his position in an open display of necromancy. Archbishop Beaton was forced to resign the Great Seal, sending it not to the king but to Angus himself. His brother, Sir George Douglas became Master of the Household, Douglas of Kilspindie the treasurer, and other members of the family allotted to more minor positions.

Margaret, moreover, immediately lost all her authority in the Scottish administration, when, in March 1526, she married Harry Stewart 'for her plesour' so it was said. Stewart, the palace guard, eight years younger than herself, as only the

---

[130] Drummond, William of Hawthornden, *History of Scotland*, p.282.

second son of Lord Avondale, had few prospects. Again it was Doctor Magnus, writing to Wolsey, who told him, with a touch of spite, that in the following month of April, when Margaret visiting her son, had asked his permission to bring her new husband with her to court, her request had been peremptorily refused.

It soon came to the King's ears that, in Stirling Castle, where his mother at this point was living, she insisted that Harry Stewart be treated with all the honour due to the husband of a queen. Furious, he sent Lord Erskine with a party of armed men to lay siege to the Castle where Margaret, surprisingly, immediately surrendered her new husband, who was marched away and imprisoned. It would seem as a form of mock punishment, however, for he soon escaped to rejoin her, this time in Edinburgh Castle which, although she was no longer the regent, was still held in her name.

On 14 June, 1526, when the king at fourteen years old, was officially declared to be of age, he was henceforth deemed to be ruling under his own authority while in reality obeying Angus's dictation.

By this time, the summer of 1526, within less than a year of his return to Scotland, Angus held complete monopoly of the Scottish government. He had forfeited the support of the lords, who had backed him against Margaret, the earls of Argyll, Cassillis, the Scottish ambassador to England, and Glencairn. All in high office were now Douglases, or their adherents. Only the young Earl of Lennox remained amongst the few men close to the king, who were not of the Douglas name.

John Stewart, 3rd Earl of Lennox, descended as he was from a younger daughter of James II, was a young man, popular with most of his acquaintances, having all of his family's charm. King James turned to him in desperation, begging him to free him from Angus in any possible way. The first chance came in July when Angus held a Justice Ayre (an itinerant court of Justice) in the Border town of Melrose, the king as usual being taken with him in proof of the authority of his rule. Lennox contrived to get in touch with Scott of Buccleuch, a powerful Border laird, whom he knew to be involved in a feud with the Homes and the Kers, both cohorts of Angus. Riding home from Melrose towards Edinburgh, Angus and the king were ambushed by the Scotts and their allies, but the well-armed men of the royal escort fought them off in a short time.

Lennox was observed, during this encounter, to be standing by the king's horse taking no part in the engagement. But once back in Edinburgh, he promised James that he would raise an army to rescue him before, unobtrusively, he left the court.

Arran, descended as he was from the elder daughter of James II, was nonetheless jealous of Lennox, the cousin, who was also his rival in line to the Scottish throne. Disgruntled by James's obvious attachment to John Lennox, but, believing Angus omnipotent, as at that point he seemed to be, he had joined him, foreswearing his loyalty to Margaret, for what appeared to him, at least in the foreseeable future, to be an unbeatable power.

But, unaware of it, as Arran would appear to have been, resistance was steadily growing against Angus, as Lennox and Archbishop Beaton, secretly in coercion with James, were working to break his power. In the last days of August, Lennox rode to the Borough Moor, land then covered with ancient oak-trees on the outskirts of Edinburgh. With him were two hundred men-at-arms and a few horsemen, leading eight spare horses, on which the king and those closest to him, known to be hostile to Angus, were to escape. The master of Kilmorris managed to get into Holyrood but someone, presumably a guard at the gate, warned Angus of his coming. King James, however, realizing what was happening, led Kilmorris through the coining-house, and out through a back door through which he managed to escape.

The fury of Angus, on discovering this, can be only too well imagined. Whatever other punishment he inflicted, he is known to have taken the young king to a house in Edinburgh, which belonged to the archbishop of St Andrews, presumably seized by Angus as a prison, for here James was held under a twenty-four hour guard, by George Douglas with forty armed men.

The story runs that the king, about a week later, was able to use his sovereign power in demanding to see his mother at the Palace of Linlithgow. He did so in the knowledge, somehow smuggled in to him, that she would find a way to rescue him there. More factually, it is known that Margaret persuaded the Earl of Lennox and Archbishop Beaton to raise an army said to have been ten thousand strong, with which Lennox marched from Stirling towards Edinburgh. Angus sent Arran to raise a force of local men, in and around the town of Linlithgow, which he then deployed, in readiness to confront Lennox on Pace Hill above the River Avon. Lennox crossed the river by a ford at Manuel Convent, actually above the bridge from which the battle takes its name. From there he led his men over a marsh to attack the flank of Arran's army on the higher, firmer, ground. He was winning, Arran's men starting to fall back, when Angus arrived, having marched from Edinburgh with a large force of men, and bringing with him King James.

In the slaughter which followed, on the hillside and on the bank of the river, James made a desperate attempt to spur his horse and ride forward into the scrimmage. But George Douglas held him back, his hand gripping the bridle, telling him, prophetically, to 'Bide where you are, sir, for if they get hold of you, be it by one of your arms, we will seize a leg and pull you in two pieces rather than part with you.'[131] Thwarted and choking with anger, James then had to watch helplessly, while in the battle the Earl of Lennox, 'his best beloved kinsman,' was wounded and taken prisoner and then murdered by Arran's natural son, Sir James Hamilton of Finnart. Later,

---

[131] *State Papers*. Letter of Magnus to Wolsey, September 4, 1526.

he must have been less sorry to learn that Harry Stewart had been wounded, and at least one of his brothers killed.

Distressed as she was by the loss of Lennox and in particular, when told of the needless cruelty shown to a man who had died for her cause, Margaret's mind was nonetheless largely obsessed by loathing, not only of Angus, but of Arran, whom she now knew to be a traitor, but also of his despicable bastard son.

It was only with the greatest reluctance that she allowed herself to be persuaded, by appeals sent to her by James, to ride from Linlithgow to Edinburgh to open the Parliament, which convened there on 20 November 1526. She did nothing to conceal her anger when, on reaching Corstorphine, she was met by Angus, with James beside him, apparently holding him by the hand, who received her with the utmost show of civility, embellished with the obsequious flattery he had learned at the court of France. James, however, showed his delight at seeing the mother who, despite her abandonment of him as an infant, he is known to have adored. Together they rode down to Holyrood, where she was given the same rooms that Albany had occupied during his time in Scotland, presumably the best in the house.

James had the room above her bedroom and it was noticed that, except when he was out hunting, he never left her side. Lord Dacre was told by his brother, at that time also at Holyrood, 'that if the Queen remains thus near her son, the whole court will have a turn, for the King since the death of the Earl of Lennox, has no affection for the Earl of Angus nor him of Arran.'[132]

This was putting it mildly. The young king was desperate, feeling himself trapped in a web of the relations of the man whom he detested most on earth. Secretly, in whispers, he and his mother consulted each other trying to decide, what in the

[132] Pinkerton, Appendix, Vol. ii, December 1526.

apparently hopeless situation, there was anything that either of them could do to overthrow the tyrants which Angus, and in particular his brother George, had become. There appeared to be no solution. Guarded day and night, there was no hope of escape.

Margaret, however, did come up with the ingenious, if not exactly practical idea, of using bloodhounds as a means of personal protection and defence. Apparently these animals were trained to sit behind horsemen, just as sheepdogs do today behind drivers of four-wheeled bikes. Writing to Lord Dacre, on 8 January 1527, she asked him to, 'get and send us three or four brace of the best ratches (harriers) in the country, less of more for hares, foxes and other greater beasts, with a brace of bloodhounds that are good and will ride behind men on horseback.'

Her main pre-occupation at this time, however, was in finally achieving her divorce. This was largely thanks to Albany who, due to family connections being on good terms with Pope Leo X, both arranged and paid for it.

Albany, on leaving Scotland, had retained the Castle of Dunbar, leaving his secretary, a man called Groselles, or Courelles, in charge of the castle as its captain to whom she refers as the dean of Dunbar.

Margaret, hoping, by now it seems forlornly, that he might yet return and marry her, told him, in this last letter that she is known to have written to him that he, of all men, was the one whom she trusted and truly loved. Had his wife died earlier, had he not now been committed to the king of France as his ambassador to Rome, Margaret might have achieved a marriage to the one man who could keep her under control.

'I give you a hundred thousand thanks, and trust the day will one day come when I may return the pleasure you have done to me, and praying you Monsieur my cousin, as the person I have more affiance in than any other man in this world, except my dearest son, both for the love of me, and to put an end to all the torments and tribulations I suffer, and for the happy advancement of all the other matters between you and me, that you will be pleased to expedite the completion of my sentence, and the process to send me into Scotland, as quickly as possible, and to supply me with the money that will be needful and requisite, till God is pleased to grant me of his grace the means of recompensing you for the said monies, and all the gratuities and benefactions you have aided me with in times past.

I am informed to-day by your servant and secretary, Nicholas Canyvet, that a captain William Stewart, with another gentleman, have been sent by you to my son with all sorts of horses and other beautiful presents, which I can assure you will be very agreeable to him, and I should have written to you for things of that kind a long time ago, if I had not been hindered as I told you in my last letters, and forasmuch as I had hope to get a full answer to my last letters by the said captain, both from the King of France and yourself. The said news (of the divorce) are to me very joyous. All the letters that you send to me can be kept in charge by your secretary, the Dean of Dunbar, or by some other equal sure and secret channel, of the subject that you have written to me in your last letters. As to any other news, I must refer you to your servant Nicholas.'

Your good cousin
Margaret

Then, in a postscript, written in her own hand, she said, 'Monsieur my Cousin, I beg you to excuse the whole letter not being written by my own hand, but have me and my business in your remembrance.

I remain to the utmost of my power.
Your good cousin.

Margaret.'[133]

Albany's reasons for helping Margaret to end her marriage to Angus, however, were not entirely altruistic, for in doing so he hoped to reduce her brother's influence in Scotland, thereby strengthening the French connection. In this he was disappointed. Angus, in control of King James, was now, in every major respect, a satellite of the English king.

A year went by before, on 27 March 1528, Angus, forcing the king to come with him, with a large party of men, advanced on Edinburgh Castle, that most famous of Scottish fortresses, to summon Margaret to surrender both it and her husband Harry Stewart in the king's name. Margaret, according to Bishop Lesley, went down on her knees before her son begging for mercy, both for her husband and his brother, James Stewart, who were nonetheless marched back as prisoners into the castle they had just left. She then made what the bishop calls 'a pacific entry' into Edinburgh with James riding beside her. Soon afterwards she went back to Stirling Castle, but Archbishop Beaton sent her a secret warning that there was a plan to kill her. It was not safe for her to stay.

Lindsay states that she fled in disguise from Stirling, having dismissed her servants and leaving the castle unoccupied, except for what must have been a skeleton staff. He also avers that, for fear of the vengeful Douglases, both she and Beaton for some time lived like gypsies, he disguised as a shepherd keeping sheep on the Burough Moor. This, in the light of Margaret's apparent disappearance, may be partly invention, contemporary historians being diverted by the controversy over religion now threatening the long established dogma of the Roman Catholic Church.

---

[133] Pie`ces et Documents Inédits, relatife `a l'Histoire d'Ecosse, In the Archives of the Kingdom o France.

CHAPTER 10

THE SCOTTISH MARTYR

The ideas of Renaissance humanism, challenging certain aspects of the Catholic Church, had begun to infiltrate into Scotland through contacts between Scottish and continental thinkers in the latter part of the fifteenth century. Then, in the early 1500s, the teachings of Martin Luther, the German priest and professor of ideology, began to influence people in Scotland. As John Knox was to write, soon to ports on the east coast of Scotland, especially to Leith and Dundee, came 'merchants and mariners, who, frequenting other countries, heard the true doctrine informed.' Some of the German princes and the kings of Denmark and Sweden were giving protection to Lutherism, and by doing so were appropriating some of the wealth of Catholic foundations. However Germany, the Netherlands and Denmark were not the only countries from which the new doctrines reached Scotland. A Frenchman, who had come with Albany, was charged with spreading Luther's principles. In 1525 the importation of Lutheran books, recognized as a threat to orthodoxy, had been banned by the Scottish parliament. But the books, and copies of Tyndale's English translation of the New Testament, still continued to be smuggled in to east coast ports, in particular St Andrews, the town which, as the seat of the primus of the Scottish Church and of its leading university, was the centre of the rapidly fomenting conflict of the Reformation.

In 1527, the Scottish Government formally supported the Catholic religion while insisting that opposition to the reform movement must be rewarded by concessions from the orthodox church. King James, in a letter to the Pope, took a firm stand, writing that he was anxious 'to banish the foul Lutheran sect' while at the same time asking him to preserve the privileges of the Scottish kings in return for his consistent loyalty to the orthodox faith.

The king had lain down his country's policy, but despite the threat of punishment for promoting, or even reading their tracts, adherents of the new reformed religion continued to gather strength. Foremost amongst its advocates was a young man called Patrick Hamilton, the suppression of whom caused the reconciliation between Angus and Archbishop Beaton.

Patrick Hamilton had been born in 1504, the second son of Sir Patrick Hamilton of Kincavil and his wife Catherine Stewart who, as the daughter of Alexander, Duke of Albany (father of the regent) a son of James II, was a sister of the 2nd Duke of Albany, thus making Patrick a third cousin of King James. Thanks to his royal connections, at the age of seventeen, he was appointed titular abbot of Fearn Abbey in Rosshire, the income from which allowed him to go to France to study at the university of Paris, where he became enthralled by the teaching of the great Protestant reformer, Martin Luther. From Paris he continued to Leuven where, by 1521, the legendary theologian Erasmus had become established. Returning to Scotland, he had enrolled at St Leonard's College in Aberdeen University where he had become, first a student and then a friend, of the humanist John Mair.

It was early in the year of 1527, that Archbishop Beaton had first realized that Hamilton's radical preaching was drawing in large congregations. Alarmed, he had ordered him to stand trial for treachery, but Hamilton had managed to escape to Germany from where, believing that the furore against him had subsided, he had returned to Scotland in the autumn. Going first to his brother's house, at Kincavel, near Linlithgow, he began preaching again, his charismatic powers of oration drawing ever growing crowds. It was David Beaton, the archbishop's nephew, who himself had just returned from Europe, who then cunningly, invited Hamilton to St Andrews where for a month, as he spread his doctrines, evidence of heresy was gathered against him. Then with the publication of

Patrick's Places, in 1528, he introduced Martin Luther's theology of the distinction of the Law and Gospel.

On Leap Year's Day, 29 February 1528, summoned before a council of clergy presided over by the archbishop, he faced thirteen charges, seven of them based on Martin Luther's ideological sermons. Hamilton confirmed their truth, after which, on examination, he was convicted on all of the charges and sentenced to die at the stake.

King James was at that moment on a pilgrimage to his father's old haunt, the shrine of St Duthac at Tain, in Ross-shire. Knowing that he might try to refute the execution of his cousin, Beaton ordered the sentence to be carried out immediately. Patrick Hamilton was burnt outside the entrance to St Salvadore's College at St Andrews, where a stone, carved with his initials, marks the spot to this day. It was raining and the faggots smouldered, causing him six hours of agony before he died, his last words being 'Lord Jesus receive my soul.'

Patrick Hamilton was dead, but he had lit a fuse in the minds of many people. Beaton was warned by one of his servants that if he proposed to execute any more heretics he should 'let them burn in deep cellars, for the reek of Master Patrick Hamilton has infected as many as it blew upon.' It is known that the king bore no blame, for he was in the power of Angus. Likewise his mother escaped all responsibility being, as it is claimed, living in hiding at that time.

One man who might have tried to save Patrick, but instead chose to stay silent, was his cousin, James Hamilton of Finnart, the illegitimate son of the Earl of Arran (he who had so fortuitously escaped with his father after the scrimmage with the Douglases in the High Street in Edinburgh). But, ambitious and aiming to use his skills as an architect in the restoration of some of the royal castles and palaces, Hamilton curried the favour of the Beatons, the archbishop and his nephew David, currently the abbot of Arbroath, as a means of advancing the connections that he hoped to achieve with the king. Members of Patrick's own family, his brother, Hamilton of Kincavel, and his sister, who was tried and acquitted for sharing his beliefs, bravely supported him. It was Finnart's refusal to do so – it would seem for self advancement rather than religious belief– that led to the bitter feud between him and Kincavel, that would finally seal his own fate.

Meanwhile what had happened to Margaret? The story that, having been warned by Beaton that she was in danger, she fled from Stirling Castle to live like a vagrant is too improbable to believe. She had now been married for two years to Harry Stewart, by whom she is known to have had at least two children, so the likelihood is that she lived with him, somewhere within Perth, the territory of his father, Lord Avondale, or in the castle of Doune, where King James had allowed Harry's brother to become the keeper at his mother's special request.

It is claimed that it was Margaret's servants who brought, not only guns and ammunition, but provisions into Stirling Castle so that by the end of May 1528 it was fully garrisoned and she able to return.[134] She certainly was there when her son asked her to exchange the castle– settled on her as part of her marriage settlement by his father –for Methven Castle, near Perth. Margaret agreed, taking the opportunity of asking her son to make Harry Stewart Lord Methven, as a favour in return. Nonetheless she seems to have been still living in Stirling Castle, in secret communication with James, when sometime between 27 and 30 May, with Angus at Falkland Palace, the young king grabbed at a chance to enact a daring plan.

The opportunity came when George Douglas, the brother on whom Angus most relied, set off to St Andrews on business. Then, fortuitously, at the same time his cousin, Douglas of Kilspindie went to visit his mistress in Dundee,

---

[134] Lesley. p.139.

Angus himself departed, to visit his mother in the family's castle, on the island of Lochleven in Fife, leaving a relation, James Douglas, of Parkhead, in charge of the king.

As soon as the sound of departing hoof-beats died away, James summoned the laird of Fernie, the forester at Falkland, and instructed him to find some local men to act as beaters and to be at the castle by seven'o'clock in the morning, for he wanted 'to slay a fat buck or two for his pleasure.' He then sent for his supper, drank a toast to James Douglas and suggested they should both go to bed early so as to be 'tymous' for the hunt in the morning.

The watch was set in the castle and all was quiet when James got up again, dressed in the clothes and bonnet he had borrowed from one of the grooms, and crept out of Falkland unseen and unheard. Reaching the stables he was joined by two trusted servants, Jocki Hairt and Zacharie Harcar with whom he rode, as fast as their horses could carry them, to Stirling. Reaching the castle, they found the gates open and the portcullis raised, as pre-arranged with Margaret, who must therefore have been in the castle.

Meanwhile, back at Falkland, Sir George Douglas had returned to find the king's bedroom door locked and after he had forced the door, an empty bed. Pandemonium ensued. Angus and Kilspindie, hastily sent for, returned to ride to Stirling, but only to be met by a herald, as they approached the town, who gave them the king's orders that no one was to be allowed within six miles of his person. [135]

Angus was defeated. The chess game played out; he had lost the king. James was joined at Stirling by the majority of the nobles of Scotland, the earls of Moray, Argyll, Eglinton, Bothwell, Montrose, Rothes and Marischal, and the Lords Maxwell and Home. Most surprising of all was that Arran, who vacillating in his loyalty as ever, now chose to join, what he clearly realized, to be the winning side.

---

[135] *Exchequer Rolls,* Vol. xv, Preface, pp, li-lv.

CHAPTER 11

INTELLIGENCE OF SECRET ORDERS.

On 6 July King James entered Edinburgh in triumph. The crowd who cheered him, riding at the head of a galaxy of nobles, now knew that Angus had gone, four days before, to his own secure castle of Tantallon. A week later, on 13th July, he was summoned for treason and when Parliament met in September, the Estates passed sentence of death and forfeiture on him, his brother George, and Douglas of Kilspindie, who were all declared guilty of 'holding our sovereign lord's person against his will continually by the space of two years… and in exposing his person to battle, he being of tender age, for the which causes they have forfeited their lives, lands and goods to remain with our sovereign lord and his successors in time to come.'[136] All three were then sentenced to banishment being put to the horn.

Angus was besieged in Tantallon, by an army, approaching from Edinburgh with drummers playing the first known regimental march, 'Ding doon Tantallon.' But the stout defences of that fortress, standing high above the North Sea, defied even the cannons that were dragged down from Edinburgh Castle to bombard the walls.

Angus and Margaret's daughter, the now thirteen year old Lady Margaret Douglas, with her aunts, fled from the sea-gate to live like vagrants until rescued by Lord Dacre, who arranged with Henry VIII, for his niece, the young Margaret, to go to England, where her aunt Mary, the Duchess of Suffolk, the former queen of France, gave her sanctuary, before she went to live, first with her cousin, Henry's daughter, Mary Tudor,

---

[136] Dickinson, Donaldson and Milne, *A Sourcebook of Scottish History,* Vol.2. p.28.

and subsequently, after King Henry had married Anne Boleyn, as her lady-in-waiting at her uncle's court. Later, Margaret would be married to the Earl of Lennox, son of the man so cruelly murdered by Hamilton of Finnart, and become the mother of Henry Darnley, husband of Mary Queen of Scots.

The siege of Tantallon continued as James brought brass guns and powder from the castle of Dunbar, still held for Albany by a custodian called Gonzolles. But even these cannons, dragged by oxen for ten miles along the road above the coast, failed to do more than lodge a few stones from the massive curtain wall surrounding the castle for a length of fifty feet. The cannonade lasted for twenty days, until the king, on realizing it was achieving nothing, ordered the gunners to withdraw.

It was as they were doing so that the master of Artillery, David Falconar, was killed, either by a shot or an arrow, fired by a marksman from the ramparts of the castle. James was so furious that he solemnly swore, that as long as he lived, the Douglases should never have the sentence of their banishment revoked.[137]

The king's almost paranoid hatred of the Douglases encompassed every member of that family. It included Angus's sister Janet, a lady famous both for her beauty and her supposed powers as a witch. Rumours surrounded the death of her husband, John Lyon, the 6th Lord Glamis, who had died only in September, reputedly poisoned by his wife. Facing accusations as a murderess, in December 1528, she was summoned on a new charge of treason, accused, together with Patrick Charteris of Cuthilgurdy, of bringing men to support her brother, in the fracas against the Hamiltons, which had taken place in Edinburgh in the previous month of April. In this instance, however, the young king, perhaps moved by the

---

[137] Buchanan, George. *History of Scotland*. P.162. (Anonymous translation Edinburgh 1752.)

beauty of the accused, calling her 'our lovittis Dame Jonat Douglas', allowed her and Charteris to go on a pilgrimage to let the scandal surrounding them to subside. In her absence all legal proceedings against Janet, for supposedly murdering her husband, were suspended before eventually, for lack of evidence against her, coming to an end.

But did James really think her innocent as it appears was claimed? Four years later she would marry again, not Patrick Charteris, her named accomplice, but Archibald Campbell of Skipness, a man like so many others charmed by her beauty, who was brother of one of the most powerful men in Scotland, the Earl of Argyll.

On 5 December, 1528, despite the intensity of James's hatred against them, an agreement was reached between the Parliament then sitting and the Douglases, that, if they surrendered their castles, they might go to England. A special proviso allowed the Scottish commissioners to inform the English government that it must take responsibility for any trouble that the Douglases might make in Scotland forthwith. Their forfeited estates were to be divided amongst men most loyal to the king, the earls of Argyll and Bothwell, Lord Maxwell, Scott of Buccleuch, and surprisingly, given his not so recent defection, the Earl of Arran.

Even more astonishing was the inclusion amongst the divided spoils of James Hamilton of Finnart, Arran's illegitimate son. James knew that he had murdered his cousin Lennox after the battle near Linlithgow, as he himself had been held a helpless captive, by his step-father's brother George, threatening to tear him to pieces if he moved. Finnart was known to be a murderer, he had certainly killed at least one other man, yet James apparently liked him to the point where Hamilton slept in his room. There is no mention of homosexuality – men in those days frequently shared beds, rare pieces of furniture when common folk slept on the floor – and James was renowned for his love of the opposite sex. But

Finnart seems to have had an inexplicable hold on him, to the extent that when a groom of Lennox's tried to avenge the death of his master, by stabbing Finnart in a dark passageway of Holyrood Palace, James had the man, recognized by his bloody dagger, carried naked through Edinburgh to be horribly tortured with red hot iron pincers until he died.

It was the fact of the groom getting into Holyrood, undetected, which caused the greatest alarm. An attack by the Douglases seemed inevitable, so that guards, fully armed, provided by the lords and the sheriff of Ayr, stood all night outside the king's chamber and even by his bed. One night, after what proved to be a false alarm, the king himself sat up in full armour, waiting for the sound of hoof-beats approaching, breaking the silence of the night. Eventually, it was Lord Dacre, as ever with his ear close to the ground, who reported that 'the Queen and the young King, removed to Stirling for greater safety.'[138]

But the expected attack of the Douglases did not come. Instead Henry VIII received both Archibald Angus and his brother George at his court, where having both sworn loyalty to him, as sovereign-paramount of Scotland, they were hospitably received.[139] Henry, calling Angus his 'dear brother-in-law', made both him and his brother, George Douglas, members of his Privy Council. He had good cause for doing so. Henry never did anything without a reason and as leaders of the still powerful, pro-English party in Scotland, he made sure of their allegiance in the knowledge that, in the event of a renewed invasion from Scotland, he would have them, and their powerful following, on his side. Also, they could be returned to Scotland as useful procurers of his purpose, if and when the opportune moment arrived.

---

[138] *State Papers*. Vol. v. Letter of Lord Dacre.
[139] Ibid. Vol. iv, September 1528.

Involved as he now was, in the first stages of trying to obtain his divorce from Catherine of Aragon, and anticipating trouble with her nephew, the Holy Roman Emperor Charles V, Henry was determined that peace with Scotland must be somehow maintained. It was to this purpose that, negotiations, which were already in place, resulted in a five year treaty, arranged and ratified at Berwick on 14 December, just ten days since Angus's official departure from Scotland had taken place.

It was from this time onwards that, with the heads of the Douglas families in England and peace with that country secure at least for the foreseeable future, James became the undisputed ruler of his kingdom. On 10 November, even before the peace treaty with England was finally signed, he made his half-brother, James Earl of Moray, 'our lieutenant general in the north parts of our realm,' giving him authority to enlist other Highland landowners in subduing the Clan Chattan, who had been raiding their neighbours without mercy, sparing only priests, women and children. Then, in the following early spring of 1529 he himself led an army, said to be eight thousand strong, to the Borders to deal with the freebooters, in particular the Armstrongs, who were terrorising the whole district where lawlessness had no bounds.

The loyalty of his subjects was of prime importance to King James. Amongst those to whom he showed favour, was Harry Stewart, his second-step-father, made both Master of the Ordnance and Lord Methven at his mother's bequest. Methven Castle, to the north of the Ochil Hills, some six miles from Perth, had been in the possession of the Scottish royal family since given to Walter Stewart and his wife Marjory by her father King Robert the Bruce. Now, in 1528, James V separated the castle and its lands of Monteith and Strathgartney, for ever from the crown of Scotland and settled them on his mother's third husband. He also agreed to grant the captaincy of Doune Castle, which stands above the confluence of the Rivers Teith and Forth, to James, the younger brother of Harry Stewart, who had been badly wounded at Linlithgow.

This however made ructions. Margaret herself was so furious at losing the rents from her dower land, that it caused the first quarrel with her husband. It was also most fiercely resented by the former custodians, the brothers William and Archibald Edmonstone of Duntreath–appointed by Albany in 1516 – that it led eventually to a running battle 'in which much blood was shed and many slain on both sides,' in the town of Dunblane.[140]

Margaret, by now living at Methven Castle, is known to have been in correspondence with her brother's former ambassador, Doctor Magnus, who had become the tutor of the ten-year-old Henry Fitzroy, the king's illegitimate son by his mistress Bessie Blount. Henry had made the boy Duke of Richmond, and endowed him with the magnificent castle and lands of Sheriff Hutton in Yorkshire

Henry Fitzroy, through the auspices of his tutor, had recently sent the harriers and the bloodhounds, that sat on the back of horses' saddles, that Margaret had asked for, to her son, his cousin King James, and Magnus now took the opportunity of sending a long letter, written in his pupil's name, calling himself 'her dear and tender nephew' and asking that 'his aunt, the Queen of Scots, would please to relent, and not utterly ruin a great noble of ancient blood like the Earl of Angus.'

Margaret, by then in Edinburgh when this missive arrived, while acknowledging the kindness of 'her dear and tender nephew', told him:

---

[140] *Genealogical Account of the family of Edmonstone of Duntreath* by Sir Archibald Edmonstone. Privately printed 1875. P.37.

'How much she marvelled that the King his father and himself, had such great regard for the Lord Angus, when we that is his natural sister sustain such great dolour and wrong. We greatly marvel, considering the offenses made to us, he has not applied him to give us good cause to continue good princess to him, which had been his high honour and special duty, having remembrance of the great honour we did until him.'[141]

The unfortunate young man then had to read a long list of the grievances suffered by Margaret at Angus's account, in particular 'the tearing away' on no less than two occasions of her daughter Margaret, 'who would not have been disinherited had she remained to her comfort.' She then directed a very direct message to Magnus, telling him that she bore no ill will to the Earl of Angus, and in proof that she only wished him well, she advised him to 'keep safely in England, out of the way of the King of Scotland, her son, and in time he may recover his favour.'[142]

In the summer of 1530, Pope Clement VII, assured of King James's ascendancy, sent an envoy to Scotland. Told of his coming, John Stewart, the 3rd Earl of Atholl, with whom Queen Margaret had long been on good terms, held what is described as 'a grand Highland hunting' in honour, both of the envoy and of the king and his mother, described by Robert Lindsay of Pitscottie as his old friend.

Lindsay's description is interesting, not only because it details the various kinds of food and drink considered to be fit for a feast at that time, but because it refers to Pitlochry, now the tourist centre of the Highlands, standing beside the main route of the A9, as a wilderness.

---

[141] *State Papers,* Vol.iv.p.533. Margaret to Magnus. Edinburgh November 21.
[142] Ibid

A palace was built near Pitlochry, made of the branches of trees and surrounded by a moat. Inside, the walls were hung with tapestry and silk and the windows covered with glass. The palace was divided into four quarters, in each of which was a circular room like a blockhouse, the height of three normal houses, the floor being covered with rushes, meadowsweet and other flowers, making it look like a garden.

The Earl overdid himself with the catering. There were 'all manner of meats, drinks and delicates, that were to be gotten at that time in Scotland… that is to say all kind of drink, as ale, beer, wine both white and claret, malmsey, muscadil, and aquavitae (whisky). Further, there was of meats, wheat bread, maise bread and gingerbread, with fleshes, beef, muttons, lambs, venison, goose, grice (pig) capon, coney, crane, swan, partridge, plover, duck, drake, bussel-cock and pawnes (blackcock and grouse) and also the stanks (ponds) round about the palace, were full of all the delicate fishes, as salmons, trouts, eels and all that could be gotten out of fresh water all ready for the banquet. Syne there were proper stewards, cunning baxters (bakers) excellent cooks and potingers with confections and drugs for the king and queen's desert. And the halls and chambers were prepared with costly beds, naperies and vessels, according for a queen, so that Queen Margaret wanted of her orders no more than when at home in her palace. The king and his royal mother abode in that wilderness at the hunting three days and nights, there being no town nearer than twenty miles on each side of them. The Earl of Atoll expended one thousand pounds per day on this regal fete in the solitude of the Highlands.'

Margaret was in her element, feted and pampered in a way that had not happened since her arrival in Scotland nearly thirty years before. She was leaving the impromptu palace, one can guess with the greatest reluctance, riding beside her son and the Pope's envoy, when, looking back, they saw the whole amazing edifice suddenly explode in flames. The envoy exclaimed in horror, turning in his saddle towards James, who explained that it was the custom of the Highland men,' 'Be they never so well lodged at night, they burn their lodging the next morn', he told the astonished Italian, who no doubt thought it one of the most bizarre experiences he had come across in this very foreign land. [143]

The same source tells that the queen and her son spent the autumn hunting in the Highlands, until, at the end of September, they stayed for the Michaelmas Festival with Archbishop Beaton at St Andrews.

Pope Clement was not the only one to send an ambassador, once it became more widely known that the young King James was the undisputed ruler of his country. Henry VIII, aware that James must be placated if peace between England and Scotland were to be maintained, sent Lord William Howard, uncle of Anne Boleyn, the woman he was determined to marry, daughter of Howard's half-sister Elizabeth Boleyn, Countess of Wiltshire. William Howard was the eldest son of Thomas Howard, 2nd Duke of Norfolk. The portrait of him as a young man, by an unknown artist, shows him wearing a black velvet bonnet with a feather stuck rakishly on one side, and a lace collar surmounting a doublet patterned in blue and gold. His long, undeniably handsome face, ends with a pointed beard, while most noticeable are the black eyes of the family, for which his niece was so famous, containing a roguish look.

Howard appeared at James's court with a train of sixty knights and esquires, all of them noted as athletes and skilled at shooting with the bow. James, who himself was renowned, both as a good horseman and notable shot, arranged competitions, watched by his mother, who gambled on the English beating the Scots. Finally, as the excitement mounted, she laid a wager with her son, that six of these Englishmen would shoot better with the bow than any of the same number of Scotsmen, be they nobles, gentlemen or yeomen, who

[143] Srickland.pp.239-40.

would shoot against them 'at riveris, the butts, or prick bonnet', whatever that old Scottish term may have meant. Margaret and James, forthwith, both laid down a hundred crowns and most importantly, 'a tun of wine was to be expended on either side.'

The site chosen was the town of St Andrews, famous for its feats of archery. The Scottish bowmen were three landed gentlemen and three yeomen: the lairds being David Arnott, David Weams, and Mr John Wedderburn, the vicar of Dundee, while the yeomen were John Thomson of Leith, Steven Tabroner, and Alick Baillie, a piper, 'who shot wondrous near, 'so well in fact that the English team was defeated to roars of applause from the Scots and in particular the king, who spent the two hundred crowns he had won from his mother, in giving all the competitors a large and magnificent feast.

Lord William's real reason for coming, however, was to offer the hand of King Henry's daughter, the Princess Mary, to the king of Scotland.

But Margaret, by this time, knew that her brother's divorce proceedings were well under way and that not even fear of the Emperor Charles could persuade him to keep the emperor's niece, Catherine of Aragon, as his queen. This meant that once Catherine was divorced, her daughter would, most likely, be declared illegitimate and therefore of no political use as a wife for Margaret's son James.

Lord William Howard returned to England to deputise for his father, the Duke of Norfolk, at the king's wedding to Anne Boleyn in May 1533. On 18 September, following her baptism of the previous week, he bore the canopy over his great niece, the infant Princess Elizabeth, before being ordered back to Scotland by her father King Henry, in the autumn of the following year. With him he took instructions to get King James's measurements from the bishop of Aberdeen, the Lord High Treasurer of Scotland, so that his uncle could get a suit of clothes made for him as a present. He was also told to try to arrange a meeting between the two kings and finally, to attempt to make a reconciliation between 'the King's dearest suster the Queen-mother of Scotland and Henry himself.'[144]

Doctor Magnus, Margaret's confessor, also added his voice in trying to persuade her to make things up with the brother who, while castigating her for her divorce, had now been divorced and re-married himself.

Despite the urgings of both men it was not until 12 December that Margaret finally put pen to paper in a letter to her brother.

'Please your Grace,

Howbeit in times bypast some misadvised persons have made unkindly report of We unto you, without cause of offence in us, we have and always sal indured and continued your most loving cystyr, ingending no less all time of our life, having sic confidence in you that ye will hold us the same. 'Your Grace is our only brother, and Owz your only sister, and since so is, let no divorce or contraire have place, nor no report of ill adviset alter our conceits, but brotherly and cysterly love ever to endure, to the pleasure of God and weal of us both. And trust no less in me than in yourself in all and sindrie things at our whole power, as pleaseth your Grace to command. Beseeching the eternal God to conserve you in everlasting grace.

Written with our own hand, the 12 day of December instant, by your Grace awn and only

Most lovyng and humble Cyster.

Margaret R. '[145]

On the same day, she wrote another longer letter to her brother's now all powerful minister, Thomas Cromwell, the main purpose of which was to convey her loving greetings to her new sister-in-law, Queen Anne, who had sent her a token

---

[144] State Papers. Vol. v. p.12. Margaret to Henry VIII, De^, B. Vol. v. p.12.

[145] Ibid. p.10. Margaret to Henry VIII. Dec. 12 1534. VIII

of friendship, probably in the form of a jewel. Addressing him as 'My Lord Sacriter' (secretary) she proceeds to tell him that Archbishop Beaton and the rest of the Scottish clergy had denounced Henry's second marriage to be unlawful in the eyes of the church, but that she herself had gone to great lengths to arrange her son, the king's meetings with Henry's envoys. She laid emphasis on the fact that, although James was still recovering from smallpox, he had travelled twenty miles a day for eight days until so exhausted that he had sent a messenger to ask her to get her husband, Lord Methven, to take the envoys to him. She had then gone with them, 'on the next morrow, being the most troublous weather that we ever travelled in, we com to our dearest son, with whom we communed and resolved, so that by the advice of us, and no other living person, determined and concluded the meeting.'

The outcome of this was, that because she had gone to such lengths to make James acknowledge the sanctity of his uncle's marriage to Anne Boleyn, Margaret now hoped to gain some financial reward.

King James's acceptance of his uncle's marriage, so censored by the Scottish Roman Catholic Church, is hardly surprising in view of the fact that he himself was bent on marrying his mistress, 'the Lady of Lochleven' in the hopes of her getting a divorce.

Born Margaret Erskine, the daughter of John, 5th Lord Erskine and his wife Lady Margaret Campbell, Margaret had married Sir Robert Douglas of Lochleven some nine years before. Their home was the castle on an island on Loch Leven in Fife, subsequently to become famous in history as the prison of James's daughter Mary Queen of Scots. Margaret already had a son by James, known as James Stewart, whom his father was to make Earl of Moray. Born in 1531, by the time of William Howard's second visit to Scotland in 1534, the boy was three years old. The rumour that James meant to marry Margaret Douglas, the Lady of Loch Leven as she became widely known, was circulating throughout Scotland where a black friar (presumably on the instruction of Archbishop Beaton) was set to preach a sermon before King James condemning his uncle's marriage to Anne Boleyn, apparently to deter him from committing a similar sin.

'Which friar, we shall not stand content with, because his report in some part concerned our dearest brother and his realm, howbeit the same was coloured and not expressly specifying his Grace nor his subjects. We shall remember him as cause requireth, but assuredly the King, our dearest son, took no manner tent (heed) thereto.' [146]

James was still undecided from taking the step of marrying his mistress, thus making their son legitimate and heir to the throne, when Lord William Howard, the uncle of Anne Boleyn, re-appeared at his court, having ridden from London, this time bringing with him the Order of the Garter as a present from King Henry to his nephew King James. The investment took place on 4 March 1535, as attested by the bishop of Aberdeen.

Lord William returned to London, with a message to King Henry from his sister, asking him for some monetary reward for the information she was about to send him, to compensate for the loss of the income of her dower lands on the Borders which, although bequeathed to Harry Stewart on their marriage, appear to have never been paid.

Queen Margaret then wrote to her brother by post to Berwick, from where her letter was carried to London either on horseback or by sea. She told him that she had managed to extract from her son, the details of the secret orders he had given to Sir Adam Otterbourne, his ambassador at Hampton Court, forbidding him to agree with his uncle's new constitution of religion, and that he meant to change the place of their intended meeting from York to Newcastle. Her letter

---

[146] Ibid. p.12.

included other details of what her son had told her of his plans, adding that Sir Adam was not to press for answer in writing, but merely to 'report cleverly' what was said. On another tack, she assured Henry that her son loved him as his 'natural father' an indication that, with still no son of his own, he might consider hers to be his heir. Finally she added 'I spake with the King my son ere I directed this letter. Please your Grace to have it close and secretly kept. By my evil hand in haste. Off Edinburgh this 16 day of March.'[147]

Lord William came back to Scotland in the following spring of 1536 to find that the king and his mother, having quarrelled, remained on bad terms. This time Margaret herself told him that her son meant to marry Lord Erskine's daughter, by whom he was already the father of a son: the popular concept being that James had found a means to divorce her from her husband, a cause of great lamentation throughout the land. But, he added, the one man privy to the secret was Sir James Hamilton of Finnart, that evil genius, who despite the fact that James knew him to be responsible for the murder of his cousin, the young Earl of Lennox after he had surrendered at Linlithgow, remained, not only his advisor in architecture, but, for some inexplicable reason, one of his closest friends.

Lord William soon discovered the cause of James's rift with his mother to be the betrayal to her brother of things he had told her in confidence. James finally lost his temper when she tried to discuss his meeting with his uncle at Newcastle.

'Her Grace hath been so very plain with him', wrote Lord William 'that he is very angry with her. Your Highness hath cause to give her great thanks. I humbly beseech your Grace that Sir Adam Otterbourne do not know that I have sartyfied your Grace that the marriage with France was broken off, or he will cause the King's Grace your nephew to be angry.'[148]

---

[147] Ibid. p.30.
[148] Ibid. p.41.

But James did find out and was so furious that he threatened to put his mother in prison. Relenting, eventually, he sent her to what was virtually house arrest in her own dower castle of Doune. From there, two days after her arrival, she wrote to her brother telling him that James had accused her of meddling with his plans to meet him at Newcastle, rather than York, because he believed the former town to be safer with its easy escape route by sea.[149]

What she really wanted, of course, was to go with him. In another letter, dated 12 May, she asked for a 'wesy' or visa, so that she might accompany her dearest son to her dearest brother to the expected congress in England, wherever it might take place. She added that she had heard that he had very important business in hand which might delay his answer, suggesting that by this time she knew, probably through Lord William, of his niece, Anne Boleyn's, disgrace and imprisonment.

On the same day Lord William's secretary, William Barlow, the Bishop-elect of St Asaph, wrote to Henry VIII, telling him plainly that his sister:

'was in high displeasure with King James... he accusing her of receiving gifts from her brother to betray him... by reason of which she is greatly discomforted, is weary of Scotland and fully determined to come to England, so that it be your Grace's pleasure... Furthermore, the King of Scotland's purpose with the divorced jantlywoman is by no means to be dissuaded, but, against the hearts of all his nobles, is like to be brought to pass, whereof no small disturbance is like to rise within the realm.'[150]

James had apparently turned on his mother telling her, that if her brother meant with her help to betray him, he would rather it was done while he was in his own country rather than

---

[149] Ibid. p. 48.
[150] Ibid.

in England. He then made sure that she had no power to interfere in his future governing of the country.

When Lord William left Edinburgh to return to England, Margaret and James were still estranged, she living at Holyrood, he at Linlithgow, some twenty-five miles away. Lord William himself was now out of favour with Henry, as were all of his family. Margaret was soon to hear that the daughter she had had with Angus, Lady Margaret Douglas as she was known, although a favourite of her brother King Henry, who called her his little Marget, for falling in love with Anne Boleyn's young uncle Thomas, was imprisoned in the Tower of London.

However, it was Lord William's secretary Barlow who, on 25 May, wrote to Cromwell, on Queen Margaret's behalf, saying, 'that she hoped to receive some comfortable answer from the king, her brother, in relief of her sorrow, which is not a little how and like to be much more grievous.'

Two months later, on 16 July, Margaret herself wrote to Henry asking him for twenty thousand marks, 'to help her out of perpetual pain, as she had done all she could to further the visit of her son to England, but he could not be induced to come.'[151]

She did not tell him, something which, due to their antipathy, she may not have known herself, that only a few days later, James would embark for France.

Wolsey, however, did hear of it and thinking that Margaret was either wilfully misleading him or else, being ignorant of her son's movements herself, was no longer effectual as a spy, sent no money, while her brother, when told of it, expressed 'mighty astonishment that wherefore she should want such heavy sums when her state was so prosperous under the estate of her son and Lord Muffin.'

---

[151] Ibid. p.59.

PART 3

CHAPTER 1

THE FRENCH BRIDE

In Scotland the coffers were empty. In the previous reign of James IV the total annual revenue had been about £thirty thousand but both Albany and particularly Margaret, had spent freely and by the year 1525-6, the total had shrunk to less than £thirteen thousand per annum. James was in fact so poor that in March 1530 he had had to borrow two thousand marks from his friend, the consistently loyal Earl of Huntly.

Plainly, under these circumstances, it was more than ever important that he should find a rich bride. The Duke of Albany, on his first return to France, at the Treaty of Rouen in 1517, had arranged a marriage for him with a daughter of the French King Francis I. Other prospects, however, had then emerged, including that of a marriage with Catherine de Medici, the Duchess of Albany's niece, the daughter of Albany's sister-in-law Madeleine de la Tour and Lorenzo de Medici, Duke of Urbino. Catherine, a great heiress, was however, a ward of Pope Clement VII, who had not wanted his protégée to be sent to far off Scotland.

Another suggestion had been that of the deposed king of Denmark, Christian II, who, keen that James should help him to regain his throne, had offered either of two daughters of marriageable age, but had admitted, due to his poverty, that he could produce no more than a dower of ten thousand crowns. James, nonetheless, had sent Sir William Hamilton of Marcniston to the Holy Roman Emperor Charles V, to find out if the marriage to one of his Danish nieces would unite Scotland with the Empire whereupon Charles, keen to affect an alliance with Scotland, had offered his own sister Mary, the widowed queen of Hungary, a suggestion unacceptable to James due to her being over thirty.

James had then written to Albany, to inform him of the emperor's suggestions, in the hopes that it might incite Francis I to make a counterbid with one of his daughters, as arranged by the Treaty of Rouen. The French king did take the bait but, unwilling to part with the third of his four daughters, the young and delicate Princess Madeleine, had instructed Albany to renew his suggestion to the Pope for a marriage with Catherine de Medici, after which James had sent his secretary, Sir Thomas Erskine of Haltoun, to Rome to arrange the details with the Pope.

It was then that Henry VIII, getting wind of what was taking place and unwilling to let James strengthen his ties with France, had prevailed upon King Francis to arrange the marriage of the Medici heiress to his own brother the Duke of Orléans.

In 1532 the Emperor Charles, keen to court a Scottish Alliance, had sent James the Order of the Golden Fleece, upon news of which, King Francis, afraid of losing good relations with Scotland, had suggested that, in place of his delicate daughter Madeleine, whose two elder sisters had already died, James should marry, either Marie de Bourbon, daughter of the Duke of Vendôme, or Marie de Guise, daughter of the Duke of Guise, or Isabeau d'Albret, daughter of the king of Navarre.

This had goaded the Emperor into attempting to outdo King Francis by offering two other royal ladies in addition to his sister, the queen of Hungary, whom James had already turned down, which, when he heard of it, had finally provoked King Henry into offering the hand of his daughter Mary to his nephew the king of Scots.

Henry's main reason for doing so was as a safeguard against France involving Scotland in renewed conflict with England. James however, had not seen Henry's eldest daughter Mary – now since the birth of her half-sister Elizabeth, robbed of her title of princess and denounced by her father as a bastard – as a suitable match. Nevertheless, anxious to remain on amicable terms with his uncle, on 12 May 1534, he had signed a peace treaty to last for the lifetime of them both and for one year beyond whichever of them should be the first to die. James had then made public recognition of the validity of his uncle's divorce from Catherine of Aragon and of his marriage to Anne Boleyn, this being why Henry, much gratified by this concession, had sent his nephew the Order of the Garter, conveyed by his much travelled envoy Lord William Howard.

It was later, in that same year of 1534, that a French ambassador appeared in Scotland with an offer from King Francis to James, of the hand of Marie de Bourbon, daughter of the Duke of Vendôme, with a dower of one hundred thousand crowns. The envoy brought with him a portrait, depicting a pretty young woman, but James was secretly informed that both Marie and her sister were 'sore made awry.' Nonetheless he decided to marry her, but only on condition that, in addition to the dowry, he received an annuity of twenty thousand livres together with the Order of St Michael. This honour, which duly arrived in Scotland in April of the following year, was the third of the great European orders of chivalry, so far conferred upon James, who forthwith had the insignia of the four European orders of chivalry, the Golden Fleece, the Garter, the Thistle, and St Michael carved over the Outer Entrance of the Palace of Linlithgow, where they can be seen today.

Then, despite the contract for his marriage to Marie of Vendôme being ratified by King Francis, on 29 March 1536, James changed his mind and decided to marry Margaret Douglas, the Lady of Lochleven, the woman he really loved. Writing to Pope Paul III, he requested a dispensation for the marriage, and by midsummer the Emperor heard that the marriage had actually taken place. But on 30 June the Pope sent a message denying the validity of Margaret Douglas's divorce.

It was shortly after this that, horrified by what had happened to Anne Boleyn, James broke off his relationship with the 'Lady of Lochleven' thus failing to legitimise their son.

The decision once made, he decided to go to France to see if the lady, who, by French law, he was pledged to marry, in anyway resembled her portrait, or was really as ugly as rumour suggested her to be.

In July he boarded a ship at Leith, but as soon as it left the Firth of Forth, the sea became extremely rough. The pilot, fearing shipwreck, asked the king to which coast should he make, whereupon the James replied 'to any thou best likest except towards England.' James then retired to his cabin to get some sleep and woke up to find himself back in Leith.

Furious, he blamed Sir James Hamilton of Finnart, that mysterious man whose sinister presence permeated his life. Hamilton had seized the tiller to make the ship reverse its course. James, told of this, believed him to have acted deliberately to prevent the chance of a French marriage, which if it resulted in children, would reduce Hamilton's own family's chance of succession to the throne.

Despite this initial set back, two months later, on 1 September, James set out again. This time it was not a single ship, but a small fleet with which he sailed. With him went a train of Scotland's nobility, the earls of Moray, Argyll and Angus and the young Hamilton Earl of Arran who, until James had a legitimate heir, was second in line to the throne. Also went Oliver Sinclair, the king's new favourite, eclipsing Hamilton of Finnart, who now, since his unfortunate attempt at navigation, was the fading star. Embarking at Kirkcaldy, they sailed into the North Sea, this time meeting fair winds before which they reached Dieppe, in the short time of only ten days. On landing, the king immediately set out on horseback for the town of St Quentin and the palace of the Duc de Vendôme.

Once there the historian, Lindsay of Pitscottie, tells of how James disguised himself as the servant of one of his own servants, in an attempt to set eyes on Marie unbeknown. But Marie had been sent his portrait, in exchange for the one of her sent to him, and recognising him, perhaps largely by his height, she went up to him, took his hand and said, 'Sir, you stand o'er far aside before addressing him as your Grace.' She then presented James to her father, who, delighted at the idea of such a handsome royal husband for his rather plain daughter, over–reached himself in providing sumptuous entertainment.

The rooms of the palace were re-decorated, the walls hung with tapestry, cloth of gold and fine silk, the floor covered with silk, the four-poster bed hung with curtains of cloth of gold, and a pall or canopy of the same material set with jewels was held above the visiting king's head while he ate, the whole building being filled with 'sweet odours, very costly and delectable to the sense of men.'

James stayed at St Quentin for eight days, being so outwardly courteous to Marie de Bourbon that the poor girl fell deeply in love with him, totally captivated by his charm. But he, for his part, could not reciprocate, finding her just as unprepossessing as rumour had led him to expect.

It may have been then that his eye was diverted from poor plain Marie to her strikingly good looking cousin, Marie de Guise, daughter of poor Marie de Bourbon's uncle, who, as tall, or even taller than himself, would have been hard to miss. Drummond of Hawthornden certainly wrote that: 'whilst James disported himself in France, he had made acquaintance with a lady rich in excellencies, Mary of Lorraine, daughter of Claude Duke of Guise, and widow of the Duke de Longueville,' which in fact she was not, the Duke, being at this time, very much alive.

Whether James did, in this instance, make plain his admiration of Marie de Bourbon's elegant cousin is unknown. Nonetheless, it is claimed that Marie de Bourbon never recovered from his rejection, dying some time afterwards, it was claimed, of a broken heart. She certainly must have known, when James left her father's court, that he was going to Lyons, where the French king was in residence with his daughter, the Princess Madeleine, on whom, so it was rumoured, he had set his heart.

Arriving at Lyons, James was met by King Francis's second son, Henri, Duc d' Orléans, the young man who, thanks to King Henry VIII's interference, had married Catherine de Medici, the great heiress, once suggested for James. Henri greeted him warmly, saying that he had come at a propitious moment to console his father, King Francis, who was greatly saddened by the death of his eldest son, the dauphin Francois, only a month before. Francois had died under suspicious circumstances, attributed to poison, for which his Italian squire, who had given him a drink just before he collapsed, had been blamed. The wretched man under torture, had at first admitted and then denied the charge, before being put to death.

Having explained to James all that had happened, of which rumours must have reached his ears, the new dauphin, Henri, took him to his father's bedroom where he knocked on the closed door. On a voice from within, demanding to know who had come to disturb him, Henri replied that it was the king of Scotland come to console him, whereupon, Francis leapt from his bed and throwing open the door flung his arms round James thanking God for His great benefits. It had pleased God, he said, to take away one of his sons, but it had also pleased him to send 'that noble Prince, the King of Scots to take his place.'[152]

King Francis, by then a man in his forties, known by the length of his nose as 'le grand nez' then proceeded to outmatch

---

[152] Bingham. C, pp.121-2

the Duke of Vendôme in the honour shown to his visitor. On James making a state entry into Paris, his host ordered the deputation from the Parlement to receive him wearing scarlet gowns, instead of the usual black, a form of deference usually shown only to the dauphin.

It was at Lyons that James first met Madeleine, the princess, who, even before her birth, had been destined by the Treaty of Rouen in 1517, when Albany (who had died in the previous July) had arranged with her father that she should marry the young Scottish king.

James was not disappointed. In fact, according to Pitscottie, he almost instantly fell in love with this frail but beautiful girl of sixteen. Madeleine, described with the pale skin and fair hair of the Valois family, apparently had her father's long nose, but it was her graceful form and the charming innuendo of her downcast eyes that made her so attractive, particularly to men. Again according to Pitscottie, the first time he saw her she was riding, in what he described as a chariot, because she was too delicate to sit on the back of a horse. As for her, it was love at first sight. She would have none other but him.

Pitscottie claims that James in fact married Madeleine largely to please her father, and to maintain the alliance with France. But be that as it may, he certainly became very attached to her, as later events would prove. Madeleine for her part, was desperate to be a queen. Her father, concerned because he had seen her two elder sisters succumb to what appears to have been tuberculosis, continued to worry about her going to Scotland, the country, so he had been told, constantly beset by storms and snow. But Madeleine assured him happily that 'At least I shall be Queen for as long as I live, that is what I have always wished for.'[153]

The marriage contract was signed at Blois, great palace of the Valois kings, on 26 November 1536, the wedding itself taking place on 1 January of the following year (according to

[153] Ibid. p.124.

the Gregorian Calendar) in the Cathedral of Notre Dame in Paris. In attendance were three kings, James of Scotland, Francis of France and the bride's uncle by marriage, the king of Navare, as well as seven red-robed cardinals of the Roman Catholic Church. James himself wore clothes of white and gold, his appearance slightly spoiled by a large bruise on his face, resulting from an accident while tilting in the lists.

The service was taken by the Cardinal de Bourbon, uncle of poor discarded Marie. Following the wedding, there was great entertainment, more jousting and banqueting than had been seen in France since the days of Charlemagne, so it was claimed. Medieval contraptions such as dragons, with fire sprouting from their noses and tails, and rivers running through the streets of towns, with ships firing guns floating down them, delighted the French public and amazed the Scottish visitors, to whom such pageants had never been seen.

Four months had gone by since James, then a bachelor, had sailed away from Fife. Now he was married to the daughter of the king of France, who treated him with all the affection he had shown to his own dead son.

James loved France. Although he never learned to speak the language fluently, he admired the country and its people, and above all its architecture to the extent that, on his return to Scotland, he was to copy it, as much as was possible with the skill of Scottish artisans. Francis himself employed the greatest European craftsmen of his day: Leonardo da Vinci being one, Benvenuto Celini another. The result was magnificence on a hitherto unprecedented scale, such as James had never dreamed of, or had thought possible to create.

The royal palaces at Blois, in the verdant valley of the Loire, and of Chambord, some twelve miles to the north-east, where the castle stood reflected in the water of the River Cosson, tributary of the Loire, were amongst those he most admired. Most of all, however did he revere the palace of Fontainebleau, where Francis had just completed the gallery connecting the royal apartments to the Chapelle de la Trinité. He had brought the architect Sebastiano Serlio from Italy to design the work, which was one of the wonders of art at the time. The Florentine artist Giovanni Battista di Jacop, known as Rosso Florentino and another Italian Francesco Primaticcio from Bologna, known as Primatice, had done the adornment of this glorious decorated gallery, the first in France, after which the School of Fontainebleau was named and which today remains regarded as the introduction of the Renaissance to France.

James, on his return to Scotland, would retain in his mind the images of those interiors, comparing them to his own castles and palaces, which, in comparison, were so austere. At Holyrood he added a new west front to the massive tower, which he had already built in 1528, and at Linlithgow Palace, the Outer gateway and the elaborate carving of the courtyard fountain exemplify the ideas of architecture which he so admired in France.

He had plenty of time to do so while, on the excuse of rough seas being dangerous for the delicate Madeleine, he stayed in France, being greatly entertained by his father-in-law, for another four months. Tournaments, balls and pageants were staged in his honour, but it was not only with the aristocracy that James became familiar but with the common folk as well. Like his father before him, James had the common touch. An agent of the Douglases, a man called John Penven, wrote an amusing account of him shopping, 'with a servant or two running up and down the streets of Paris buying every trifle himself, and every carter pointing at him and saying, 'Yonder goes la roy de Escosse.'[154] The items bought included white plumes for his own bonnet, and a headpiece for his horse in a tournament, and a great pointed diamond costing eight thousand seven hundred and eighty-seven francs ten shillings Scots.

---

[154] Ibid. p.128.

Penven also throws interesting light on other of James's activities, most notably that he was still in correspondence with Margaret Douglas, the Lady of Lochleven, for whom the diamond may even have been bought. He also says that Sir James Hamilton of Finnart, once James's amanuensis, was still out of favour. It seems that on the voyage to France, Penven had either overheard or been told of James telling one of his attendants, 'If I would but once look merely upon the Earl of Angus, Sir James would droop, for by the wounds of God, for all Sir James's bragging, the Earl of Angus and he never met but Sir James turned over the back seams of his hose.' This remark, meaning that Hamilton of Finnart, knowing that James hated Angus, had consistently turned his back on him, was taken to signify that the king, once he had seen through the duplicity of Hamilton, had, at least to some extent, revised his opinion of Angus. Penven went so far as to suggest to Henry VIII that he should write to King Francis, asking him and his daughter Madeleine, to influence James in his favour. But this proved ineffective. James had no further use for Hamilton. The man so long his close confidante, was eclipsed and all but forgotten, his place as chosen companion taken over by Oliver Sinclair.

One person ignorant of James's plans at that time was his mother, with whom he remained on bad terms. Margaret was living at Methven Castle when she wrote to her brother to complain of his treatment of her daughter, Lady Margaret Douglas, who, because she had become betrothed to Lord Thomas Howard without first gaining her uncle's consent, had been imprisoned (as was Thomas Howard) in the Tower of London. There, she had been put in rooms, where, from the windows, as an added means to terrify her, she could see traces of Anne Boleyn's blood still staining the grass below.

On 12 August 1536, just before her son, without telling her, was embarking for the second time for France, Margaret wrote a long letter to her brother blaming him, for first encouraging

Margaret's romance with Thomas Howard and then punishing them both. Demanding that her daughter be immediately sent to Scotland, she assured him that if this was done that her daughter 'would never trouble him more.' She ended her letter by bewailing her perennial shortage of money and what she described as the 'ill-treatment' meted out to her, not only by her son, but by her third husband, Lord Muffin, as Henry contemptuously called him.

Lord Herbert of Cherbury, in his life of Henry VIII, believed that the real reason for her displeasure was not concern for her daughter, but annoyance that Margaret's incarceration put a stop to her own plans to travel down to England to her brother's court where, of all things extraordinary, she intended to remarry Angus, incredible as that may seem.

This was too much even for Henry, used as he was to his sister's erratic behaviour, he could not believe that she actually planned to remarry the man she had so much reviled. Bewildered he wrote to her, asking 'his dearest sister' for an explanation of what can only be described as her *volte face*.

'Dearest sister

'You shall understand, that like-as we would be right sorry to see our good brother and nephew should not use you in all things as beseeemeth a natural and kind son to use his mother, so you may certainly persuade yourself, that in case we should certainly perceive that you were treated otherwise than on your honour and the treaty of your marriage doth require, there shall, want no loving and kind office which we think may rend to your relief. But dearest sister, by the report of Sir John Campbell, whom you recommended as your special friend, it appeared to me that you were very well handled and be grown to so much weal (wealth) quiet and riches, and, on the other side, by your account given our servant Berwick (the herald) it appeared otherwise. These tales be so contrary to one another, that we may well remain doubtful which of them we may believe. Perceiving also, by other information received from you, concerning your trouble and evil handling, both by our nephew, your son, and by the Lord Muffyn, that either your state varies, or else things have not been well understood.'[155]

This is the first indication that now, after only two years of marriage, Margaret was intending to divorce Harry Stewart, the man with whom, for the second time in her life, she had made a precipitous marriage, so she had claimed, for love. The complications of the whole affair increase its mystery, but it is thought that her new paramour bore the name of Stewart. One fact, that may give the clue to his identity, is that of her asking her son to give the captaincy of Doune Castle to James Stewart, the landless younger brother of Harry. This was done supposedly in compensation for his being badly wounded and left for dead at the battle near the Bridge at Linlithgow, when Margaret's own small army had been defeated and she herself taken to Edinburgh by Angus in 1526. From this it may be taken that the legend of her falling in love with her husband's younger brother and wishing to make him her fourth husband, may carry some truth.

King Henry certainly hated Lord Methven, believing him to be loyal only to King James, for which reason he sent Sir Ralph Sadler to spy on him during James's absence in France. Sadler went to Scotland and returned laden with letters from Margaret to her brother concerning her decision to divorce this third husband who, according to all contemporary sources, had been consistently loyal to herself.

Next appeared Harry Ray, the Berwick herald, sent ostensibly to find out what was happening during the king's absence, but in reality to discover what his mother was about. Their interview was conducted in secret. Ray, as an English herald in Scotland, wore the royal arms of England on his

---

[155] *Letters of the Kings of England.* Ed. J.O. Halliwell. vol.i. p.275. *Henry VIII to Margaret Queen Mother of Scotland.*

breast, so Margaret told him to discard his uniform for a hat, such as worn in Scotland, and a heavy cloak. Thus disguised, he was led by a man he knew, who happened to be in Margaret's service, through the private apartments of Holyrood where, at nine o'clock at night, he had a secret meeting with Margaret in a darkened corner of a gallery.

The first thing she said to him was that she was very surprised to have had no answer from her brother to the letters she had sent with Ralph Sadler. Would he, she asked him, refer the matter to the Duke of Norfolk, to which the herald replied by telling her bluntly that Norfolk had asked him to get him some news. She told him that James was immensely popular, all of Scotland was loyal to him, 'There is not one lord in Scotland that will speak to the King, my son, good counsel towards England unless it be he take it of himself.' Throughout the land there was great anxiety, she told him, all the Lords and the Council believing that English ships had gone to the western seas to seize her son's ship on his return. The Lords had sat in counsel 'for what reason I know not' but upon their rising they had sent the Rothesay herald to France to arrive before the departure of King James, presumably to warn him of the threat of capture at sea. She then told Ray that he was to 'oversee' the country of England as he went through it and report back to her son.

Harry Ray departed but next evening was summoned again so that, muffled once more in a Scottish plaid, with his bonnet well down over his ears, he was again conducted to the dark corner of the gallery where he waited for the queen.

'There shall be nothing done in this realm' she told him, 'but that the King my brother, and my Lord of Norfolk, shall have knowledge of it. The Lords and all the commonality of Scotland do suspect that ye will make war against them, and if it be so, let my Lord of Norfolk make sure of the Commons.'[156]

---

[156] *State Papers*, Vol. v, p.63.

From this enigmatic speech, Ray translated a warning that the people of the north of England, destitute of support from the monasteries which King Henry had sequestered from the church, about to rise in rebellion in what would become known as the Pilgrimage of Grace, were beseeching help from Scotland. Ray asked her if she was certain of their numbers to which Margaret replied that she was not, but then added:

'I pray you show this unto him, and also if ye intend war, say, that I pray my Lord of Norfolk that he makes no war until I and Harry Stewart be divorced. For if the war should be before the said divorce were made, the lords of Scotland will suffer him to have my living.' [157]

Once again, in this fairly conclusive evidence of what Margaret intended, her main concern was to safeguard the income from her dower lands, given to and then retrieved from Angus and now, in an age when a woman's property automatically belonged to her husband, in danger of being confiscated by Lord Methven.

Margaret heard no more of what was happening in England until, in the middle of May, a dispatch arrived from Cromwell asking her for news from Scotland and sending her a present of cramp rings, of which King Henry, who is known to have suffered pain in his ulcerated legs, had made a collection. That he did so suggests that Margaret, who would have worn these medieval rings on her fingers, had been suffering from arthritis or cramp.

Henry VIII had actually sent his ambassador Ralph Sadler to James when he was in France, to confront him over the reports sent to him by Margaret, on how badly her son was treating her. Almost unbelievably, Margaret was now intending to divorce her third husband so that she could marry a fourth, on the grounds that the body of her first, King James IV had never been recovered leaving doubt that he was

---

[157] Ibid.

actually dead! It was this absurd supposition that finally decided James V, to put an end to his mother's ridiculous allegations as soon as he saw her again.

CHAPTER 2

A TIME OF JOY AND SORROW

James finally left France, it would seem with great reluctance, at the beginning of May 1537. He went loaded with presents. King Francis, in addition to the promised dowry of one hundred thousand livres, gave him twelve warhorses, with full equipment for each and several suits of gilded armour. Madeleine, for her part, was told to choose as many lengths of cloth of gold, velvet, satin, damask and taffeta from the royal wardrobe, and whatever jewels she liked to complete her trousseau.

The parting was a sad one. Francis probably guessed that he would never see his frail and lovely daughter again and during the course of his visit, expensive as it had been, he had come to regard James as a son. But back to Scotland they had to go. James had been away for nine months. He knew, from what envoys from there had told him, that many urgent issues awaited his return.

In addition to all the other presents, his father-in-law had given him two ships. One was the *Salamander,* named after the mythical reptile that was the personal emblem of the French king, and the other the *Morsewer,* which may have been translated as 'Monsieur' or even 'Morse,' which means a sea-horse. These two ships, together with James's own vessels, sailed in convoy from France, first into the Channel and then through the North Sea up the east coast of England.

Becalmed off Yorkshire, an incident occurred which could have been dangerous had Henry's ships been searching for them, prowling like sea-wolves to intercept, as Margaret, by Penven, had been warned. The alarm was raised aboard as a rowing boat was seen to approach, but it proved to be a party of Catholic gentlemen, who came to offer the allegiance of the

Catholics in England, would James lead an army from Scotland to depose their heretic King Henry, now defying the Pope in proclaiming himself head of the church. James spoke kindly to them but could not give a firm answer before, as the wind rose, the ships once more got under way without meeting any of the hostile English men-of-war.

Soon they were in Scottish waters, the Isle of May and the unmistakeable shape of the Bass Rock coming into sight as they sailed up the Firth of Forth, the low hills of Fife on their right. The tide was with them, carrying them upstream, as, on 19 May, they slipped into a safe anchorage in the port of Leith.

Madeleine, on landing, made a charming gesture, much applauded by the waiting crowd, which, on first sight of the sails out at sea, had gathered to see this reputedly fabulous French princess come ashore. There were cries of joy and admiration as, on stepping from the gangplank to the shore, she picked up two handfuls of Scottish earth and kissed it, the soil clear to see on her lily-white hands. [158]

Meanwhile, at Holyrood, Margaret waited in expectation, for word from the look-outs straining their eyes to the east for a sign of the royal procession expected to arrive. Now aged forty-eight, she had done her best to look magnificent in a new robe adorned with as many jewels as she could possibly find and probably, as in one of her portraits, with a snood, made so fashionable by Anne Boleyn, holding back her lovely red-gold hair, streaked as it now was with grey. Warned what to expect by the envoys, of the extravagantly beautiful dresses, worn not only by the young queen, but of the French ladies in her entourage, and determined not to be outshone, Margaret had extracted £two hundred from her brother, for which she would write and thank him on 7 June. 'That she might appear queenly, for the honour of England, in the eyes of the royal daughter of France.' She also took the opportunity to thank

---

[158] Pitscottie. Vol.i.p.369.

him for sending Ralph Sadler to see her son in France 'to complain how ill she was treated in Scotland' and explained that she had spoken to her son, who had sent his own ambassador, in the form of David Beaton, the politically ambitious nephew of the archbishop of St Andrews, who was currently abbot of Arbroath, to Henry, who she hoped that 'he would take kindly to' despite his being an ecclesiastic, 'for he is great with my son… and this being done your Grace will be kinder to the realm of Scotland for my sake.'[159]

Now, on that day in May, as she waited for the son she had not seen for nearly a year, Margaret expected to see him come riding astride his saddle, his bride on a pillion behind, just as she had done with his father on their entry into Edinburgh thirty-four years ago. But instead, as they drew into sight, she saw that James rode alone. Behind came a horse-drawn litter from which stepped a sixteen year old girl, who, judging from the extreme palour of her undoubtedly lovely face, was clearly very far from well.

All was consternation as Madeleine entered the palace leaning heavily on James's arm. Obviously the long sea journey had been too much for her, the banquets, tournaments and other celebrations arranged to welcome her, would have to be temporarily postponed. So too would her state entry into Edinburgh and the coronation, meticulously planned by James's old mentor Sir David Lindsay, the man who had been as a surrogate father, carrying him piggy-back and sleeping beside him as a child.

Thoroughly alarmed by Madeleine's obvious weakness, James also cancelled the progress through Scotland, on which he had planned to take her, to meet his people and for them to see their new queen. Desperate to find a remedy for her illness, he decided to take her to the Abbey of Balmerino in Fife, renowned for having the best air of anywhere in the kingdom.

---

[159] State Papers. vol. v. June 7, 1537.

But Madeleine never reached Fife. On 7 July, not quite seven weeks after her arrival in the country for which she longed to be queen, she died, at Holyrood Palace, it is said in James's arms.

James, who must have grown to love her in the short time they had together, was deeply saddened by her death. Moreover he worried that the good relationship he had built up with her father might now be severed by what had occurred. Writing to King Francis on the evening of the day on which Madeleine died, he told him:

'Monsieur,

Howbeit there is nothing in the world more grievous than the occasion which I have for writing to you this present letter – that occasion being the passing of your daughter, my most dear companion, which befell this day after long sickness – yet I would in no wise desire to be negligent in apprising you thereof. And where it not for the great comfort and confidence I have in you, that you will forever remain my good father, as I wish never to be anything but your good and humble son, I would be in greater grief than yet I am and I assure you that you will never find any fault upon my part, who will bear myself ever towards you as a son bears himself to his father.'[160]

Saddened, as undoubtedly he was, James did not grieve alone. Sir David Lindsay, who had to tell the tailors stitching away, that the magnificent robes for the coronation must all now be 'turnit into sable,' described the national mourning in an elegy.

'Provosts, bailies and lordis of the town
The senators in order consequent
Clad in silk of purple black and brown,
Syne the great lordis of the Parliament,

---

[160] Bingham. C. James V, King of Scots. p.133.

With many knightly Baron and baurent
In silk and gold, in colours comfortable,
But thou alas turnit into sable.
Under a pall of gold she should have past,
By burgis borne, clothed in silkis fine,
In the fair Abbey of the Holy Rude
In presence of ane mirthful multitude.'

Foremost amongst those who regretted the premature death of James of Scotland's young wife, was his mother, who, in the short space of her life at Holyrood was reported to have been on noticeably good terms with her son. At that time all was going well with Margaret. She believed herself about to be rid of Harry Stewart, having discovered that, not only did he have a former wife, widow of the eldest son of the Earl of Sutherland, but several children of much the same age as those which their own marriage had produced. This, she believed, was evidence enough to guarantee her divorce. Convinced that she held a trump card, in her letter to Henry, of 7 June, she told him:

'Pleaseth your Grace to know, that my divorce and partition is at the giving of sentence, and proved by many famous folk, to the number of four-and twenty provers. An' by the grace of God, I shall never have such a trouble again.'[161]

Alas for her false hopes. James, on being told what was happening, immersed as he was in grief at the end of his own marriage, firmly vetoed his mother's plan of ending hers. Margaret incandescent with fury, wrote to the Duke of Norfolk (son of he who had brought her to Scotland) telling him she thought it :

'Great unkindness that when ye do send in this realm, that ye will not write or send to speak with me, that I may hear from you, and you to hear how I am entreated. For since the departure of Master Sadler, I have gotten no word, neither

---

[161] *State Papers*. vol v. p. 104.

from the King's Grace my brother, nor yet from you, which are greatly to my comfort to hear from.

And dearest cousin I must make my complaint to you, how I am heavily done in this realm, for I have obteynet my cause of divorce betwixt me and the Lord of Meffen, and it is so far past that the judge has concluded and written my sentence, ready to be pronounced this twelve weeks bypast, but the King has stoppen the same, and will not let it be given contrary to justice and reason. And he promised, when I gave him my Mains of Dunbar for a certain sum of money, that I should have my sentence pronounced.'[162]

It would seem that it was at this point that James, infuriated by what he considered, with some justification, to be her most unreasonable behaviour, and suspecting her of betraying state secrets, had put her under some form of restraint, probably house arrest. She certainly told Norfolk that 'As for me, I am holden in much suspicion for England's sake that I dare send no Scottish man.' Instead, she asked him to send some trusted servant of his own, to whom she might speak in private and pleaded with him that he would listen to the Berwick herald, Harry Ray to whom, in that secret corner of Holyrood, she had told of the unnatural cruelty shown to her by her son.[163]

James was probably too pre-occupied to pay much, if any, attention to his mother's allegations of her ill treatment at his hands. It was now nine years since, in the December of 1528, while still pontificating against the Douglases and driving the head of the family, his detested step-father, from the country, he had ordered the charge of treason against the latter's sister, the famously beautiful Janet, Lady Glamis, for lack of evidence against her, to be dropped. Supposedly the poisoner of her first husband, Lord Glamis, she was now married to Archibald Campbell of Skipness, brother of the Earl of Argyll.

---

[162] Ibid.
[163] Ibid. p.103.

Suspicion, however, had always clung to her and on 17 July 1537, just ten days after the death of Madeleine had left James distraught with sorrow, Janet was brought to trial on the two charges of trying to poison her husband and of being in treasonable correspondence with her brothers, the Earl of Angus and the master of Douglas, as his brother George was known. James, in his state of bereavement, his mind perhaps confused, remembered his original suspicion of this woman whose lovely face had concealed what, at the time had been claimed, was treachery against him but which, for lack of evidence, had never been proved.

There must have been some reason for doubt. James may have contracted an illness for which the cause was unexplained. Now, in this renewed instance, of her reported betrayal in an attempt to kill him, he ordered her to be held a prisoner, together with her husband and their young son, in a dungeon of Edinburgh Castle. There was little or no evidence against her but the king, in a mood of what seems unjustifiable vengeance, inspired by his loathing of her kindred, ordered her servants and some say members of her family to be tortured, until they confessed to Janet's sorcery and attempts to end the life of the king. Convicted she, like Patrick Hamilton, was sentenced to die by burning, the fact of her being a woman, and exceptionally beautiful, making no difference to the excruciating agony of the death to which she was condemned.

Her execution took place on 17 July on the esplanade of Edinburgh Castle where her son, although just a little boy, was forced to watch her die. The cruelty shown by James on this occasion, although even in those times abhorrent to many who believed Lady Glamis to have been unfairly, if not wrongly, charged, can only be attributed to his long standing obsessional hatred of the Douglases, for whom the sister of Angus, the man he most detested, paid the price. Seen in the light of the present day, while the totally vindictive cruelty of James's actions is hard to excuse, perhaps it is only fair to realize that, not only did he live in a country where barbarous

298

actions were rife, but the very recent personal tragedy of losing Madeleine may, at least to some extent, have temporarily unbalanced his mind.

Then the purge of the Douglas family continued, involving even remote relations of Angus. Five days after the death of his sister Janet Glamis, the master of Forbes, whose wife was Angus's niece, was executed on a charge of plotting to shoot the king, following which, in September 1540, James Douglas of Parkhead, accused of plotting to murder the king with the Earl of Angus, and the (by then) late James Hamilton of Finnart, 'within the fortalice of Tantallon', was summoned for treason and sentenced to death and forfeiture by Alexander Cunningham, a sheriff's messenger, who pronounced 'And that I gave for doom.'

In the second week of October 1537, an envoy, riding post haste from London, brought the news that, on the 12th, King Henry's third wife, Jane Seymour, had born him a son. This was the moment when Margaret's skills as an actress were never more severely tried. With the birth of two daughters to Henry by two of his previous wives, and the long length of time before his third had even become pregnant, Margaret had become increasingly convinced that it was her son, albeit she was at odds with him at the time, who, as Henry's nephew, would succeed to her brother's throne.

Now those hopes were dashed, unless of course the child, as so frequently happened, failed to survive. She herself had lost three babies before even James was born, and his poor little brother Alexander had lived but a very short time.

Pretending to be delighted, Margaret took up her pen to write to Thomas Cromwell, the lawyer who, having engineered both Henry's divorce from Catherine of Aragon and his establishment as head of the Church of England, was now the first minister of the realm.

Addressing him as her 'truly and beloved friend' she told him that:

'I commend me heartily to you, and has received your writing from the King my brother's servant, and 'the joyful tidings you have written to me, that God has had the grace to send a prince to the King's Grace my brother, the which I assure you, next the welfare of the King's Grace my brother, is the thing in the world most to my grace and comfort, praying God to preserve him in health and long life, as I shall daily pray for.'

Then, obsessed with her own predicament, she added:

'Be the King my dearest brother in good prosperity, I trust I cannot be evil. But ye shall understand I have been and is yet heavily troubled, as any jantlewoman may be, and I trust no princes are in that sort entreated.'[164]

A few days later, on 30 October, Margaret wrote again to Cromwell, complaining of her son's cruelty, but she did add that she 'was comforted to understand' that, following the death of Lord Thomas Howard, her brother had released her daughter, Margaret Douglas, from imprisonment in the Tower.[165]

Then in yet another letter she poured out her fury against her husband who had had the effrontery to reveal to her son that she meant to go to England to remarry Archibald Angus. Because of this, although she had given the judge no less than forty-four famous proofs as a reason for divorce between her and Lord Meffin (as she habitually misspelt his name) her son had undutifully stopped the divorce. 'And this Harry Stewart, causes him to believe this of me! I had liever be dead, for I am holden in great suspicion.'

By this time she was living somewhere in Dundee, not in the palace to which she felt entitled, but in a house where she appears to have been kept under arrest. She was allowed to write, however, for on 1 December she sent a letter, taken by

---

[164] Ibid. p.120. Dated October 14 1537.
[165] Ibid. p.120. October 14 1537.

Sir Thomas Erskine of Haltoun to her brother, to tell him of her son's approaching marriage to a second French lady, this time the widowed Duchess of Longueville, Marie of Lorraine.[166]

---

[166] Ibid. p.126. December 1.

CHAPTER 3

'SPOUSIT WITH GREAT GLORY'

This time James did not sail to France himself, sending instead the young and aspiring churchman David Beaton to act on his behalf. This nephew of James Beaton, the archbishop of St Andrews, main antagonist of the Reformation in Scotland, was now, as the abbot of Arbroath, like his uncle, a pillar of the Roman Catholic Church.

It was King Francis who had suggested the daughter of Claude of Guisse-Lorraine, Duc d'Aumale, as a replacement for his own daughter Madeleine, to the man whom he still regarded as a son. James had in fact met Marie on his visit to France, where, on seeing her at the French court, he had at once been struck by her presence, given largely by her physical height. A head taller than most of the women and even some of the men, she moved with a grace that was eye-catching and almost impossible to miss. More importantly, as he was later to discover, she was already the mother of one son and pregnant with a second child, which proved to be another boy.

A friend both of Madeleine and her sister Margaret, Marie, the duchess de Longueville, had attended the wedding of Princess Madeleine to King James in January 1537. Present at many of the festivities, she had been pregnant, with her second son, when James and Madeleine left France in the following May. Tragedy had then followed when her husband, campaigning for King Francis, had died suddenly at Rouen in June. Marie was to keep his last letter to her, written on the night before his death, until the end of her life.

James's ambassador, David Beaton, had completed the arrangements of his betrothal to the Duchess Marie, on 22 October, a fortunate piece of diplomacy as events were soon to prove. It was only two days later, on 26th, when Henry's third wife, Jane Seymour, died of complications following Prince Edward's birth. Her funeral was hardly over before Henry was announcing in public that he intended to marry again, the lady of choice in this instance being none other than Marie of Guise. He was a big man, he said and wanted a big wife. Forthwith, Lord William Howard and the bishop of Winchester were directed to arrange the marriage while Sir Peter Mewtas was sent to put the proposition to Marie of Guise herself.

The eldest daughter of Claude of Lorraine, Duc de Guise, and his wife Antoinette de Bourbon, daughter of the count of Vendôme, Marie had been born on 22 November 1515, in Bar-le-Duc, the castle described as resembling an eagle's nest, perched on a precipitous rock above the little river Onain, a tributary of the Saux before it joins the Marne. Educated at a convent, she had been taken away by her uncle, at the age of fourteen, to be introduced to the court of the French king, at which, on her first appearance, she was present at the marriage of Francis 1 to Eleanor of Austria. In August 1534, Marie, herself, at the age of eighteen, had been married to Louis II d'Orléans, duc de Longueville, like the dauphin Henry, a second son, who had succeeded to the great wealth and titles of his family on the death of his brother at the battle of Pavia. Besides being a ducal peer in his own right and heir to his father's Dukedom of Normandy, he had held the hereditary office of Great Chamberlain of France.

The marriage, although arranged, had proved a particularly happy one. The young couple lived in great state in the family's palaces of Amiens, Rouen, and Chateaudun. A widow at the age of only twenty-one, Marie gave birth to her husband's posthumous child in August 1537. Named Louis, after his father, he died when a few weeks old. Marie had only just left her lying-in-chamber when ambassadors from both Henry of England and James of Scotland, arrived with offers of marriage from the two sovereigns they served.

A clever woman, whose head ruled her heart, Marie favoured the English, rather than the Scottish proposal, in the knowledge of it being a better match. But King Francis would have none of it. The historic alliance with Scotland, so recently augmented by the visit of James, was very dear to him. He had no wish to make a new treaty with England and was furious to discover that Marie of Guise, with the backing of her family, intended to contravene his will. They were, none the less his subjects, bound to abide by his rule, thus Marie found herself with no choice other than to submit to marriage with his protégée, the Scottish King James.

King Francis wasted no time. He had a marriage contract made out, which included a dowry of one hundred and fifty thousand livres, as great a sum as if she had been his daughter. The Scots, for their part, as was customary, promised Marie the jointure of the castles of Stirling, Dingwall and Threave, together with the Palace of Falkland, should she outlive the king.

Despite these promises Marie herself was devastated. Her younger son had just died as a baby, and she did not wish to leave her older boy, whose great inheritance she intended to manage until at least he came of age. Her father, seeing her distress, is said to have tried to delay her departure, but Beaton was adamant, writing to James on 22 October, that Marie was strong and fit to travel. The marriage contract was finally completed in January 1558.

It was not until the following spring, that James sent Lord Maxwell to France to act as his proxy at the marriage, which took place in the great Cathedral of Nôtre Dame on 18 May. How many amongst those attending must have remembered that other wedding, when James in person had married Madeleine, just seventeen months before.

The ceremony once solemnised, Marie, now entitled queen of Scotland, was given into the care of Lord Maxwell, a Border laird who was not above raiding his neighbours himself, but, thanks to his desertion of Angus to the king, was now High

Admiral of Scotland, Warden of the West Marches and provost of Edinburgh. Together with him and the guard of honour, sent by her new husband from Scotland, as well as with a party of French noblemen, Marie travelled from Paris to Dieppe. There she found Annebaut, the admiral of France, waiting to escort her, with a convoy of French ships to protect the vessels sent from Scotland from possible English attack. Her departure, sad enough in itself as she was leaving her little boy behind, is said to have been marred by a fierce quarrel between Lord Maxwell and David Beaton– by now so much a Francophile that he could easily have been mistaken for a Frenchman–who had just been presented to the bishopric of Mirepoix, during his sojourn in France. It is also claimed that Henry VIII, piqued because his nephew was marrying the bride that he wished for himself, refused a request to let Marie land on the coast of England should the sea become very rough.

This it certainly did. Lindsay of Pitscottie says that 'as soon as the wind served, he (Lord Maxwell) shipped the Queen and syne pulled up sails and sailed to Scotland the nearest way. But because the Cardinal (Beaton) got no charge in the Queen's home-coming, and was not letten in the ship with her, he was discontented with the Lord Maxwell, quhilk gendered hatred thereafter.' He adds that 'the Queen landit very pleasant in a part of Fife called Fifeness, near Balcomie.'[167]

Sir David Lindsay of the Mount, in his ode on David Beaton, who in fact was only created a cardinal in the following December, makes him claim full credit for arranging Marie's marriage to King James.

'Through me were made triumphant marriages,
That to King James brought profit and pleasance,
When Magdalene our Queen, first daughter of France,
With riches great was into Scotland brought;
After whose death, to France I passed again,

---

[167] Pitscottie. vol.i.p.375.

The second Queen homeward I did convoy,
That lovely Princess Mary of Lorraine,
Who was received with great triumph and joy,
So served I our right renowned Roy.'

In fact the pilot on the ship, mistaking Balcomie for St Andrews, had got it wrong. James was waiting at St Andrews some ten miles away. Marie landed in Scotland on Trinity Sunday, which fell that year on 12 June 1538. On coming ashore, expecting to meet James, but soon being told of how the mistaken place of landing had occurred, she was taken to Balcomie Castle, seat of the laird of Learmont, Master of the Royal Household, where his lady sent all her servants scurrying about to light fires and find comforts for the unexpected guests.

Meanwhile James, told of her arrival, shouted for his horse and followed by all the peers and prelates, gathered at St Andrews to do honour to his new queen, he spurred it along the coast to where, as he neared Balcomie, catching sight of the masts of the anchored ships, he knew that he would find her there.

The descriptions of the wedding and the tour through Scotland, which James undertook to show the people his new bride, written by the two contemporary historians, John Lesley, the bishop of Ross, and Robert Lindsay of Pitscottie, must have been taken from hearsay, both being boys of eleven and eight years old respectively at the time. They do not reflect upon Margaret, who, now at the age of forty-nine, still out of favour with her son, was, much to her fury, excluded from the festivities.

But they do throw light on the conditions of the country, so much reviled apparently abroad, where, so Marie had been told, 'Scotland was but a barbarous country, destitute and void of all commodities that uses to be in other countries.' But now she confessed she saw the contrary… At these words the king was greatly rejoiced and said to her 'Forsooth, madam, ye shall see better ere ye gang, will God.'[168] It also shows that Sir David Lindsay of the Mount, he who had cared so devotedly for James when a little boy, was still a strong influence in his life.

Together James and Marie rode back to St Andrews, at that time the most civilized city in Scotland, seat of the country's oldest university, established over a hundred years before, during the reign of the first James of Scotland. As the centre of the arts and sciences, as well as of learning in Scotland, St Andrews was known throughout the world.

The records of the Scottish Exchequer do not give evidence of material bought for making Marie's clothes, which presumably she brought from France. But she must have made a striking figure sitting upright, tall and graceful, on a side-saddle riding by the king's side. James himself was decked out in 'ane hat thrummit with gold', decorated with ostrich feathers and a ruby, which, according to the Treasury Account, cost him three crowns.

They were certainly an attractive couple, Marie, elegant and beautiful from all contemporary accounts, while James was described by Bishop Lesley as:

'a man of personage and statue convenient, albeit mighty and strong therewith. Of countenance amiable and lovely, specially in his communication, his eyes grey and sharp of sight, that whomsoever he did once see and mark, he would perfectly know in all times thereafter. Of wit, in all things quick and prompt, of a princely stomach and high courage in great peril.'[169]

Lindsay of Pitscottie gives a vivid account of the royal pair entering St Andrews where:

'And first she (Marie) was received at the New Abbey gate, upon the east side thereof there was made to her a triumphant arch, by Sir David Lindsay of the Mount, Lyon

---

[168] *Letters of James V*,p.295.
[169] Bingham, Caroline. *James V King of Scots*.p.145.

Herald, which caused a great cloud come out of the heavens above the gate and open instantly, and there appeared a fair lady most like an angel having the keys of Scotland in her hands, and delivered them to the Queen, in sign and token that all the hearts in Scotland were open to receive her Grace.'

There followed speeches and an exhortation made by Sir David Lindsay to the queen to serve her God and obey her husband before Marie was received into her palace, which was called the New Inns, specially redecorated for her arrival. Then came the wedding in the magnificent cathedral of St Andrews, the second largest in Europe, where the nobility and churchmen, from the archbishop to the lowliest friar, waited in full finery, while organs (there seem to have been more than one) bellowed and choir boys chanted, their voices ringing to the rafters.

While Marie must have been wearing the robes, which were part of her trousseau, an entry in the Exchequer Rolls shows that James was dressed, much as for his first wedding, in a white coat of Venice satin, laced with silver, the silk lining of which cost two shillings.

From the great western entrance of the cathedral, Marie and James were brought in solemn procession to the high altar, where the blessing of the marriage, made by Lord Maxwell standing proxy for the king in Nôtre Dame, was given by David Beaton, acting this time as coadjutor of St Andrews for his uncle, now very old and frail, whom, as primate, he was about to succeed.

'And there the King's Grace and the said Marie were spousit with great glory, where the Archbishop of Glasgow and many of the noblemen of Scotland were present,' wrote Lesley describing the scene of which he must have been told.

Following the wedding, according to Lindsay of Pitscottie, 'the king received the Queen in his palace to dinner, where was great mirth all day, till time of supper. On the morn, the Queen passed through the town, she saw the Blackfriars, the Greyfriars, the old college and the new college and St

Leonard's (and she met) the provost of the town and the honest burgesses, and when the queen came to her palace and met with the king, she confessed to him that 'that she never saw in France, nor no other country, so many goodly faces in so little room, as that day in Scotland,' for, she said 'it was shown unto her in France that Scotland was but a barbarous country, destitute and void of all commodities that used to be in other countries,' but now she confessed she saw the contrary 'for she never beheld so many fair personages of men, women, young babes and children as she saw that day.' At these words of the queen the king greatly rejoiced and said to her 'Forsooth madam, you shall see better, please God. Ere you go through Scotland, you will see many good-like men and women, with other commodities that will be to your contentment."[170]

The historian continues to relate how the King and Queen stayed at St Andrews for a fortnight after their wedding, while great merrymaking continued in the form of games, jousting, running at the lists, archery, hunting, hawking, dancing and what he calls masking (presumably masked balls) with all other princely disportes.

Leaving St Andrews, James took his new wife to Falkland Palace, the hunting lodge in which, above all his other residences, he seems to have found most happiness and it was here, that inspired by what he had seen in France, he added extensions built in the French Renaissance style. Proof that Marie shared his love for this place seems to lie in the improvements made to the gardens and the park, home of a herd of red deer, and the addition of a tennis court shortly after their marriage. It may have been even on this first visit, that James had the name Marie carved round the pilasters of this castle, of which both he and the wife, to whom he soon became devoted, relying on her strong character for support, are known to have been so fond.

---

[170] Pitscottie, vol.i.pp.278-80.

Nonetheless, they could not stay at Falkland for ever, much as they would have liked to do so. James next took Marie to Stirling, most central and secure fortress of his realm. The castle held many memories for him of his childhood there, under the care of Lord Erskine. It was here that the Duke of Albany, had besieged the castle, bringing the famous cannon Mons Meg from Edinburgh, and where his mother had defied the regent so bravely, before disappearing with the step-father he hated, leaving him with his little brother Alexander, who had also suddenly vanished, taken away from him by death, when bewildered, he had been too young to understand.

James had only just achieved his majority when, with the help and advice of his mother, who had known the original plans, he had continued the rebuilding program of his father. Then, it had been on the urging of Sir James Hamilton of Finnart, that manipulative genius of his youth, that he had begun his own outstanding achievement in the construction of the royal palace, built by masons imported from France. That work was still in progress is shown by the portrait of Marie being amongst the basso reliefs with which the ceiling of the banqueting hall was decorated.

After spending several days at Stirling, occupied by business and pleasure, James took Marie to Linlithgow Palace, on which, in preparation for her arrival, he had already spent four hundred crowns. Marie, used as she was to the French palaces, was nonetheless impressed, telling her new husband that she had never seen 'a more princely palace.' From there they made an excursion to Dundee and into Perthshire, where everywhere the new French queen was royally entertained and much admired.

But despite the extent of her welcome in Scotland, Marie was secretly home-sick for France and all that she had left behind, including her little son, as was revealed by the French lady, who had come to Scotland with Madeleine as her governess, and together with other of her attendants, who had remained in Scotland following her death, on James's second marriage was now dismissed. Travelling through England and taking the chance to visit London, possibly, like so many visitors of today going to the Tower, she was asked by one of Henry VIII's officers how the new queen liked Scotland, to which she replied, with a sad smile, that 'the Queen of Scotland loved France the best.'

As for the dowager Queen Margaret, some time had passed since Margaret had heard from her brother. However, the expected arrival of her son's new wife from France provided an excellent excuse to ask Henry for money to buy wedding presents, or to send them some gold or silver plate.

On 16 October 1538 she wrote to him, making her requests.

'Dearest Brother

Pleaseth your Grace to consider now the coming into this realm of the lady, spouse to your nephew, our dearest son, and with her comes sundry strangers, for the which, as it pleaseth your Grace, we think to address us at this time, according so far as we may, to the honour of your Grace and our noble progenitors.

Wherefore, an please your Grace to be good brother to us, as to support part with money and some silver-work as pleaseth best your Grace to do, for we may be chargeable to your Grace before all earthly creature. Beseeching your Grace in our most humble manner, of your Grace's pardon here unto, and that it pleases your grace to advertise me by this bearer of your Grace's will anent the same, in writing. And if it please your Grace to do such pleasure and honour to me, your Grace's only faithful sister, your Grace shall more and more deem the same merited as in my possible power. Almighty God preserve your Grace eternally.

By the evil hand (writing) of your Grace's humble sister,
    Margaret R.'[171]

---

[171] *State Papers,* vol. v. p.119. Dundee, October 16.

Margaret followed this up with another appeal to her brother, through the auspices of the Rothesay Herald, promising him:

'never again to be 'cummersone to your Grace, but to guide myself within bounds to your pleasure and my honour.'

But this, like another similar missive, failed to extract either sympathy or money from Henry, he being otherwise engaged in dealing with the subjection of a possible rising of the Catholics in the north of England and the alleged adultery of his fifth wife, Katherine Howard. That there was also trouble fomenting in Scotland, he knew from the Duke of Norfolk sending news from Harry Ray, the Berwick herald, to Cromwell from Edinburgh.

According to Ray, all Scotsmen had heard a proclamation that they should be ready for war. A secret friend of the banished Earl of Angus, who was an officer in the Scottish Ordnance, had told him that six great cannons or culverins and sixty smaller guns had been refurnished, or newly cast in Edinburgh Castle. All the guns would be ready twenty days after Easter. Ray had also heard a sermon, preached by a friar of the Scottish queen in Linlithgow, while his Scottish friends assured him that if England made peace with France, all three countries would be at peace.[172]

It is said to have been the question of Marie of Guise, her new daughter-in-law, asking why she had not heard from her brother, which set Margaret writing to Henry yet again. After first reproaching him for his negligence, she proceeded to tell him that her son was in good health and that there was 'great love' between him and his new wife. Surprisingly, in view of Margaret's known irascibility, according at least to her own word, she was on very good terms with Marie.

'Your Grace shall understand that, since her coming to this realm, I have been much in her company, and she bears her

---

[172] *State Papers* Henry VIII, vol. 5. Part 4 (1836) pp. 153-6. Norfolk to Cromwell. 29 March 1539.

very favourably to me, with as good treatment as may be, and hearty. And she asked of me when I heard any word out of your realm from your Grace? I said it was but a short time since I hear from you. Now, dearest brother, since there is here another Princess than I, (your only sister) I beseech your Grace that it may be seen and understood that you will be a kind and loving brother to me, for that will be a great reason to the King my son to do the like.'[173]

Surprisingly, considering that they were both strong- minded women, Margaret and her new daughter-in-law remained, if not exactly friends, at least on compatible terms. This was largely due to the diplomacy of Marie, a sensible woman, endowed with such good common sense, that she saw the advantage of maintaining a good relationship with her mother-in-law, difficult and unpredictable, as she is known to have been. Possibly she relied on Margaret to put her wise to the ways of Scotland, when James went off campaigning in the spring of 1540.

Marie gave birth to their first child, a boy, 'fair and lifelike to succeed us,' on 22 May 1540. A week later, the king went aboard a ship at Leith to begin his tour of the northern parts of his kingdom, where, in the previous year, a man called Donald Gorme, claiming the hereditary Lordship of the Isles, had risen in rebellion. With the king went Archbishop David Beaton, created a cardinal by Pope Paul III in 1538, his cousin the Earl of Arran, his friend the Earl of Huntly and the man who had ousted Arran's illegitimate half-brother, Hamilton of Finnart as his favourite, Oliver Sinclair, who, on the voyage was made Sheriff of Orkney and governor of Angus' former stronghold, Tantallon Castle.

Having rounded the north of Scotland and visited both the Orkney and Shetland Isles, he made for the Outer Hebrides,

---

[173] State Papers, vol.v. May 1540.

where, as in Skye and the Inner Hebrides including Islay, he took hostages of local chiefs to effect the good behaviour of their people. Then, with his captives, on board his fleet of ships, he came up the Firth of Clyde, to land at the royal castle of Dumbarton sometime in the middle of August.

In January 1541, when Queen Marie was again pregnant, James organized her coronation. A new crown was made for her, partly of gold worked by the miners she had imported from France, to work the gold mines of Crawford Muir. Most notably, no mention is made of the presence of Margaret, the queen mother, either at the ceremony, or any of the following festivities.

CHAPTER 4

'THOUGH I BE FORGOTTEN IN ENGLAND, NEVER
SHALL I FORGET ENGLAND.'

Sir Ralph Sadler came to Scotland again in February 1540,
sent to Scotland by Henry VIII, for three main reasons. Firstly,
to discredit Cardinal David Beaton by producing intercepted
letters, written by him to his agent in Rome. Secondly, to try
to persuade James to follow his uncle's example by seizing all
the abbey-lands and church property, and thirdly, to make his
'master's hearty commendations to both the queens here.'

King Henry's ambassador found Margaret installed in her
winter quarters in Holyrood Palace where he reported her as
being 'broken in spirit and infirm in health.' The latter may
have been true. The former certainly was not. Furious on
discovering that her brother's dispatches did not include a
letter to her, she told him:

'Though I be forgotten in England, never shall I forget
England. It would have been a small matter to have spent a
little paper and ink on me, and much would it have been to my
comfort. Were it perceived that the King's Grace, my brother,
did better regard me, I should be better regarded by all parties
here.'

From this it seems plain that she was still on bad terms with
James who suspected her, with some reason, of betraying
secret information to her brother. In another letter, written
from Stirling on 12 May, she told Henry :

'I trust you will stand my friend and loving brother in that
I get no hurt in nothing that I write to your Grace, nor that you
will write nothing concerning me, your sister, to the King my
son, without I be first advertised, and that it will be with my
advice. Praying your Grace, dearest brother, that I will please
you to do this for me, your sister, and I am and shall be ever

ready to do your Grace's will and pleasure. But I am afraid that I put your Grace to great pain and travail to read my oft writing and my evil hand. Praying your Grace to pardon me of the same, and that it will please you, dearest brother, to keep secret any writings that I send, for otherwise I may do me great hurt, which I trust your Grace will not do to me, your sister, seeing I am remaining in this realm, as God knows, whom preserve your Grace.'

Displeased as she was by her brother's lack of attention, Margaret did confess to 'how well she was treated, and made much of by the new Queen.'[174] Marie of Lorraine was in fact the mistress of tact, so much so that she managed to persuade Margaret to drop the divorce case against Harry Stewart, for after her arrival in Scotland, nothing is heard of it again.

That Margaret was then living in Stirling Castle with Mary of Lorraine, who was waiting for the birth of her second child, is shown by a letter in the State Paper Office, dated March 1 1540 in which, rather unusually, she asks for help, not for herself, but for a priest who, afraid to travel back through England without permission, had asked her to approach her brother on his behalf. She describes him as:

'a poor religious man, Friar Joachim, sometime of the Holy Sepulchre of our Lord Jesus in Jerusalem, and now Monk of the Abbey of Our Lady of Grace, situate betwixt the cities of Jerusalem and Damascus, lately come to Scotland with patent letters of the Patriarch of Jerusalem, to collect alms for the ransom of the abbot and monks of St Basil, violently taken and holden in prison by the Saracen infidels of those parts.'[175]

It was in Stirling Castle in April that Mary of Lorraine gave birth to a second son, giving her husband another male heir to his throne. But James was not with her at the time of the boy's birth. Instead he was at Linlithgow Palace, involved

---

[174] *Sadler's State Papers, Embassy to Scotland in 1540*, vol. i.p.10.

[175] *State Papers*, Royal Letters

with one of the most pressing and complicated issues that marked the start of the decline of both his mental and physical health.

The core of the trouble revolved around the person of Sir James Hamilton of Finnart, that enigmatic character, still known as the 'Bastard,' son of the 1st Earl of Arran, whose despotic nature had at first revolted and then for his skills in both flattery and capability, apparently captivated, at least to some extent, the mind of King James.

One of the main reasons for the extent of the sovereign's poverty, which had necessitated his search for a bride with a large dowry, had been the cost of the building projects on which, on achieving power, he had embarked. In charge of them was none other than Sir James Hamilton of Finnart, now following his father's death, the guardian of his ten year old half-brother James, 2nd Earl of Arran, head of the Hamilton dynasty. Hamilton in this capacity, ranked amongst the most influential men in Scotland.

His relationship with King James seems based on his competence as the architect of so many and varied additions to the royal castles throughout Scotland, which had won James's admiration to the point where, in 1530, he had given him land in Lanarkshire and made him, not only Master of Works but Steward of the Royal Household.

That Hamilton made himself obsequious, in the hopes of retaining favour, seems shown by the fact that, in 1536, he is known to have acquired horses, hounds and hawks for the king who then ordered Patrick Lord Gray, who was somehow in his debt, to pay him eight hundred and fifty Scottish marks.

However, it was on the first, ill-fated voyage to France, in July 1536, that James had become suspicious of him when, while he himself was sleeping in his cabin during the storm, Hamilton, on the excuse of imminent danger, had seized the tiller from the steersman and headed back to Leith. His excuses for doing so had seemed genuine enough at the time – the sea was so rough that they might well have perished in the storm–

but James, perhaps at the instigation of Oliver Sinclair, his new favourite, immediately began to wonder if Hamilton had not acted deliberately to prevent him getting married in France. Hamilton, who is believed to have tried to stop James's marriage to Princess Mary of England, certainly had a reason for trying to prevent his attempt to find a wife. In 1513, in the event of his father failing to have legitimate children, he had been declared his heir. His father did then have another son, the unquestionably authentic half-brother, of whom Hamilton was now in charge. But children died so frequently that it was not impossible that he might yet inherit the earldom, in which case, if James himself did not have children, Hamilton, through his descent from James II, might one day find himself king of Scotland.

Meanwhile, while harbouring his secret ambition, despite his fall from favour, Hamilton continued to work on the restoration of the royal palaces on which, with his skill as an architect, he had already begun. He had started work on the renovation of both Linlithgow Palace and Blackness Castle. At Linlithgow, the master mason, Thomas French, received £forty a year, 'gratis Ja. Hamilton.' The palace was finally completed round the great central courtyard. In the following year of 1537, the accounts of the Royal Exchequer prove that the treasurer had awarded Hamilton £133-6s-8d for the money he had spent on Linlithgow Palace, where, as the keeper, he was responsible for renewing the stone-work in the front façade, and building both the outer gate house and the elaborately carved fountain in the court-yard. Also, he had transformed Blackness Castle on the south side of the Forth, where, by strengthening the fortifications, he had turned the 15th century fortress into the most advanced artillery fortification in Scotland.

At Falkland Palace, Hamilton, at James direction, completed the south range where the courtyard has five windows, each flanked by a pair of medallions carved in stone representing personages who are supposed to be James V, his two queens and his most important nobles. This work, which is in fact a Renaissance screen, has been described as 'a display of early Renaissance architecture without parallel in the British Isles.'[176]

His greatest achievement, however, was in the completion of the monumental construction, begun during the reign of James IV, of the Royal Palace in Stirling Castle where, with the assistance of the Master of Works, John Scrymgeour, and the French masons brought from France, he constructed what is probably the greatest and most lasting triumph of the fourth and fifth James's reigns.

Already in place were the buildings, commenced in the time of James's grandfather, James III, on the designs of his favourite, the architect Thomas Cochrane, whose life had ended so ignominiously on Lauder Bridge. His was the inspiration of the Great Hall, the Gate House and the Chapel Royal. James IV had begun the Royal Palace, which his son now completed. Again the winged faces and the panels of thin foliage on square columns and the winged angel faces on the cornice, supporting the parapet which oversails the wall face, are suggestive of the Valois Palace of Blois, where Hamilton had been present when James signed his marriage contract with Princess Madeleine, during his sojourn in France.

Further examples of Hamilton's work can be seen today in the medallions painted on walls at Falkland, and ceilings in Stirling where, in the Presence Chamber, the heads of the kings and queens of Scotland are thought to include those of James, wearing a bonnet and his mother Margaret Tudor in a pedimented English hood and with a little greyhound in her arms.

But always suspicion of his loyalty lurked in the king's mind and shortly after his return from his northern expedition, proof of what he feared came to hand from, of all people, one

---

[176] Moncrieffe of that Ilk, *Falkland Palace*, pp.4,19.

of the same family name. The cruel and despotic death at the stake of Patrick Hamilton had never been forgotten by those of his relations, who waited for a chance of revenge.

Chief amongst them was Patrick's older brother, Sir James Hamilton of Kincavel, now the sheriff of Linlithgow, who had long been at feud with his cousin Hamilton of Finnart, blaming him, at least in part, for causing his brother's death. Now he denounced him for plotting against the king's life and for being in treasonable communications with the Douglases.

King James was waiting on the south shore of the Forth for a boat to take him over to Fife, when a young man appeared saying he was Kincavel's son. He had come, he said, at his father's behest, to warn James that Hamilton of Finnart 'attended only the occasion when he might suprize him and breaking up his chamber doors assassinate him.'[177]The youth then went on to mention some rumoured association between Hamilton of Finnart and the Douglases, which was all James needed to hear. Giving the young man a ring to prove to the Council, then sitting in Edinburgh, that he was acting on his authority, he boarded the boat and set sail across the Firth of Forth.

Hamilton was subsequently arrested by Sir Thomas Erskine of Haltoun, Sir James Learmont, Master of the Household, and Sir William Kirkcaldy of Grange the Treasurer. Risking no delay, to allow the king to change his mind, on 16 August 1540 they brought Hamilton to trial.

It was proved that he had murdered the Earl of Lennox, after Lennox had surrendered following the battle by the bridge at Linlithgow in 1526, while James had sat fuming and helpless to intervene, his horse held back by Sir George Douglas. Why otherwise would Finnart have been paying six priests to 'do suffrage for the soul of the deceased John, Earl of Lennox, for no less than seven years, three of whom sang continually in the College Kirk of Hamilton and the other three

---

[177] Bingham. pp.174-5.

in the Black Friars of Glasgow.' [178] Amongst other charges brought against him were those of twelve years earlier which, despite the fact that, together with his father the Earl of Arran, he played such a leading part in the action called 'Clear the Causeway' which drove the Douglases out of Edinburgh, do imply collusion, with certain members of that family, in a plot to kill the king.

'At the time it is said he was with Archibald Douglas of Kilspindie and James Douglas of Parkhead at the chapel of St Leonard near Edinburgh after the forfeiture of Archibald Douglas, formerly Earl of Angus, George Douglas of Pittendreich his brother, and the said Archibald Douglas, his father, and also during the siege of Tantallon Castle in consultation with the said Douglases. How he would enter by the window near the upper part of the bed in the king's palace near Holyrood Abbey, and how there he would commit the slaughter of the king. And for common treason and conspiracy against the king, his realm and lieges, therefore it was given that this James forfeited his life, lands, rents and possessions to the king as his escheat, to remain width him in perpetuity.' [179]

Found guilty of such points of the indictment as was laid against him, Hamilton was summarily sentenced to death by the axe. It is said that he demanded trial by combat with his accuser, which was refused, and he died swearing his innocence of any conspiracy against the king. [180]

The execution of Hamilton, unpopular as he had been with many who had resented his covetousness when in favour with James, shocked the nobility of Scotland, many of whom thought him innocent of the crime for which he was killed. If

---

[178] Ibid. p.175.

[179] *Acts of the Parliaments of Scotland.* vol.2. (1814) Latin, December 1540. See also Wikipedia.

[180] Drummond of Hawthornden, *History of Scotland*, pp.333-5.

Hamilton, once such a favourite in high position, could be accused of treachery, who in Scotland was safe? According to Drummond of Hawthornden, many men, in fear for their own lives, left the court.

As this was happening, James became paranoid in his belief that those around him were converts to the reformed religion and as such were in league with Henry VIII. 'Neither was he herein far mistaken', wrote Drummond, who continued to tell how, overcome with worry, the king became increasingly melancholy and withdrawn. Worse still, he began to suffer from appalling nightmares resulting, so it was surmised, from guilt over Hamilton's death. George Buchanan, another contemporary historian, writes that among the king's most frightening dreams 'there was one more remarkable than the rest, which was much talked of, that, in his sleep, he saw James Hamilton running at him with his drawn sword, and that he first cut off his right arm, then his left, and threatened him shortly to come and take away his life.' This nightmare came to be endued with particular significance as a result of the great misfortune that shortly afterwards occured.

James was in Linlithgow Palace in April 1541 when a messenger came galloping from St Andrews bringing him the dreadful news that his eldest son, just eleven months old, was dangerously ill in that town. Riding a fast horse, he probably had himself ferried across from Queensferry to Inverkeithing, this being the shortest route. Once in Fife, he rode flat out for St Andrews but arrived to find that the little boy was dead. Then, while he was still trying to come to terms with this tragedy, another courier appeared to say that the younger boy, Prince Arthur, just weeks old, was seriously ill in Stirling Castle, where on arrival, he found that he too had died. Pathetic entries in the accounts of the Royal Exchequer show money spent on white taffeta 'of twa threads,' wherewith to hold the candles at my Lord Duke's baptism on 24 April with soon afterwards another entry for 'ane cape of lead' bought from Andrew Yare at Stirling for fourteen shillings, which my Lord Duke was buried in'. The two little princes were laid side by side in the royal vault at Holyrood, and while the whole country mourned, James himself was inconsolable believing that the right and left arms, which in his dream Hamilton had cut from his body, represented his two sons.

Nothing speaks more of the strong character of Mary of Guise, in that it was she, who, despite her own overwhelming grief, comforted James telling him that 'they were young enough and God would send them more succession.'

With them, at that very sad time in Stirling, was Margaret, the queen mother, who wrote to her brother Henry VIII, describing all that had happened under a charge of secrecy.

'Pleaseth you, dearest Brother, here hath been great displeasure, for the death of the Prince and his brother, both with the King my son and the Queen his wife, wherefore I have done great diligence to put them in comfort, and is never from them, but ever in their company, whereof they are very glad. Therefore I pray your Grace to hold me excused that I write not at length of my matters at this time, because I can get no leisure, but I trust ye will stand my friend and loving brother, and that I get no hurt in nothing that I write to your Grace, nor that you will not write nothing that belonging to me, your sister, to the King my son, without I be first advertised, and that it be with my avise. (consent)

Praying your Grace, dearest brother, that it will please you to do this for me, your sister, and I am, and shall ever be ready, to do your Grace's will and pleasure. But I am afeard that I put your Grace to great pain and travail to read my oft writing, and mine evil hand, praying your Grace to pardon me of the same, and that it will please you, dearest brother, to keep secret any writings that I send, for other ways it may do me great hurt, which I trust your Grace would not do to me, your sister, seeing as I am remaining in this realm, as God knows, whom preserve your Grace.

Written at Stirling the 12 May.

Your loving Sister,
Margaret R.'
To the King's Grace, my dearest Brother. [181]

Inspired by the courage of his wife and perhaps, in some degree comforted by his mother, James forced himself to return to public life. Together with Marie, both wearing black for their dead children, they began a tour of the main cities of the north of Scotland. Beginning at Perth, where the queen was very honourably received, they continued to Aberdeen where they stayed for fifteen days as guests of James's old tutor, Bishop Gavin Dunbar, Chancellor of Scotland and founder of the new university to which they paid a visit as also to several schools. Pageants were laid on to entertain them, and elaborate speeches of welcome were given by the scholars and fellows of the colleges and schools in Greek, Latin and other languages, most of which, it must be presumed, that neither of them understood.

The royal couple returned to Edinburgh from Aberdeen to receive Sir Ralph Sadler, sent by King Henry to revive the proposal that a meeting should take place between him and his nephew, King James on English ground. When Sadler arrived, in August 1541 Cardinal Beaton was in France whither he had gone to attempt to achieve 'the extirpation of heresy from Scotland and the re-establishment of the Catholic faith within the dominions of Henry VIII, by a coalition between King Francis, King James, the Emperor Charles V and the Pope.'

At that time Henry greatly feared an invasion from the combined forces of the triple alliance, but when the French king quarrelled with the emperor, by negotiating with the Turks, Henry sided with the emperor while James remained loyal to France. Under these circumstances the threat of renewed war between Scotland and England was resumed, and

---

[181] *State Papers*, vol. v.

it was for this reason that Henry had sent Sadler to Scotland to suggest a meeting between himself and James at York.

James, still waiting for Beaton's return from France, agreed. Henry then travelled to York where he waited with growing impatience for twelve days. Told that it was the Scottish king's clerical advisers – in other words Beaton– who had advised him not to go in case his uncle should persuade him to adopt the Reformation, Henry, by now seething with anger, said with scorn, 'We would be loath to put him to so great pains, seeing he cannot without leave of others do it'. James himself made the excuse of trouble on the Borders for failing to attend the meeting but Henry, furious at being publicly humiliated by waiting at York for the nephew who did not appear, was convinced that he had done so as an act of deliberate provocation into declaring war.

CHAPTER 5

'KEEP SECRET ANY WRITINGS'

Meanwhile, Queen Margaret was doing all in her power to prevent another war with England. Normally by nature optimistic, ready to confront all challenges that confronted her, she was now downcast to the point of despair. Everything that she had fought for and tried to create during her time in Scotland was falling apart before her eyes. Her long term ambition of an alliance between the country in which, through circumstance, she found herself forced to live and that of her birth which she still thought of as her own, was now doomed, inevitably, to failure. Her son was as obtuse as his father, in refusing to see the fallacy of adhering to an association with France, ill-fated over the centuries, as that had proved to be.

Foremost in her mind was that last night with her husband, the fourth King James at Falkland Palace, when he had showed her the hiding place of that glittering pile of Louis d'Or, sent by the French King Louis to bribe him to lead an invasion into England. How fatal had that proved to be? If James had only sided with her brother, how much stronger and richer could Scotland have been in the present day? Now, forty-four years later, it was all happening again. Margaret could only foresee disaster, and thanks to the killing power of the cannons being cast in Edinburgh Castle, slaughter of men's lives on an even more calamitous scale.

That she was still in secret communication with her brother is proved by her last letter, written on 12 May, in which she asks him specifically 'to keep secret any writings that I send, for otherwise it may do me great hurt.' She was then still at Stirling, living with her son and his wife with whom she had such a good relationship that she became, not only 'a zealous observer of Roman Catholic rites but is said to have lived decorously for the brief residue of her days'.

This is so unlike her that, reading between the lines, it seems her spirit had gone. Margaret, forever English at heart, could only visualise how the country where she now remained with so much reluctance, would once again be torn apart.

Sometime, during the late summer or autumn, she left Stirling to return to Methven Castle, for it was there that, on Friday 20 November, she was struck with palsy, or more prosaically had a stroke, sometime in the afternoon.

She was not alarmed until the following Tuesday when, following what sounds like another stroke, she sent for James who was at Falkland Palace. Knowing then that she was dying, she summoned priests, who proved to be friars, probably from the local Blackfriars Priory of the Dominican Order, in Perth.

Plainly her conscience worried her concerning Archibald Angus, for she instructed the friars, to whom she confessed, 'to sit on their knees before the King, her son, and beseech that he would be good and gracious to Lord Angus.'

She then exceedingly lamented and asked God to have mercy that she had offended the said Earl as she had.[182] She then asked her confessors to solicit her son James V, for him to be good to the Lady Margaret Douglas her daughter, and that he would give her what goods she left, thinking it right because her daughter had never had anything of her. She had failed so far to make a will, and now she knew that she had neither the time nor the memory to do so before she died.

As it was, her son reached Methven to find her already dead. With him came his now constant companion Oliver Sinclair and John Tennant, two gentlemen of his privy-chamber, who he told to lock up all his mother's possessions. Margaret left in ready money, only two thousand three hundred marks Scots, it being the Berwick Herald, Harry Ray, sent by King Henry to find out if his sister was really dead and

---

[182] Ibid. November 1541.

if so whether she died intestate, who faithfully reported these details on his return. [183]

James V gave his mother the most magnificent funeral. Riding behind her coffin at the head of a long procession of clergy and nobility, he himself laid her head in the coffin when she was buried in the Abbey Church of St John, belonging to the monastery of St Johnston, the original name of Perth. Her coffin was placed in the vault of James I, and his wife Joan Beaufort, founders of the monastery where in the royal residence attached to it, James himself had been murdered just over one hundred years before. On its demolition by a mob, during the Reformation in 1559, it is said that these bodies were moved to the east end of St John's Church. The graves are believed to be marked by a large blue marble slab, carved in two compartments, with the royal crown of Scotland over each and ornamented, in honour of the French connection, with fleur-de-lis.

Of Margaret's three husbands two survived her, one the Earl of Angus living in exile in England, at that time with their daughter Margaret, at the court of Henry VIII, the other Harry Stewart, to whom the barony of Methven was confirmed by James V, and who would be killed at the battle of Pinkie in 1547. The orphaned son and daughter of Margaret and Methven, were then brought up by the Mistress of Sutherland, she who had been named by Margaret as the co-respondent in her failed attempt at divorce. Following Margaret's death, Stewart married her and apparently had children in addition to those who, so Margaret claimed, had been born before his marriage to her had taken place.

---

[183] Ibid. Letters of Harry Ray.

ENVOI

On 24 August 1542, the year following Margaret's death, Sir Robert Bowes, captain of Norham Castle and the English Warden of the East March, with Archibald Earl of Angus and his brother Sir George Douglas, invaded Scotland with a force three thousand strong. They were defeated by a Scottish army, commanded by the ever loyal Earl of Huntly at Hatton Rig, near Kelso. Huntly took many prisoners, but Angus and his brother, riding fast horses, escaped.

King Henry then ordered the Duke of Norfolk to raise an army for a full-scale invasion of Scotland. James, informed by spies that it numbered forty thousand men, knowing that his own soldiers would be hopelessly outnumbered, sent commissioners to York to try to negotiate a truce. But they met with no success. Norfolk, together with Angus, invaded the Borders to loot and burn indiscriminately, leaving the country people destitute, as winter inevitably approached. James could get no help from France, King Francis now being at war with the Emperor Charles V. In desperation for assistance, both he and Cardinal Beaton appealed to the Pope, asking him to send men and armaments to defend Scotland from an English invasion expected before the summer was out.

The king marched south with an army but, just as when Albany had asked them to do so, many of his commanders, all men of the nobility, converted to the Reformation, claiming that their king was asking them to fight on the orders of the Pope, refused to cross the Border into England.

James could not force them to obey. Deeply depressed and humiliated, he marched back to Edinburgh, saying publicly that the Scottish nobles 'neither loved his honour nor desired his continuance amongst them.' In desperation he turned to Oliver Sinclair, believing him to be the only man on whom he could rely.

Following this, the recalcitrant nobles were banned from the king's counsels, the only men left in consultation being his illegitimate son, the Earl of Moray, Cardinal Beaton and inevitably his continuing favourite, Oliver Sinclair of Pitcairns, 'the most secret man living with the King of Scots.' Sinclair, related to the earls of Caithness and Roslin, who had been made keeper of Tantallon in 1540, since receiving the tack of Orkney and Shetland, had been given many other gifts.

On 21 November, King James, with the cardinal and Moray, left Edinburgh and marched towards the West March with an army that has been variously estimated at fourteen thousand to twenty thousand strong. Beaton and Moray took up a position in the East Lothian town of Haddington, while the king went on to Lochmaben, in Dumfries, with part of his force intending to cross the Solway Moss at low tide. The rest of the army, under the command of Oliver Sinclair, took a more easterly route.

It was Oliver's division of the army, which, on 24 November, fought Thomas Lord Wharton, the English Deputy Warden on the Solway Moss, a marshy area near the River Esk. According to John Knox, the king had decreed that Sinclair should take command in his absence, but it was only when the action was about to start, that it became generally realized, that James himself was not there. This was Oliver's moment. Raising the king's banner, he had himself hoisted onto men's shoulders 'and there with sound of trumpet was he proclaimed general lieutenant... There was present the Lord Maxwell (Scottish Warden of the Marches) to whom the (command of) the regiment properly appertained... There was also present the Earls of Glencairn and Cassillis, with the Lord Fleming and many other lords, barons and gentlemen of Lothian, Fife, Angus and the Mearns'.[184]Led by Maxwell they revolted and refused to accept Sinclair's command. Uproar

---

[184] Knox. vol. 1. p.86.

broke out, and there was total disorder, as men broke ranks, the soldiers throwing down their pikes, the horsemen their spears. Many were taken prisoner including Lord Maxwell and Oliver Sinclair himself, reported to be 'fleeing most manfully' in what became known as the rout of Solway Moss.

It was evening when, at Lochmaben Castle, on a promontory at the south end of the loch, the king heard the news of the disaster. Ill as he was, those with him thought that he suffered a seizure, so unexpected and terrible was the shock. Lying in bed he muttered continually, always the same words, 'Oh fled Oliver? Is Oliver tane?'

Leaving Lochmaben he rode back to Edinburgh where, again according to Knox, so great was his humiliation that he could not look anyone in the face. He then rode to Tantallon where he was claimed to have had a mistress, in the keeping of Oliver Sinclair's wife.[185] Be that as it may, James then rode on to Linlithgow where Marie of Guise was in the last month of her pregnancy with their third child. But he could not rest anywhere, so distraught was his state of mind.

Onwards he went, across the Forth to Halyards in Fife, where lived his Treasurer, Sir William Kirkcaldy of Grange. Lady Grange tried to comfort him but to her kind words he merely told her that 'My portion of this world is short, for I will not be with you in fifteen days.' Convinced of his approaching death he told his servants, asking him 'where he would have provision made for this Yule', 'I cannot tell, choose ye the place, but this I can tell you,'ere Yule day, ye will be masterless and the realm without a King.'

Leaving the hospitable Kirkaldys he went on to Falkland, where, physically and mentally exhausted, he at once went to bed. On 7 December, at Linlithgow, Mary of Guise gave birth to their child when, told that it was a girl, knowing that the Stewart dynasty had descended from Marjory, daughter of Robert the Bruce, who had married Walter the Steward, as reported by Lindsay of Pitscottie, he so famously said 'it came with a lass, it will pass with a lass.' Then, turning his face to the wall, on 14 December, just a week after the birth of the daughter who would live to become Mary Queen of Scots, he died.

---

[185] *Letters and Papers of Henry VIII,* vol. xvii, No, 1194.

Index